THE METAMORPHOSIS OF A SOCIAL CLASS IN HUNGARY DURING THE REIGN OF YOUNG FRANZ JOSEPH

PETER I. HIDAS

EAST EUROPEAN QUARTERLY, BOULDER
DISTRIBUTED BY COLUMBIA UNIVERSITY PRESS
NEW YORK

1977

EAST EUROPEAN MONOGRAPHS, NO. XXVI

Peter I. Hidas is Professor of History at
Dawson College, Westmount, Quebec

Printed in the United States of America

EAST EUROPEAN MONOGRAPHS

The *East European Monographs* comprise scholarly books on the history and civilization of Eastern Europe. They are published by the *East European Quarterly* in the belief that these studies contribute substantially to the knowledge of the area and serve to stimulate scholarship and research.

1. *Political Ideas and the Enlightenment in the Romanian Principalities, 1750, 1831.* By Vlad Georgescu. 1971.

2. *America, Italy and the Birth of Yugoslavia, 1917–1919.* By Dragan R. Zivojinovic. 1972.

3. *Jewish Nobles and Geniuses in Modern Hungary.* By William O. McCagg, Jr.

4. *Mixail Soloxov in Yugoslavia: Reception and Literary Impact.* By Robert F. Price. 1973.

5. *The Historical and Nationalistic Thought of Nicolae Iorga.* By William O. Oldson. 1973.

6. *Guide to Polish Libraries and Archives.* By Richard C. Lewanski. 1974.

7. *Vienna Broadcasts to Slovakia, 1938–1939: A Case Study in Subversion.* By Henry Delfiner. 1974.

8. *The 1917 Revolution in Latvia.* By Andrew Ezergailis. 1974.

9. *The Ukraine in the United Nations Organization: A Study in Soviet Foreign Policy, 1944–1950.* By Konstantin Sawczuk. 1975.

10. *The Bosnian Church: A New Interpretation.* By John V. A. Fine, Jr. 1975.

11. *Intellectual and Social Developments in the Hapsburg Empire from Maria Theresa to World War I.* Edited by Stanley B. Winters and Joseph Held. 1975.

12. *Ljudevit Gaj and the Illyrian Movement.* By Elinor Murray Despalatovic. 1975.

13. *Tolerance and Movements of Religious Dissent in Eastern Europe.* Edited by Bela K. Kiraly. 1975.

14. *The Parish Republic: Hlinka's Slovak People's Party, 1939–1945.* By Yeshayahu Jelinek. 1976.

15. *The Russian Annexation of Bessarabia, 1774–1828.* By George F. Jewsbury. 1976.

16. *Modern Hungarian Historiography.* By Steven Bela Vardy. 1976.

17. *Values and Community in Multi-National Yugoslavia.* By Gary K. Bertsch. 1976.

18. *The Greek Socialist Movement and the First World War: The Road to Unity.* By George B. Leon. 1976.

19. *The Radical Left in the Hungarian Revolution of 1848.* By Laszlo Deme. 1976.

20. *Hungary between Wilson and Lenin: The Hungarian Revolution of 1918–1919 and the Big Three.* By Peter Pastor. 1976.

21. *The Crises of France's East Central European Diplomacy, 1933–1938.* By Anthony Tihamer Komjathy. 1976.

22. *Polish Politics and National Reform, 1775–1788.* By Daniel Stone. 1976.

23. *The Habsburg Empire in World War I.* Edited by R. A. Kann, B. K. Kiraly, and P. S. Fichtner. 1977.

24. *The Slovenes and Yugoslavism 1890–1914.* By Carole Rogel. 1977.

25. *German-Hungarian Relations and the Swabian Problem.* By Thomas Spira. 1977.

To Helen

Contents

INTRODUCTION ix

1 THE LIBERAL CENTRALISTS AND
THEIR HUNGARIAN POLICIES 1

2 THE DEFEAT OF THE LIBERAL CENTRALISTS 28

3 THE IMPACT OF GOVERNMENT POLICIES
ON THE ARISTOCRACY 46

4 THE GENTRY IN OPPOSITION 64

APPENDIX 86

NOTES 92

BIBLIOGRAPHY 118

INDEX 137

Introduction

The morning snow which fell on the streets of Pest-Buda on 15 March 1848 quickly melted away as the March winds penetrated Hungary from the West. The bourgeois revolutions of Paris and Vienna and the daring legislative activity of the Magyar gentry and aristocracy at the Pozsony Diet brought the citizens of Pest, young and old, German and Magyar, to the threshold of a revolution of their own.

By the autumn of 1848 the Revolution turned into a civil war of the Empire, with Germans, Croats, Serbs and Magyar aristocrats besieging Hungary. The determined stand of the Hungarian *Honvéd* Army in 1849 forced Franz Joseph to request Russian intervention. In April, the Hungarians, led by Lajos Kossuth, severed their connection with the House of Habsburg and transformed the Civil War into their War of Independence. The combined strength of two Imperial armies and the hostile nationalities proved overwhelming for Hungary. In addition, Kossuth was gradually abandoned by the very people for whom he had conducted the struggle, the Magyar gentry.

Meanwhile in Vienna, the Habsburgs decided to take their chances with Prince Schwarzenberg's cabinet which professed a liberal economic and centralist administrative program. Between June 1849 and April 1853 the Liberal Centralists were in power. This period, unfortunately, still remains a neglected field of historical investigation.

Péter Hanák, senior researcher at the Historical Institute of the Hungarian Academy of Sciences, wrote in 1964:

> Only relatively few scholars [in Hungary] have expressed an interest
> in the internal politics of the neo-absolutist period (1849-1867).[1]

Those few Hungarians as well as Austrians and other historians who did, have found few features in the regime and its politicians praiseworthy. By focusing on constitutional and legal developments and unanimously condemning the aristocracy, Hungarian historians have concentrated primarily on the negative aspects of the Liberal Centralist Era. Austrian historians have often joined this chorus in reviling the period for its bureaucratic sterility or, in turn, have praised the reform administration and blamed the Hungarians for Liberal Centralist failures without paying much attention to the internal conditions of Hungary in the early 1850's. The three groups of historians transferred some of the attributes of the Absolutist Centralist Era (1853–1860) to the Period of Liberal Centralism (1849–1853).

Oscar Jaszi, former Hungarian politician turned historian, claimed that Schwarzenberg's regime did not differ on substantial points from the system of Metternich since his Government germanized, centralized, extended the former police and spy system and surrendered the Empire to Catholicism.[2] The marxist and nationalist Hungarian György Szabad characterized Schwarzenberg's Administration as one of "unlimited absolutism."[3]

Of the Austrians, Joseph Redlich referred to the regime as simply "fraudulent"[4] while William Lingelbach called it a "polyglot polyarchy of pitiless reaction."[5] Victor Bibl censured the Viennese Administration for its continued reliance on the army, clergy and nobility.[6] Eva Priester held them responsible for introducing Josephinian forms without Josephinian content.[7]

After a general condemnation the critics' main target has always been the March Constitution. According to Albert Berzeviczy, writing in the 1920's, only Franz Joseph and Stadion regarded the March Constitution seriously.[8] Szabad rejects all notions that the Cabinet wanted to make the Constitution operative.[9] The Austrian Heinrich Friedjung accused Schwarzenberg of temporarily retreating into a sham constitutional position.[10] The promulgation of the new Imperial Constitution, wrote Redlich, opened an era of "conscious fraud."[11] The French historian Louis Eisenmann bluntly stated that the March Constitution was just an excuse for the dismemberment of Hungary.[12] In Professor Robert Kann's view the Government, except for Count Philipp Stadion and his collaborators, never seriously contemplated putting into practice the March Constitution.[13] The Canadian historian Stanley Pech depicted the Viennese Cabinet as generally conservative and contemptuous of the principle of constitutional government.[14]

The Minister President of the Cabinet, Schwarzenberg, was singled out by Gyula Szekfű as the man who prevented the realization of the provisions of the liberal March Constitution.[15] There is no concrete evidence in support of Kann's view that Schwarzenberg promoted uncompromising absolutism in unison with Kübeck and Bach[16] or, as Szabad believes, that the Minister President was "the most important inspirer of absolutism."[17] The same is true about Redlich's statement

that Schwarzenberg was impatient to "cast off the mask of liberalism."[18]
It is correct, however, that he did speak ill of the March Constitution
to receptive audiences such as Tsar Nicholas I of Russia or the Magyar
aristocrats.[19]

Schwarzenberg's Ministers, primarily Bach, were often attacked by
historians. Lingelbach said that Bach was an "advocate of absolutism
and reaction."[20] In Professor C. A. Macartney's judgment the Minister
of Interior turned the Government into an instrument of the Court's
Hungarian policies. Szekfű accused Bach of working for the withdrawal of the March Constitution;[22] the marxist Hungarian Imre
Révész of serving Catholic interest without reservation.[23] The American expert of the Period, Kenneth Rock, wrote recently:

> Bach functioned ably and energetically but despised by his former
> German liberal associates and by the disdainful aristocrats, he
> lacked the force, perhaps the will and certainly the authority of
> either the Minister President or his predecessor at the Ministry of
> the Interior to implement a genuine constitutional program.[24]

Friedjung condemned Bach's agrarian policies as mere political tac-
tics[25] and the American Andrew Brenman maintains that he had no
nationality policy at all.[26] Could this Bach be then the same person
whom A.J.P. Taylor called a dictator who used his power for revolutionary ends in the hope of an early realization of the March Constitution[27] which K. Tschuppik identified as "the final fruit of the
Revolution?"[28] The émigré Hungarian László Révész also praised
Bach for his effective application of the social principles which were
incorporated in the April Laws of 1848.[29] Eisenmann credited the
Minister for the lessening of social antagonism between the nobility
and the peasantry.[30] Kann claimed that between 1849 and 1854 Bach
was the executor of the revolutionary inheritance,[31] who until late in
1852 [the March Constitution was officially cancelled on 1 January
1852] as Taylor explained, did not give up the hope of crowning his
administrative work with a centralized liberal constitution.[32]

Count Leo Thun, another key member of the Schwarzenberg Cabinet, considered large numbers of schools and freedom of teaching
politically dangerous,[33] according to a university textbook which was
introduced in Hungary in 1973. Szekfű claimed that the school reforms of the absolutist period were prepared by domestic development
and European educational achievements, which "any other government would have executed—probably better."[34] Berzeviczy's views[35]
are less hostile to Thun while the analyses of Oszkár Sashegyi present
a more composite picture of Thun's educational policies.[36]

In general, the leading Austrian statesmen of the period were highly approved by the Austrian historians R. Charmatz,[37] H. Fournier[38] and Friedjung, the Hungarian Oszkár Sashegyi and Hanák[39] and the American George Barany[40] and Andrew Brenman. Most Austrian historians, including Robert Kann, viewed the Hungarian influence within the Habsburg empire as detrimental. Ivan Zolger[41] was anti-Hungarian and Friedjung, a staunch defender of the Habsburg ideal, and Karl Renner, an opponent of dualism, had little tolerance for Henrik Marczali's legalistic arguments on behalf of Hungarian autonomy.[42] But the executions in 1849 horrified friends and critics alike. The Government was accused of pursuing a course of deliberate, merciless, bloody and inhuman revenge and sanctioning Haynau's "lust for vengeance."[43] Gábor G. Kemény[44] and Zoltán Kramar[45] even invented the execution of thousands of brave freedom fighters by the allegedly blood-thirsty Haynau. Professor Miskolczy[46] and other writers sympathetic to the Dynasty, especially those Imperial historians who wrote when Franz Joseph still reigned over his Empire, always exonerated the Emperor from any responsibility for the executions.[47] Macartney joined their ranks when he divorced the Emperor from his oppressive governmental agencies.

> Under him [Franz Joseph] we hear little of the censorship, police espionage etc., which had been so notorious a feature of his grandfather's reign.[48]

In all fairness one must also quote another opinion of Professor Macartney:

> Francis Joseph, too must bear his share of the responsibility. If he had human scruples, he swallowed them.[49]

The Schwarzenberg-Bach Administration's Hungarian policies are judged variably by historians, except for the reign of Field Marshal Haynau which is universally condemned. In the 1950's Marxist Hungarian historians Aladár Mód,[50] Vilmos Sándor,[51] Iván Berend, György Ránki[52] and György Szabad spoke of colonization of Hungary by the Austrian upper bourgeoisie. The Viennese Government worked deliberately for the alienation of gentry and peasantry, commented Szabad before a freer spirit began to characterize Hungarian historiography in the 1960's.[53] These historians followed earlier Hungarian patriotic authors[54] who found Austria guilty of obstructing the development of agriculture in Hungary. The Government would serve, wrote Jaszi, "the cause of economic progress only so far as it was not opposed by the interest of the great landed proprietors."[55] Szekű developed the thesis of colonial dependence and Austria's deliberate blockage of Hungarian industrialization.[56]

Once historians began to pay more attention to economic developments during the Liberal Centralist Period, the brighter aspects of the Schwarzenberg-Bach Administration came to light. Formerly, in Hungary only a few, like Menyhért Lónyay,[57] Károly Keleti[58] and Ferenc Erdei[59] dared praise the achievements of the regime. More recently Péter Hanák suggested about the reign of Franz Joseph:

> Hungary was not a "dependent" country at least not in the sense by which dependence is associated with oppression, usurpation, or the notion of a semicolonial status.

To overcome her economic backwardness

> Hungary gained more advantages than disadvantages from her connection with the Austro-Hungarian empire.[60]

Hanák's views are shared today by Oszkár Sashegyi but opposed by the Hungarocentrist Szabad. Several studies of the American scholars Barany, Kenneth Rock and Brenman present a more realistic image of the era. Their task was difficult since a positive approach has often been discredited by both friendly and hostile commentators of the post-revolutionary reforms. Victor Tapié noted: Franz Joseph's

> reign marked a period of general technical progress, better living conditions for the majority of his subjects, the embellishment of cities and the blossoming of intellectual life and of the arts, achievements which, in another age, would have been accredited to his own person.[61]

Contrariwise, here is Lingelbach's characterization:

> All political life ceased, and intellectual torpor marks the period while material conditions became steadily worse.[62]

In failing to separate economic and constitutional developments, most treatments of the Liberal Centralist Period remain confusing.

Ideological considerations whether in favor of or against the Hungarian aristocracy, mar many historical studies dealing with this dominant segment of the Magyar ruling class. Hungarian historians represented the aristocrats as self-serving, unpatriotic and unrealistic politicians.[63] In Andics' mind the aristocrats were traitors and reactionaries—an assertion she was determined to prove in three bulky volumes.[64] Lajos Lukács tells us that the aristocratic leaders were hated and their program was alien to the aims of the nation.[65] Domokos Kosáry wrote that the activities of the Old Conservatives, the political wing of the aristocracy, were confined to the social, literary and scientific field.[66] Adhering to theories on class struggle, Szekfű,[67] Jaszi,[68] Emil Niederhausser,[69] Pál Sándor[70] and Szabad[71] advanced the thesis that after 1848 the Viennese Government, representing only the interest of the Austrian ruling class, extended special economic favors to the Hungarian aristocracy.

Karl Renner criticized the Old Conservatives for their endless pre-occupation with constitutional questions; [72] Redlich for considering themselves solely qualified to act as the political Magyar nation;[73] Kann for their "exclusivism" and "prolix" and "sterile" proposals.[74] Redlich added that the aristocrats

> pursued purely class politics and desired nothing more than the restoration to power in Hungary of their old aristocratic regime.[75]

As a result, wrote Tschuppik,[76] the Old Conservatives were without power in their own country and their program was opposed by the united lesser nobility and peasantry together with a small but active bourgeoisie. William Rogge suggested that they were "heading straight back toward the Middle Ages."[77] In harmony with the above views is Macartney's passage:

> [Hungary's] own aulic magnates regarded the land reform as sheer spoliation and from the outset adopted the attitude which soon hardened into the "Old Conservative" policy of pulling every wire within their reach to have the bulk of the April Laws undone.[78]

Recent American doctoral dissertations accepted the by now traditional condemnation of the aristocracy. Sylvia Medgyesi's notions that the Conservatives did not understand the intelligentsia and the nobility for whom "the tragic hero was Lajos Kossuth; the lost ideal, the republic of April 14, 1849."[79] Zoltán Kramar echoes Rogge's ultimate jibe on the "Middle Ages."[80] According to Brenman, the magnates were "unappreciative of the substantial role given them in railroad and industrial concessions."[81]

It is again the ever maverick Taylor and the most scholarly Sashegyi who provide the contrast. Taylor has no doubt that the Old Conservatives had the solid backing of the Hungarian nation in general,[82] while Sashegyi affirms the powerful impact of conservative forces between 1849 and 1867.[83]

The Hungarian historians, however, who usually reject the feasibility of the Old Conservative program, glorify with the same breath the Magyar gentry, its leadership of the nation and its passive resistance to Vienna. Ferenc Toldy, writing in the late 1850's, spoke of the Magyar civilizing mission in Eastern Europe and thus supplied the gentry with an "ideology" in preparation for a compromise with the Dynasty.[84] Gusztáv Wenzel developed the idea of Magyar manifest destiny.[85] György Gracza portrayed the passive resistance of a unified Hungarian nation.[86] Berzeviczy and Szekfű toned down the unqualified exhaltation of the middle nobility but those who wrote after them ignored their moderate approach. The standard way of characterizing the post-revolutionary era was to speak of passive resistance of all

Hungarians led by Deák and the Magyar gentry. Florence Forster's paragraph exemplifies this trend:

> The Hungary that emerged from the disaster of 1849 was at least a united Hungary; the nation which now looked to Deák as their guide and counsellor in the new campaign of passive resistance was no longer weakened by class distinctions nor hampered by the cumbrous relics of an obsolete feudalism.[87]

Zoltán Ferenczi, a biographer of Deák, in the absence of concrete evidence to prove where the former Minister of Justice stood politically in 1849 exclaimed in desperation that there was no need for justification because Deák had explained everything in 1848.[88] Szekfű interpreted Deák's silence from 1849 identically.[89] Strangely, Marxist Hungarian historians ignored the sharpening class struggle between the nobility and the peasantry and viewed the Hungarian social scene through red, white and green-colored glasses.[90] The uniformity of opinions must have motivated Kann to refer to Deák as the

> silent though unshakeable pivot of passive national resistance to the centralist reforms of Bach and Schwarzenberg, as well as the intellectual focal point of the movement for restoration.[91]

Medgyesi even invented the existence of a Party for her hero.

> The tactic of the Opposition Party, led by Deák was beginning to win more adherents during 1851. This passive resistance was marked not only by a refusal to serve the government, but even by a refusal to support the government by the payment of taxes.[92]

In the presence of these confusing interpretations, it is the intention of this study to clarify the situation in Hungary during the Liberal Centralist Era. This aim can be best achieved by examining, firstly, the desired and actual impact of the Liberal Centralist Administration on Hungary, and, secondly, the political, cultural and socio-economic activities of the Hungarian ruling class in response to Vienna's policies between 1849 and 1853. Once a differentiation is made between the Viennese Liberal Centralists and Absolutist Centralists, their attitude towards Hungary, the power-relationship between these groups and the two components of the Hungarian ruling class, the aristocracy and the gentry, a better understanding of the complex situation in existence during the Liberal Centralist Era becomes possible.

The undertaking of such an enterprise can now be initiated because of the availability of new sources. After the Second World War the National Archives of Hungary began the systematization and establishment of a special section for documents concerning the political administration and the civil service of the post-Világos era in Hungary. The organization of the collection, which besides Hungarian material, contains documents received in the 1920's from the Viennese archives, was finally completed in the mid-1960's and a guide to it was published by Oszkár Sashegyi.[93] Due to Sashegyi's archival organizational work, the rich collection of *Stimmungsberichte,* a set of public opinion reports sent regularly, at first bi-weekly and later monthly, to central authorities by local officials, local police, gendarmerie and army officers, became easily accessible.

The Simor Collection of Manuscripts in the National Széchenyi Library, also located in Budapest, which contains the private post-revolutionary correspondence of two prominent clerics and which has not yet been subjected to scholarly analysis was partially explored by the author of this study.

The multi-volume collection of documents from the *Haus-, Hof-, und Staatsarchiv* and the *Verwaltungsarchiv* was published almost at the same time as Sashegyi's volume. This outstanding collection of Friedrich Walter contains new material from the post-revolutionary period dealing mainly with governmental policies.[94] Sashegyi's rich compilation on workers and peasants and Andics's on the aristocracy and the Catholic Hierarchy were valuable to my research. The reading of the daily press of the early 1850's, primarily the *Pesti Napló*, in addition to Dávid Angyal's document collection on the press give a fascinating insight into power-relations during the Period. With the aid of these works, a re-orientation in the anarchy of opinions about the Liberal Centralist Period can now be undertaken.

None of this labor would have had any chance of success without the advice and constant encouragement of Professor Emeritus Milos Mladenovic, McGill University, Dr. Oszkár Sashegyi of the National Archives of Hungary and my wife, Helen. I wish to share with them any praise that the book may earn but for shortcomings responsibility rests entirely on my shoulders.

I

The Liberal Centralists and Their Hungarian Policies

In the middle of the nineteenth century the Habsburgs were struggling against national liberalism by using a tempered version of the same ideology in the interest of the survival of the Dynasty and its power. The revolutionary governments of 1848 in Vienna and Pest-Buda had to be replaced by a viable, potentially popular government and not by a resurrected Metternich regime.

The traditional pillars of the Empire showed cracks in 1848; the clergy became nationalistic, the bureaucracy liberal or, at least, enlightened, and the army undisciplined. To sustain the Empire, reforms became necessary. The clergy had to be placated and the Imperial Bureaucracy reassured that Joseph II's revolution from above could be continued with substantial modifications to suit the times, that is, without interference from the aristocracy but with sufficient social support to deter the national-liberal intellectuals of Vienna, Prague and Pest-Buda.[1] Prince Felix Schwarzenberg devised such a program for the Dynasty and formed a cabinet for its execution. The middle classes of Cisleithania[2] provided the initial social base for the Habsburg restoration and rejuvenation.

> After the troubled years 1848 and 1849, the world of big business, and also that of the petty bourgeoisie and the artisan class, needed an assurance of tranquility: the former therefore encouraged the establishment of a strong government and efficient administration, which the latter accepted as necessary for the security of their political ideal.[3]

The Austrian middle classes viewed with satisfaction the Dynasty's efforts to dominate in Germany. They were willing to forsake direct participation in state affairs. In return, the Habsburgs consented to modernize the Empire provided that their power and the territorial unity of their domains remained basically intact and their imperial ambitions fulfilled. Blessed by both the middle classes and the House of Habsburg, the new Administration of Schwarzenberg decided to build centralized constitutional monarchy for seventy million Germans and Austrians. Schwarzenberg's chief concern was economic and political union with Germany under Habsburg leadership. He wished to make Austria a Great Power dominant in Central Europe. To achieve this aim the Empire had to be strengthened and transformed into a modern state through efficient administration and government inspired economic growth.[4] Between 1848 and 1851 Schwarzenberg and his Cabinet reasoned that liberal economic policies and the establishment of a centralized constitutional monarchy might provide a foundation for their imperial goals in Germany. There is evidence that, at this time, Schwarzenberg earnestly believed in measured constitutional and popular liberties. When he presented his Ministry to the Imperial Parliament, the *Reichstag,* in Kremsier on 27 November 1848, his address, coauthored by several Cabinet members, was a lyrical and possibly earnest profession of faith in liberalism and constitutional monarchy.[5] He spoke of his desire for an empire with a constitution, equality of nationalities, termination of secrecy within the state administration, communal autonomy to form the basis of a free state, legal compensation for loss of corvée or *robot* and the separation of the judicial system from administration. At the Cabinet meeting on 26 May 1849 Schwarzenberg further expounded the views that the Government should represent the interest of all social classes and offer tangible material advantages in addition to an orderly state. The Government wanted to provide the legal pre-conditions for prosperity to gain the loyalty of the citizens.[6] A week later the Minister President forwarded one of his key ministers', Alexander Bach's, Cabinet approved memorandum to Franz Joseph. They wanted to eliminate all anti-centralist institutions without offending ethnic or local customs and traditions. Instead of relying on one class, the Government planned to opt for an equitable socio-political stance in search of a broader and, consequently, securer social base for policies to be carried out by its own civil servants.[7] Bach was determined to deny power to the aristocracy but an attempt was made to obtain the cooperation of the *Reichstag.* The Cabinet groped for sympathetic support from the "correct thinking" middle classes, which dominated Parliament, because they perceived that recognition of bourgeois interests would give stability to the Government's rule.[8]

The Imperial Parliament, which opened in Vienna on 22 July 1848 and later transferred to Kremsier, did not reflect a balanced representation of the peoples of the Empire. There were only Cisleithanian delegates, Hungary remained unrepresented. Most Slavic members, who formed a majority in the *Reichstag,* were of middle class origin. Among the parliamentary delegates from Bohemia-Moravia, there were very few aristocrats, peasants or clergymen.[9] German representatives were also mainly of bourgeois origin, whose views ranged from Left to Center and Right, that is, from radical liberalism to progressive conservatism. Count Stadion led the Center, a small group of Tyrolese, Lower and Upper Austrian delegates. He was also influential with the Right whose support was, however, insufficient to prevent the majority from drafting highly objectionable parts to what the Government otherwise considered an acceptable Constitution.[10]

Both the *Reichstag* and the Cabinet worked for democratic-bourgeois constitutionalism and for the preservation of the House of Habsburg and its European Great Power position, but they differed in their interpretation of democratic rule and the constitutional role of the Emperor. The Parliament's constitutional draft, completed at Kremsier, democratized the state on both provincial and central levels, while the Government favored a stronger central power and democratization on the lower levels of administration. The Kremsier Left wanted a constitutional monarchy in the proper sense of the term, while Stadion favored greater executive and legislative power for the Monarch. There was, nevertheless, continuous meaningful dialogue between the Parliament and Schwarzenberg's Cabinet for about two months. In January, 1849, commenting on Chapter One of the Kremsier Draft, which endorsed popular sovereignty, Minister of Interior Count Philipp Stadion suggested that participation in government was not the right of the people but a favor bestowed by a gracious ruler. The *Reichstag* rejected Stadion's interpretation.[11] Once Parliament disputed the sovereignty of the Monarch, the Government saw no other option but to dissolve it.

Their failure at Kremsier, however, did not mean the complete failure of liberalism or that the Government would turn a deaf ear to future bourgeois representations. The middle classes were compensated with an octroied Constitution and an "enlightened conservative bureaucracy tinged with liberal doctrines."[12] Although this alternative Constitution, composed almost in its entirety by Stadion, was never officially adopted for the whole Empire, it should not be treated as a sham constitution. The Schwarzenberg-Bach Administration began the gradual implementation of the Constitution and most of the Cabinet Ministers attempted to safeguard its spirit until they were gradually overwhelmed by internal reaction, court intrigues and an unfavorable international political climate.

On 4 March 1849 Franz Joseph signed the Constitution and the members of the Cabinet countersigned to validate it in strict conformity with Article 18 in Chapter Two of the same Charter.[13] The First Chapter described the Empire as a constitutional monarchy (Article Two) within which all peoples were equal and had inalienable rights to sustain and cultivate their respective languages (Article Five). The Seventh Article ordered the elimination of all existing internal tariff walls and the establishment of a tariff union. Vienna was to remain the Imperial capital (Article Three) from where power would be exercised over the Crownlands (Article Two) which were allowed to continue the use of their emblems and colors (Article Eight).

The Second Chapter dealt with the Emperor's rights and duties. He was to take an oath to the Constitution (Article Thirteen) and was to have the laws which he issued countersigned by his Ministers (Article Eighteen), but otherwise the Sovereign was not responsible to any Imperial institution (Article Fourteen). The Emperor was to appoint the Ministers (Article Nineteen), declare war and peace, contract treaties with foreign powers (Article Seventeen) and give pardon and grant amnesty.

Chapter Three outlined the rights of citizens. It introduced a uniform legal system and established the institution of citizenship (Articles Twenty-Three and Twenty-Four), equality before the law (Article Twenty-Seven), and personal freedom for all individuals residing in or entering Austrian territory (Article Twenty-Six), in addition to freedom of movement and emigration. The Articles from Twenty-Nine to Thirty-Two elaborated on property rights, especially on the right of compensation and free trade for all.

Chapter Four elaborated on the elective principle and the autonomy of municipalities. The jurisdiction of the Crownlands was extensibly circumscribed in Chapter Five and most affairs of the State were referred to the central Government (Chapter Six). The next two chapters commented on the Imperial and Crownland Assemblies and Crownland Constitutions. In Chapter Ten (Article Eighty-Seven) the Emperor was authorized to issue laws with the approval of his ministers whenever the Assemblies would not be in session and delay would be harmful. The Constitution made provisions for the establishment of an advisory body—the Imperial Council or *Reichsrat*—to aid the Crown (Chapter Eleven). Chapters Twelve and Thirteen stipulated the separation of administrative and judicial bodies, the independence of judges, the use of juries, especially in cases of political and press violations, and the central control of the judiciary. The laws of Hungary were to be maintained except when they contradicted the provisions of the Imperial Constitution (Article Seventy-One), but the territory of Hungary was limited to Inner Hungary[14] (Articles Seventy-Two, Seventy-Three and Seventy-Four). Finally, the *de jure* introduction of the Constitution was temporarily postponed.

All in all, Count Stadion's constitutional edifice promised to bring the Empire's industrial, commercial and professional classes to the threshold of political power. These groups reasoned that they would not be neglected in the future, because many of Schwarzenberg's Ministers were of middle class origin. The leading members of the Cabinet, the Liberal Centralist Bach, Bruck and Krauss believed in the rejuvenation of Austria through the creation of a centralized state with a modern economy.[15]

A close friend of Stadion, and his eventual replacement in the Cabinet, was Alexander Bach.[16] Between 1849 and 1853 he became the executor of Stadion's political testament. His prime concerns, however, were not political liberties, but administrative, economic and social reforms. His policies were "to give rising industry and commerce, as well as within limits the economically more prosperous parts of the professional classes ('property and intelligence') a chance to make their political weight felt more decidedly."[17] Until 1852 Bach would not relinquish the hope of applying Stadion's Constitution.[18]

Another believer in the Constitution was Charles Louis von Bruck, the son of a commoner and a successful industrialist, who joined the Administration in 1849. He, like Bach, intended with middle class support to initiate a new commercial policy in Austria and later within Greater Germany through the creation of a common market.

Philipp von Krauss and Ferdinand von Thinnfeld, other members of the Cabinet, also expected the economic and subsequent political rejuvenation of the Empire. Krauss favored the issuance of laws that would foster the emergence of a strong and affluent peasantry.[19] A. Paton, a contemporary English journalist who toured Austria and Hungary in 1850, was impressed by the progressive economic measures planned for Hungary as they were outlined to him by Thinnfeld. During his stay in the Imperial capital where he witnessed the presence of talented individuals in the sphere of public administration, he became convinced about the liberalism of the Viennese Government.[20] Paton's views were confirmed by a Hungarian journalist who, in addition, stated that even the police had its large share of liberal bureaucrats.[21]

Since all domestic opposition, military and political, had been overcome or, at least, brought under control by the late summer of 1849,
the Schwarzenberg-Bach Administration was unhindered in their
effort to create suitable conditions for the expansionist foreign policy
program in Germany. The key to success lay mainly with Hungary. It
was thought that if Hungary would support modernization emanating
from Vienna, the other nationalities would agree to limited autonomy.
This was not an unreasonable assumption, because an agreement on
the nationality question was already reached by Slavs and Germans
at Kremsier and their solution was included with some modifications
in the March Constitution. The basic question, then, was, how to
rejuvenate Hungary for the benefit of the Empire as a whole and the
Hungarian population.

The Liberal Centralist Government attempted to realize its main
objectives in Inner Hungary from 1849 to 1853. The Administration
governed in the spirit of the Constitution. The Charter, however, was
not officially implemented with the justification that a premature
introduction would be impractical as long as the maintenance of the
state of siege was necessary. During this time the Government wished
to integrate Hungary into the Empire using both Constitutional principles and oppressive methods.

From June 1849 to December 1850, Hungary was under military
rule. This regime was to lay the groundwork for a permanent administrative system. The Imperial Army was to retain control until the
Government was firmly established and the threat of a new uprising
would disappear. Nevertheless, the Military did not have a free hand.
On 4 June 1849, Baron Geringer, Councillor in the Ministry of Interior
and Bach's trusted official, was appointed Commissioner in charge of
the civil administration in Inner Hungary.[22] Geringer and General
Haynau, who had become military governor of Hungary just five days
earlier, were to apply Bach's program to Hungary with "carrot and
stick."

The new policy could not be enforced until the armies of Kossuth
were defeated. The primary task was, therefore, to pacify Hungary.
Austrian victory came quickly with Russian intervention.[23] The main
Hungarian Army of General Görgey surrendered at Világos on
13 August 1849. To prevent a new uprising and to consolidate discipline in the Imperial Army, the Government decided to punish the
revolutionary leaders as well as the soldiers of Kossuth, the honvéds
and, specifically, those officers who had defected to the Hungarians.
Franz Joseph and his Cabinet were determined to treat the Magyar

leaders with severity and punish the most dangerous revolutionaries. The young Emperor personally accepted the arguments of Schwarzenberg for the necessity of expiation and a terror striking example.[24]

> He [Schwarzenberg] wanted to punish the compromised ones with the greatest severity and said that many heads were yet to fall as the tallest poppies drop when mowed,

wrote General Kempen in his diary on 26 July 1849.[25]

The Cabinet selected General Haynau to bring Hungary under martial rule. He was well qualified for the task because of his successes at suppressing local rebellions in Lombardy. During the first three months of his tour Haynau was preoccupied with the conduct of war so the full demonstration of Austrian power had to be delayed until the establishment of military courts and the complete defeat of independent Hungary.

On 1 July 1849 Haynau informed the Hungarian population of his appointment. He reminded the people that the state of siege, imposed in October 1848, had not been lifted and that, as a result, all political crimes committed since that date would come under the jurisdiction of summary military courts. He promised severe punishment to ex-members of the Hungarian revolutionary Parliament, National Defense Commissioners and those persons who would attempt in any way to impede the progress of the Imperial Army.[26] Three days later Haynau ordered the establishment of military courts in Hungary and Transylvania.[27] Seven courts were soon set up, the main ones in Pest-Buda and Arad.[28] Although the authorities promised death sentences even for the wearing of national colors, very few executions took place before October 1849.

Foreign powers exerted pressure on Austria not to persecute the Hungarian insurgents after Világos. Palmerston instructed the British Ambassador in Vienna to investigate extreme Austrian cruelties.[29] England cautioned the Austrian Cabinet repeatedly. So did Russia. Tsar Nicholas I thought it politically wise to promise amnesty to the rebels. General Paskevich, Commander of the Russian interventionist forces, also urged Austria to give amnesty to those rebel officers who wished to join the allies.[30] The French Foreign Minister de Tocqueville urged moderation as well.[31]

The Austrian Government rejected all interference in the internal affairs of the Empire, but by the end of August 1849 the Cabinet began to yield. Haynau was informed that no execution could take place without the consent of the Cabinet. However, Schmerling, Minister of Justice, later modified the minutes of August 31 by deleting

the original third paragraph which made Cabinet approval manda-
tory. He rewrote the lines to read that "if a death sentence had been
carried out, such a case must be reported to Vienna."[32] The Cabinet
raised no objection.

Vienna gave Haynau extra time to carry out the original policy of
reprisal. The General planned to hang the prominent rebels and shoot
former Imperial officers.

> I would hang all the leaders, shoot all the Austrian officers who had
> entered the enemy's service, and have reduced to the rank of private
> all those Hungarian officers who had earlier served us either in
> civilian capacities or as sergeants. I accept the responsibility for this
> terrible example to the Army and to the world.[33]

During the autumn months Haynau and his military courts delivered
a dreadful blow to Hungary. Death sentences were pronounced and
actually carried out on 114 individuals, 89 of whom were former
Imperial officers.[34] Moreover, an additional 386 persons were sentenced to death but their sentences were commuted to prison terms.
No less than 1,765 people were imprisoned.[35]

From the Austrian point of view, captured Hungarians who had
forsaken their allegiance to the legitimate sovereign were not to be
granted the treatment accorded to prisoners-of-war. The Emperor
himself believed that military honor called for exemplary expiation.[36]
The situation in the Army gave substance to his conviction. According
to intelligence reports, many young officers of Haynau's Third Army
were of radical disposition and in conflict with their ultra-conservative
generals and senior officers.[37] Albeit the maintenance of military discipline remained vital in post-revolutionary Austria, the Cabinet at its
meeting of 26 October 1849 concluded that they had made their point.
The position of August 31 was reiterated to protect Austria's good
name and to prevent senseless revenge or reprisal.[38] Haynau's courts
continued sentencing many ex-officers and revolutionaries, but the
observant newspaper reader of the times could safely conclude that
the worst was over; the dailies duly reported how Haynau commuted
all death sentences to prison terms.

The executions did not start with the Imperial rule. During the
Civil War, Hungarian revolutionary tribunals had 154 suspects executed. In the Pest district alone 123 persons had been shot without
benefit of trial. Kossuth's Transylvanian courts sentenced 478 individuals to death and an additional 4,834 were massacred by his supporters.[39] From the fall of 1848 to the summer of 1849 military courts
active near the Southern Front ordered the execution of 467 persons,

mainly Serbs. On 22 March 1849 the Hungarian General Mór Perczel's firing squads shot 45 Serbs.[40] "There were insane people," wrote the radical daily *Pesti Napló* in 1850, "who parodized terror during the revolutionary period, but even the parody was horrible because it took many innocent lives."[41] From the humanist point of view the terror of the Counter-Revolution emerged favorably in comparison with the terror of the Revolution.

To prevent a new uprising, Haynau had to decide the fate of the former *honvéd* officers, soldiers and national guardsmen. Public security was seriously endangered by wandering and often armed veterans of the Revolution. On 20 August 1849 Haynau ordered that all former members of Kossuth's Army be redrafted and removed from Hungary.[42] Eventually, Haynau decreed the enrollment of all *honvéd* officers as well as of common *honvéds* and national guardists into Imperial units stationed outside Hungary. Their drafting proved to be an impossible task, since towards the end of the Civil War the revolutionary armed forces numbered about one hundred thousand. There were no local administrators or *gendarmes* to assist the Third Army's military police in carrying out this task. Even when a new administration was established, the recruitment of former *honvéd* officers was sabotaged by some village officials.[43] Many *honvéds* went into hiding or resumed civilian life far from their original residence. A few thousand fled to the Ottoman Empire.

According to various estimates, forty to fifty thousand *honvéds* were finally enrolled, but many were considered a part of the regular Hungarian contribution to the Imperial draft.[44] As the regime consolidated, the Army released most veterans of the Revolution who were actually a potential hazard to army discipline. In 1850 Haynau liberated all national guardists and *honvéds* over the age of 38, only sons and those who supplied substitute or paid the Treasury 500 forints. The defenders of Fortress Komárom, the last revolutionary stronghold, and 3,000 refugees who had been repatriated received amnesty.[45] Deserters were exonerated by the Minister of War before the end of 1850.[46] The Emperor pardoned those officers who had left the Imperial Army without the retention of their ranks.[47] However, punitive enlistment remained in force against *honvéd* officers who were enrolled as ordinary soldiers in various Imperial regiments where they eventually became a particularly volatile element.[48]

In addition to the consolidation of army discipline through executions and the removal of rebels from the scene through temporary drafting, the Army attempted to control the population and purge the civil service of disloyal elements. The free flow of information was to be restricted. Foreigners could not enter Hungary without a special army permit.[49] The Military supplied local authorities with information and requested their cooperation concerning the possible influx of foreign and émigré revolutionary publications.[50] Local archives were searched for subversive materials. Minutes of Protestant church meetings compiled during the Revolution were designated for destruction.[51] The Army introduced compulsory internal passports or travelling certificates to control the movements of potential troublemakers, foreign agents and the population in general. Anyone on a journey had to register with local authorities within 24 hours of arrival.[52] Any person found without valid passport was arrested, jailed and then either drafted or deported to his place of domicile. Round-ups were common in Pest and Buda and received widespread coverage in the local press.

At times the Military equated control with interference in the daily lives of the population or with plain terror. The wearing of *honvéd* uniforms, the use of revolutionary colors and symbols and the sporting of Kossuth beards were forbidden.[53] All firearms, including hunting rifles, were confiscated. Angry generals occasionally ordered the flogging of non-cooperative local officials and punished entire cities with heavy fines.[54] To the great embarrassment of the Government, Haynau was determined to punish the Hungarian Jewish community *en bloc* by fining them for their support of the Kossuth regime.[55] An elderly bishop was put into irons and at Arad a baroness was publicly flogged for hiding a *honvéd* officer.[56] Hungarian historians used this latter incident, allegedly ordered by Haynau, to denigrate the regime. Oscar Jászi blamed Haynau and spoke of "carefully selected brutalities" and "whipping of women."[57] No historian of the period, however, reported any flogging of ladies except for the case at Arad. Personal responsibility even for this action was denied by Haynau in an interview.[58] Nevertheless, excesses were visible. The Cabinet, anxious to eliminate all extreme measures, deprived the Army of its major role in pacification. Only the military courts kept temporarily their jurisdiction over civilians.

On 1 September 1849 Haynau ordered all civil servants to appear within three months before one of his military courts to give an account of their activities during the Revolution.[59] As the counties were reorganized all new applicants for governmental positions were screened. Politically compromised ones were rejected. Instead, representatives of non-Magyar nationalities were encouraged to apply and

individuals who had been purged by the Kossuth regime were rein-
stated. Teachers, clergymen and members of the legal profession were
also obliged to appear before the courts. The military prosecutors
paid special attention to judges of the revolutionary courts in order
to establish whether they had voted for death sentences during the
Civil War.[60] The purge of the state apparatus had nearly been completed in 1849 when Haynau transferred its administration to civilian
courts.

The purge was just one aspect of the administrative work in Hungary. Bach did not want to see a military dictatorship. Rather he used
Haynau's firmness to maintain tight control over the Hungarians
while his civil servants oriented themselves and gradually took charge
of Hungary. The Army was loyal to the Crown but not necessarily to
the Liberal Centralist Cabinet. The aristocratic officer corps despised
the reformers and the generals resented the curtailment of their powers
over civilians.

Schwarzenberg and his Ministers urgently needed a loyal and efficient administration and a law enforcement agency for the projected
modernization of Hungary. The Cabinet submitted a proposal, based
on Bach's plan for the administrative reorganization of the Empire,
to Franz Joseph, suggesting a new political regime for Hungary. The
draft was accepted and the patent was issued on 25 October 1849.[61]
The Law intimated that the ancient Hungarian Constitution had been
destroyed by the Revolution and emphasized the unity of the Empire
and the equality of the nationalities. The executive power remained
in the hands of the Commander-in-Chief of all troops in Hungary
(Haynau). He was to safeguard public order and security, administer
military laws and all activities related to the state of siege. An Imperial
Commissioner (Geringer), directly responsible to the Minister of the
Interior (Bach), was to work with the Commander. Geringer became
the head of the Hungarian civil administration, the guarantor of state
security, the coordinator between the various local branches of the
government and their corresponding Viennese ministries.

Inner Hungary was divided into five military districts, namely:
Sopron, Pozsony, Kassa, Pest-Buda and Nagyvárad, each governed
by a military commander. The equivalent civil position was that of the
ministerial commissioners who, according to Bach, were to lessen the
impact of military rule and supervise the uniform introduction of the
new system.[62] They were responsible to the Imperial Commissioner
and the Minister of the Interior. Each military district contained two
or three civil districts, which, in turn, consisted of three or four

counties. The civil districts were administered by District Chief Commissioners who formed the backbone of the administration. Bach entrusted them with eliminating all traces of the revolutionary regime and securing the support of the population for the reforms. The chief commissioners were to pay special attention to municipal affairs, public schools, charitable institutions, cultural affairs, public health, the state of jails and the development of agriculture, industry and transportation. County Chiefs and other civil servants were appointed on their recommendations. The counties were further subdivided into boroughs. The Borough Commissioners were to establish residence at the borough seat, which was to be centrally located for the convenience of the population. Following the census of 1850, Geringer planned to reorganize the boroughs, giving a clear majority in each to one of the nationalities, but where that could not be realized, a special office was to be created to safeguard the interest of the national minorities.[63] The official language of administration was the language of the locality. District commissioners used German among themselves and for correspondence with the Military and authorities outside Hungary.

The judicial system also had to be remodeled because the civil servants of the districts, counties, boroughs and municipalities were forbidden by the March Constitution to administer justice to the population. After the failure of the Revolution there was no active court system in Hungary for months except for the Imperial military and summary courts. A provisional court system began to take shape from November 1849. The press regularly listed the names of the new appointees to the various district and other courts.[64] The seat of a new supreme court with a special Hungarian section was instituted in Vienna. On behalf of the Minister of Justice, a commissioner toured the country and with the assistance of local officials selected judges for the courts.[65]

To modernize Hungary, together with the rest of the Empire, Bach wanted reliable, efficient and progressive judicial and civil administrators. Geringer, in September, 1849, ordered the formation of a Disciplinary Committee to examine the behavior of administrators and pensioned officials during the Revolution. For the Membership of this Committee he chose loyal Hungarians acquainted with the branches of the government under scrutiny. The serious cases were transferred to the military courts.[66] Considering that most Hungarian administrators remained active during the Revolution and the fact that an enlarged civil service became necessary for the execution of the reform program, the purges had to be limited in scope.

Political reliability was not the only prerequisite for entering public service. An administrator was expected to be an expert in his field and familiar with local conditions and language. Anyone who, for example, on concluding his university studies, wished to work for the state in a position which required legal training, was obliged to take a state examination. However, since the Government needed many qualified officials in Hungary, the examination requirements were temporarily eased, although, in 1850, for the theoretical part of the entrance examination, the candidate still had to travel to Vienna, Prague or another designated city *outside* Inner Hungary.[67] The contemporary Hungarian press praised the introduction of the new testing device as a limit on nepotism and an instrument for the advancement of middle class talent.[68]

Geringer did not welcome civil servants who were unfamiliar with the Magyar parts of Hungary.[69] The few administrators who were transferred from other Crownlands were urged to learn the local language. Bach himself studied Hungarian and planned to address Hungarian delegates in their own tongue.[70] Geringer told the county chiefs to send their orders to Magyar municipalities in Hungarian in conformity with the March Constitution.[71] In 1850, in a speech at Pest, he admonished local authorities to teach and lead the people, live amongst them and be aware of public opinion. Geringer exhorted them to avoid bureaucratic methods and adopt simple and systematic business procedures in their work.[72]

The Imperial Commissioner realized that proper execution of administrative reforms ultimately depended on the cooperation of the civil servants. However, as long as the nobility maintained its stranglehold on the local administration of Hungary, the success of all reforms remained in jeopardy.

Since neither the Army nor the new Hungarian civil service could be completely trusted to carry out the planned modernization, Bach introduced to Hungary his own internal security agency, the *gendarmerie*. The Army was unwilling and also unable to maintain law and order without military dictatorship. In the tradition of seigneurial justice, the aristocratic and gentry administrators did not always apply the law equally. In addition, the Hungarian county police, the *pandúrs*, were politically unreliable and often acted as receivers for local highwaymen.[73] The active supporters of the regime and the new administrators needed protection, a feeling of security, and a trustworthy and competent law enforcement agency close at hand.[74] In that the improvement of public security had long been an item on the programs of many Austrian reforms and since there was an obvious need for an absolutely loyal instrument, it was not surprising that one of Bach's first acts as Minister of Interior was the creation of the *gendarmerie*.

Originally the Empire had 16 regiments comprising 2,500 mounted and 12,000 foot *gendarmes*. Together with their officers they numbered 15,573.[75] In many parts of the Empire the organization of the *gendarmerie* proceeded slowly. On 31 December 1850 the *Bote für Tirol und Vorarlberg* complained of the shortage of recruits.[76] The first *gendarmerie* regiment commander for Hungary, Count M. Pálffy, began his work in June, 1849.[77] By December, 1849 there were three regiments, the fifth, sixth and seventh, 1,500 in strength.[78] Recruitment was intensive but only partially successful. Many Magyar soldiers and officers had to be transferred from line units to the new security forces.[79] In order to maintain a high morale, these cadres of the army were now, as *gendarmes*, well paid, housed, armed and clothed.[80] Until the *gendarmerie* units familiarized themselves with local conditions they coordinated their police work with the *pandúrs* and the Army.

In January, 1850 a provisional law regulated the organization and jurisdiction of the *gendarmerie*. Bonuses were promised for convictions obtained following arrests. Heavier sentences brought higher bonuses.[81] At first, political work was emphasized but by the end of 1849, regular police duties became equally important. Good use was made of the large number of denunciations. Stool-pigeons were recruited from the population. The *gendarme's* integrity and reputation among the peasants soon superseded that of the *pandúr's*.[82] The internal security force became the protectors of the counter-revolution and the new reforms. The *gendarmerie* mitigated the rule of the Army and the Hungarian ruling class. The Force provided an improved climate for the orderly modernization of Hungary's economy.

The civil service, the judiciary and the *gendarmerie* together formed the necessary framework for the Liberal Centralist economic program. A healthy economy was to be the ultimate weapon in the pacification of the Empire. Without it the internal conditions for Schwarzenberg's foreign policies could not be met. In the field of economic rejuvenation, however, the Administration faced seemingly insoluble problems.

The Civil War had been an enormous drain on the financial resources of the Empire. In 1848 and 1849, in addition to increased military expenses, the royal coffers were deprived of incomes normally originating in Hungary and Italy. The national debt increased in one year from 914 to 1,358 million guldens.[83] The problem was not the amount. In mid-century the per capita national debt of England was eight times greater and France's double that of Austria. The Habsburg Empire had only started its industrial revolution and now the sudden rise of state indebtedness posed a threat to the Government's reform program by placing an intolerable burden on the Treasury and ultimately on the taxpayers. Once the Civil War and the Revolutions were terminated, the budget deficit was almost halved, but the Army still received 124 million out of a total income of 191 million guldens.[84] The Government's foreign policies and the pacification of the Empire were costly enterprises.

The Cabinet's difficulties multiplied in Hungary where there was no indigenous class of entrepreneurs and no modern transportation and communication system. Moreover, the Civil War and the Russian Intervention had caused much material damage throughout the country. The Government, nevertheless, began the task of rejuvenation in 1849 as soon as the pacification of Hungary was completed. The most forbidding barriers obstructing the development of capitalism in Hungary were lifted, thus opening up an era of prosperity and paving the way for a modern economy.

The first task was consolidation. In 1848 radical changes had taken place in property relations. The Hungarian diet freed the serfs, gave them land and liberated them from most feudal obligations. The villeins received free land while in Cisleithania the peasants were obliged to pay one-third of the cost of compensation to their former lords. In Hungary, the *robot* was redeemed exclusively from state funds.

During Hungary's War of Independence Imperial commissioners assigned to Russian and Austrian troops advised the Hungarian population that there would be no return to the pre-1848 property arrangements and that the Government would assist the people in retaining the fruits of the Revolution.[85] The Imperial patents of 7 July 1849 and of 25 September 1850 and Haynau's address of 9 July 1849, in conformity with Article 87 of the March Constitution, further clarified the situation.[86] The Government repeatedly reassured the peasants concerning the legality of their newly acquired liberties and lands.

The Liberal Centralists wished to enhance the economic position of the nobility as well. Advance compensation payment for lost *robot* was promised to all landlords. Only public and private institutions, including the churches, and persons who had emigrated illegally or been convicted or accused of high treason did not receive advances.

For the latter two groups ultimate compensation was not excluded. From the end of 1849 cash advance payments were to be paid. Thirty forints was allotted for each full serf section and five forints for the lot of a cottager, that is for his *robot* obligation, making a total of seven million forints.[87] A Crownland fund was set up to assign advances and compensation. The capital was guaranteed by the state at five per cent annual interest. The advances were charged against earned or future interest payments on compensation.[88] Back taxes were deducted from the advances and mortgage holders were entitled to interest payments. Therefore, Haynau's insistence on strict political clearance as a condition for obtaining advances could not be observed without threatening the investments of the Austrian upper-middle class, the major mortgage holders in Hungary.[89]

Payments were disbursed slowly due to complicated administrative procedures and because many former landlords would not apply for the advance in fear of police investigation.[90] As a result, by 1851, only a million forints had been distributed in Hungary—much to the displeasure of both the former landlords and the Viennese Cabinet. Bach launched an investigation as early as October, 1850 and then instructed Geringer to improve the regulations concerning advances and eliminate completely the political reliability clauses to expedite a rapid flow of cash.[91] This was necessary because the change from the Kossuth currency to an Imperial one resulted in financial losses for many Hungarians.

To regain Magyar confidence in the Austrian currency was an essential part of the Liberal Centralists' consolidation drive. On 14 November 1849 the editor of the Pest daily, *Figyelmező*, wrote:

> The Hungarian people is still calm. It is time, nevertheless, to appeal
> to the Head of State. The Government should be interested in
> noticing signs of trouble, e.g., the currency situation.

It is true that the introduction of the exclusive use of Austrian currency and the cancellation of 62 million Kossuth forints,[92] not backed by reserves, did create jolts in the economy but there were no visible signs of social or political trouble as the *Figyelmező* would have one believe. As far back as 3 October 1848, Vienna had declared the issuance of monies its exclusive right. When the independent Hungarian Government printed a new currency it was immediately discounted by the business community and the cautious segments of the population began hoarding the old gold and silver pieces still in circulation. In 1848, Kossuth's Minister of Interior threatened currency speculators and black marketeers with summary courts in an attempt to maintain the value of the money. Nevertheless, the decline of the Kossuth forint could not be halted. The merchants of Pest gradually abandoned its use and the population slowly followed their example.[93] In 1849, during the spring offensive of the Hungarian revolutionary armies, there was renewed confidence in a Kossuth victory. Consequently, some of the worthless currency remained in the hands of optimists, causing difficulties in trade and payment of debts and taxes after Világos.

The monetary policies of the Liberal Centralist Government aimed at both destroying the economy of Revolutionary Hungary and creating a stable financial base for Imperial Hungary. "I proclaimed the Kossuth money illegal," wrote Haynau to Radetzky. "This order is essential to cut their throats."[94] The Imperial Minister of Finance had explained earlier to the reluctant Field Marshal Windischgrätz, military dictator of Hungary in early 1849, that the circulation of Hungarian bank notes must be disallowed because their continuous use would provide a dangerous weapon for the enemy and would place an unwarranted burden on the loyal Crownlands and the Imperial bank.[95] By July, 1849 Kossuth bills were not accepted as legal tender in territories under Imperial rule. Windischgrätz allowed the temporary circulation of small Kossuth bills with one or two forints face value. In March and April of 1849 the population could convert them at par into Austrian funds. All larger denominations were declared worthless.[96] As the Imperial troops penetrated Hungary, their generals ordered the public to burn the illegal bills.[97] Haynau threatened those who hid Kossuth money with a jail term of two to six months duration.[98] The *Figyelmező* complained that the nation was paying for the sins of the money printers.[99]

In March 1849 Emperor Franz Joseph ordered the issuance of new Hungarian bills, forints, based on the incomes of that country. Haynau began the forced circulation of assignets in July, while the next month witnessed the appearance of small change notes in place of the customary copper coins.[100] The new currency was pumped into the monetary veins of Hungary in the form of advances to former landlords and salaries to civil servants, army officers, judges, teachers and clergymen. The Pest merchants received half a million forints in government loan for the establishment of a credit fund.[101]

The Government forwarded more funds for emergency aid to towns and for the financing of public works. Baron Krauss, Minister of Finance, gave half a million forints for the restoration of Buda.[102] The city of Pest received several subsidies to cover current operational expenses.[103] When the Government realized that the Tisza Valley Company was unable to operate without financial and managerial support, it sent Hungarian experts to re-organize the firm and allocated the Company half a million forints for a five year period for flood prevention and the re-chanelling of sections of the Tisza River.[104] In 1850, similar works started on the Kőrös River.[105] The new Liberal Centralist currency reforms and other monetary and investment policies brought the currency crisis to an end by 1851.

The Government further stimulated the Hungarian economy with tax concessions. During the first quarter of 1850, the tax contribution of Hungary amounted to less than one million forints, while in previous years her share of the expenses of the central government had been approximately five million forints for each corresponding period.[106] Only gradually were taxes collected in the other Crownlands also introduced in Hungary. In March, 1850 a land and house tax was levied on the net income of the owners. From November of the same year, incomes for taxation purposes were based on the 1844 classification and not on current higher revenues.[107] To ensure a more equal distribution of the tax burden, a rather light income tax was proclaimed. It provided for a tax-free zone under a yearly income of 600 forints, a one per cent tax on incomes from 600 to 1,000 forints, followed by a one per cent increase on every additional 1,000 forints up to ten per cent maximum.[108] In 1850, a total of 11 million forints was collected in direct taxes in Hungary and 61 million in the whole Empire. In indirect taxes Vienna received 96 million forints of which only twelve million came from Hungary. The increase from the pre-1848 level was merely one-eighth, while direct taxes were four per cent higher than the Empire average.[109] No intent of "tax exploitation," to use Professor Szabad's phrase, is traceable in interpreting the above data.[110] Rather the Liberal Centralists encouraged a rapid growth of the Hungarian economy in the expectation of more taxpayers with higher taxable incomes.

In addition to administrative and economic rejuvenation, the Cabinet introduced a modern educational system in Hungary. Education was one of the principal concerns of nineteenth century liberals. They believed in man's perfectibility and viewed education as the means by which it could be furthered.

Liberal Centralist educational policies were drafted in this vein. A unified, nationality-oriented, universal, government financed and supervised school system was created which remained in force with modifications until 1945. The Minister of Religion and Public Education, Count Leo Thun, laid the foundations for the new regime. In October, 1849 he outlined for Geringer the basic principles for a reformed Hungarian school system.[111]

The right to supervise all forms of education and teaching was to belong to the state. Inspectors were to make sure that high standards were maintained in all institutions. The education of children from the ages of six to twelve became compulsory. Students did not have to attend a school of their own religion. The schools, however, had to consider the needs of nationalities. In the elementary grades the language of instruction was to be in the mother tongue of the majority of the pupils, while in the gymnasia or high schools, any one of the languages spoken in the Empire could be used, even bilingualism was allowed.

There were to be both public and private schools. Public schools were those which operated on a government designed level, gave standard examinations and issued certificates. The students of private schools might obtain similar certificates if they submitted to examinations at the public schools. Educational institutions under the Ministry were to be of three types: elementary, secondary and post-secondary.

The four-year elementary schools were to be administered jointly by the municipalities and the local parishes. The gymnasia were to be established according to religious affiliations, although the curriculum would be prescribed and supervised by the state. Textbooks were selected by the gymnasia. The principal of the eight-year high school, with the assistance of a teachers' council, managed the school. The hiring of subject specialists was ordered.[112] The earlier low standard six-year gymnasia, and the law and philosophy faculties of academies were either eliminated or combined with the new gymnasia or incorporated with the universities. Some of the less effective academies were to be down-graded to a gymnasium level and certain high schools transformed into junior gymnasia.[113]

Thun strove to free the universities from politics and have them concentrate on scholarly research and high quality teaching.[114] To secure academic freedom of teaching a professor could choose his own text books. With the establishment of private professorial chairs the students were given their freedom of selection. They could register and pay for the courses they preferred because fees were abolished. The private professors' income was dependent on class enrollment or, as Thun hoped, on his scholarly expertise.[115] Both Law Schools and Arts Faculties were reformed and a new engineering faculty was established at Buda.[116]

Geringer was responsible for the application of Thun's principles. He appointed inspectors to implement the school reforms in each administrative district. Thun wanted politically reliable, energetic, well-educated and respected inspectors, and had instructed Geringer to consider also the religious affiliation of the population in selecting these officials. Later, each major religious group was to have its own inspector who was to purge the faculty and the student corps, close substandard schools, set up new schools, eliminate the forced use of the Hungarian language in non-Magyar areas, collect statistical data, 'supervise existing schools and propose reforms based on Thun's principles. Unremunerated school councillors who were members of the local community were to support the work of the inspectors. Each district had a school board, chaired by the ministerial commissioner and the inspectors. Every board was to establish one or two state gymnasia. Experienced Hungarian educational experts were consulted about reforms and the press was also permitted to debate publicly the new measures and proposals.[117]

Geringer ordered that all schools be opened in the autumn of 1849. The Civil War and Intervention had made teaching impossible for almost a year. Soon over half of the school age children attended classes.[118] The number of schools increased by 2,000. Roman and Greek Catholic teachers' training was reorganized and the first normal school for girls was founded. The Government pressured the municipalities to improve the financial position of elementary schools and teachers. The reforms raised the level of instruction in both the humanities and the sciences. The establishment of school libraries and other educational facilities set high standards for decades. The first science-oriented high schools were also launched in the early 1850's.[119]

The achievements were accomplished with the assistance of the Churches which retained effective control of the schools. Secularization of the system was attempted in 1848 but the independent Hungarian Parliament refused to pass the proposed educational reforms in fear of antagonizing the Churches. A shortage of qualified instructors, especially among laymen, placed an additional barrier in the path of a state sponsored school system. The problem was inherited by the Schwarzenberg-Bach Cabinet. The Imperial Government reluctantly accepted clerical participation in education. The Liberal Centralists maintained Josephinism[120] wherever and as long as they could. Rejuvenation in Hungary could not be successful without the active support or, at least, the tacit consent of the Hungarian churches.

The "carrot and stick" policy seemed most appropriate in dealing with the Magyar Churches which, without exception, backed Kossuth in 1848. The time had not come for the restoration of the Catholic Church to the position from which Joseph II had ousted it and where years later Franz Joseph wanted to place it again.

At the Cabinet meeting of 3 July 1849 Bach reported on the affairs of the Hungarian Churches. He insisted on purges, the court-martialing of at least three Catholic bishops and the dismissal of the Primate of Hungary. The Emperor had initially supported strong measures and not even the protests of the papal nuncio could alter the policy of retribution.[121]

During the troubled summer of 1849, the Imperial firing squads executed nine priests in Csanád County and two in Szatmár for their active support of the Revolution. The Bishop of Nagyvárad was sentenced to death but Haynau commuted his sentence to 20 years imprisonment at the Fortress of Olmütz. A Protestant pastor was hanged near Pozsony for agitating against the Government. The Bishop of Rozsnyó received a six-year sentence. In March, 1851, there were still 31 Roman Catholic clergymen in jail.[122]

Blackmail accompanied vengeance. Windischgrätz demanded one million forints from János Hám, Primate of Hungary, as a token of loyalty to the Empire. The request for the "offering" was repeated to Hám by Archduke Franz Karl, father of Franz Joseph.[123] Haynau demanded 2.3 million forints reparation from the Jewish communities of Pest, Buda and Old Buda.

Government harassment of clerics was not unusual and the liberal press was let loose on the Catholic Hierarchy. The clergy was ordered to read regularly the government's political and administrative announcements from the pulpit.[124] Rabbis and ministers received similar directives.[125] The *gendarmes* raided church premises in search of compromising documents.[126] The liberal Hungarian press lashed out with impunity at the Catholic Hierarchy. Geringer approved the plans of Ferenc Szilágyi, editor of the semi-official *Magyar Hirlap*, which promised to expose the "guilty and shameful role of the Hungarian clergy."[127] The editors of the *Pesti Napló* demonstrated their radical anti-clericalism by their frequent attacks on the high clergy. The *Pester Zeitung* demanded the exclusion of priests from politics and at one time castigated the Primate for his attempts to block the secularization of the Pozsony gymnasium.[128]

The Church was outraged by the anti-clerical campaign. Their supporters at the Imperial Court and within the Cabinet began to press vigorously for compromises and for the restoration of the Catholic Church as one of the main pillars of the Empire. The Bishops' Conference, held in April 1849 in Vienna, demanded restoration of Catholic privileges.[129] The Cabinet refused to comply but Thun was "convinced that a modern society could not be strong without solid religious foundation"—and supported the bishops.[130] He was prepared to sacrifice Josephinism, at least partially, to gain clerical support for the Government so that a loyal and more powerful clergy might prevent the repetition of 1848. Thun, in a report written in April, 1850 to Franz Joseph, elucidated the beneficial impact of a powerful clergy on the internal peace of countries. He recommended in the name of the Cabinet and in accordance with existing laws, which secured the equality and independence of established Churches, that certain steps be taken immediately to permit a freer operation of a loyal Catholic Church.[131] The Rescripts of 18 and 23 April 1850 allowed free communication between bishops, congregations and the Holy See. To publish Papal Bulls and Encyclica the Church no longer needed the approval of the Government. The Emperor thus relinquished his ancient *ius placeti regii*. The bishops could discipline the clergy, including the imprisonment of clerics, and lay authorities were obliged by law to cooperate. Franz Joseph promised to name bishops only on the recommendation of the Church. The bishops appointed teachers of theology and religion. The Government, however, maintained the right to veto such appointments on grounds of political reliability.[132] The Rescripts gave new rights to the Church and strengthened the hand of the Hierarchy over the lower clergy without completely eliminating government influence especially in personnel matters. The limits of compromise were drawn by Franz Joseph. He remained ". . . Josephinian enough in his view of the Church's relationship to the Crown, demanding (and receiving) from it service which made it another of the main props of his rule."[133]

In Hungary such a role was not unattractive to the Catholic Hierarchy, although a complete identification with the regime was rejected because the clergy jealously guarded its independence from the Viennese Hierarchy. Furthermore, such a stance would have meant the alienation of the faithful in Hungary. Nevertheless, both parties recognized mutual dependence. In a two part article in July, 1849 the semi-official *Figyelmező* pleaded for cooperation between state and Church. "If you oppose the state, you are threatening the Church." "Let us put aside all accusations since we are all guilty and let the Church teach the people to become good citizens."[134]

The Liberal Centralists agreed but with reservations. János Hám, Primate of Hungary, was forced to resign for having given support to the Kossuth regime, and for his hesitation in pledging financial support in 1849 to the Imperial Army. Intrigues at the Court and in high clerical circles also prompted his resignation. At Bach's insistence, the Cabinet replaced him with the talented and ambitious royalist János Scitovszky, Bishop of Pécs. Loyal bishops gradually occupied the vacant Hungarian sees.[135] Other measures were also undertaken to promote the allegiance of the Catholic clergy. Both Hám and Scitovszky were decorated with the Order of St. Stephen.[136] In July, 1850 Franz Joseph halted all court proceedings against clerics. Their cases were referred to the bishops.[137] Thun decided to placate the lower clergy too. He made the payment of their salaries a governmental responsibility and raised their yearly income.[138] To further conciliate the priests Geringer discontinued the use of the pulpit for public announcements.[139]

The Protestant Churches were also approached tactfully. In their case, in the interest of rejuvenation, the Liberal Centralists would have been contented with their depoliticization, because Bach and Thun considered the Protestant Churches of Hungary the politically least reliable and their two and a half million followers hot-headed, easily excitable people.[140] The struggle between Protestant Hierarchy and lay church leaders had always enabled the Habsburgs to interfere with Protestant autonomy. The Schwarzenberg-Bach Administration pursued the old policy in a bid to control the Churches without seriously altering Law XXVI/1790–1791 concerning autonomy and the Laws by which the Diet of 1847/8 granted the Protestant Churches equality with the Catholic Church.[141] The Protestant Churches were not subjected to the reparation payment as were Catholics and Jews. The Calvinist Hierarchy was allowed to retain its power. The four Lutheran leaders who had actively supported the Kossuth regime were removed and replaced by more reliable pastors, who were to represent not only the Magyar ministers but also the German and Slovak majority in the Lutheran Church. In his Order of 10 February 1850 Haynau forbade the participation of lay persons in the leadership of the Protestant Churches. The exclusion from leadership of the financially independent and politically active laity augured well for Vienna. Not to alienate the loyal laity, Haynau did not exclude the use of trustees and deans as advisors or the holding of general district meetings, provided they were authorized by the local military commander and were held in the presence of a governmental commissioner.[142]

The Government, however, was not satisfied with makeshift arrangements. Two distinguished royalist pastors, K. Kuzmany and J. Kollar were soon invited to work out a new settlement between the

State and the Protestant Churches. The press discussed various options and published certain proposals. As in 1848, the Protestant clergy simultaneously aimed at becoming an established religion and remaining autonomous. Both Baron József Eötvös, Minister of Religion and Public Education during the Revolution, and Thun failed to reach agreement with the Protestants, whom neither Minister found politically wise to antagonize.[143] Moreover, Franz Joseph failed to stand by his Ministers due to Court pressures emanating mainly from Archduchess Maria Dorothy, widow of the once popular Palatine Joseph, on behalf of Lutherans.[144] Franz Joseph gave audience to a Lutheran delegation in December, 1850.[145] His friendly reception must have encouraged them to reject governmental proposals which included new restrictions on their autonomy. Thus, in the absence of a settlement, Haynau's provisional order remained in effect. The Government, nevertheless, aided the Protestant clergy financially and authorized a year's extension to implement Thun's school reforms. The military also proved lenient in authorizing general meetings of congregations.[146]

The Government took positive measures to gain the support of the Jewish communities in Hungary. The Pest-Buda and Viennese press openly discussed rumors that one of the reasons for Haynau's dismissal was his strict measures in 1849 against the Jewish congregations of Hungary's capital. No official denial was issued but at the time the Cabinet proceeded to alleviate Haynau's action. The Minister of War spread the burden of the reparation, 2.3 million forints, to half a dozen other Jewish congregations. On 22 October the Cabinet ordered all Jews of Hungary to participate in the payment of the reparation. Finally, on 30 June 1850, the amount was reduced to one million forints. With this money the Government established a Jewish religious and school foundation under the jurisdiction of a state supervised Jewish agency.[147] Bach's commissioners blocked or reversed measures which the city fathers of Pozsony and Buda had introduced against Jews. Geringer appointed several Jewish businessmen as executives of the newly formed chambers of commerce and crafts. The Cabinet ordered two dozen Trencsén County villages to pay 318,000 forints in compensation to the Jewish citizens whom they had robbed in 1848.[148]

The Government also encouraged the development of Jewish education and even consulted the rabbis on the waning religious interest of Jewish youth.[149] University authorities at the Pest medical school were reminded that the exclusive use of Hungarian was both unconstitutional and unfair to the non-Magyar nationalities.[150] At this time German-speaking Jewish students comprised a substantial proportion of the student body.[151]

Bach's administrators rigorously enforced Chapter Three of the March Constitution which, just like the Jewish emancipation law of 1849, granted citizenship, freedom of movement and equal property rights to the Hungarian Jewry. The Austrian high clergy and the Court restrained their anti-Semitism and temporarily recognized the new policy of pacification and rejuvenation.

The Liberal Centralists were so certain about the self-evidently progressive and convincingly just nature of their program that they remained utterly confident that eventually the majority of Hungarians would agree with them and support modernization. In true liberal tradition they flinched from the muzzling of the press, the gauge of public opinion and the outlet for educated views. The Government recognized the value of a free press with a high degree of credibility which they could use for a sophisticated propaganda campaign on behalf of liberal centralism. Newspaper licenses were issued with the sole proviso that the editors support the March Constitution. Control was exercised by the imposition of legal liability of editors and owners and the provision for subsidies. These control factors, however, never stifled the aggressive Hungarian journalists.

The first Hungarian daily of the new regime was the *Figyelmező*. It actually began to appear on 19 July 1848 but was banned in December by the revolutionary Defence Council for its outspoken opposition to Kossuth. The paper was revived in January, 1849 and the editor, Károly Vida, received Windischgrätz's financial support in return for the promise of a constitutional monarchist stand. When Geringer noticed deviation from this program, the paper's emphasis on Hungarian state rights, he eliminated the subsidy and in August withdrew his support completely. The *Figyelmező* was in print again when Vida secured the backing of Primate Scitovszky and Vince Szentiványi, District Chief Commissioner of Pest. Vida pledged once more to support the March Constitution. The *Figyelmező* now refrained from attacking Bach, supported the Cabinet, built up hope for the realization of all provisions of the March Constitution and championed Magyar nationality and language rights. Its opposition to the state of siege and absolutism in general was overlooked by the authorities. When Vida, however, got on the bandwagon of the Old Conservatives, the political wing of the Hungarian aristocracy and began writing against Bach and his system, the Government prohibited further publication.[152]

Well before the elimination of the *Figyelmező*, Geringer had searched for a Hungarian political paper to print official announcements, to fight rumors and to popularize government measures. In order to receive a publication licence the anti-clerical author, Ferenc Szilágyi, promised to write the history of the Revolution of 1848 to demonstrate the greatness of the House of Habsburg and the futility of separatism. His *Magyar Hirlap* became the semi-official mouthpiece of the Administration. Throughout 1850 the paper maintained its endorsement of the March Constitution. It opposed the Old Conservatives and the Catholic Hierarchy, but otherwise never ceased criticizing the regime or advocating Magyar superiority over the other nationalities of the Empire. Geringer was more successful with the German-language publication *Pester Zeitung*, which systematically championed Vienna's Hungarian policies. But it never achieved popularity among the Hungarian reading public. Finally, an independent, liberal, but not separatist daily, the *Pesti Napló* emerged. In authorizing publication, Bach requested the editor, through Geringer, to respect the equality of the nationalities and support the March Constitution. The paper sustained a liberal political line until it was taken over by the Old Conservatives in the autumn of 1850. By then, 19 Hungarian papers were being distributed in Hungary and Transylvania.[153] They were seldom suppressed, although the editor of the daily *Hölgyfutár* was arrested for publishing the revolutionary poem "The Hussar Family" and Szilágyi had to stand trial for printing the anti-regime poem "The Prisoner."[154] The freedom of the press can best be illustrated by a few representative quotations from the contemporary Hungarian press.

The *Hölgyfutár* preferred to give literary form to its political spikes at Haynau's suppressive work.

> Now the census is taken, humanity is registered, but inhumanity will surely receive no special mention.[155]

> Nowadays, more than the usual number of people turn grey. All considered, are not the blind fortunate?[156]

> Around Kalocsa the flood causes terrible damages, near Bácska the situation is the same, as if the plentiful water would like to wash away the blood.[157]

A Csongrád correspondent of the *Pesti Napló* actually threatened the Government with revolution.

> Hungary is now somewhat weakened. She bows in the face of Power but people should believe that they are giving unrealizable advice when they propose to the government germanization and absorption

> [of Hungary] ... so the government on a stormy morning may dis-
> cover that Hungary ... therefore [act] carefully and intelligently.[158]

In the face of a press which gradually turned from liberalism to chauvinism and used its power to discredit the regime, Geringer still preferred friendly persuasion, although his efforts and methods were often proved ineffective.

Neither did the Government hinder the work of the Hungarian theatres. Novelist Pál Gyulai complained in 1850:

> The nation suffers proudly in her chains. She does not crawl in the
> dust ... there is no free press but there is free theatre.[159]

The Liberal Centralists decided to demonstrate their good will towards Hungarians by other means as well. From early November, 1849 amnesties, reduced sentences and individual pardons were granted. Franz Joseph personally contributed a large sum to the maintenance of the Hungarian National Museum. In December, 1849 Haynau established a pension fund for crippled soldiers and non-commissioned officers of both the Imperial and *Honvéd* armies.[160]

From 1849 Cabinet policies were based on the eventual implementation of the March Constitution. The first obstacle in the path of the Liberal Centralists, the Kremsier federalists, were dispersed forcibly when they refused to compromise. Hungary's independence was not negotiable. To prevent the separation of Hungary from the Empire the Schwarzenberg Administration, after some hesitation, invited Russia to assist their armies in dislodging Kossuth from power. The third obstacle, the Military, or rather, the threat of military dictatorship, was removed through political maneuvering—both Windischgrätz and Haynau were valuable soldiers but political dilettanti. Windischgrätz was dismissed for mismanaging the Civil War and Haynau was recalled from Hungary for disobeying orders. By the autumn of 1849 the Liberal Centralists could launch their program for a modern, liberal and united Empire.

In Hungary, after the crushing of the independence movement the Cabinet offered the population an improved standard of living and the benefits of a well organized and efficient Imperial state apparatus. They wished to consider the interest of the whole population, Magyars and non-Magyars, ex-landlords and former serfs, Catholics, Protestants and Jews, and invite them to participate without the sharing of political power in the process of economic, social and cultural rejuvenation of Hungary—within the Empire.

II

The Defeat of the Liberal Centralists

During the autumn of 1850, the Liberal Centralist Administration reached the height of its power. The Cabinet began implementing some of the democratic features of the March Constitution. In Austria proper municipal elections were held and many candidates who were supporters of the March Constitution gained seats on city councils.[1] In Inner Hungary, at the end of 1850, similar elections took place in Pozsony and six other towns.[2] Meanwhile, in Vienna it was rumored that Bach planned the 15 March 1851 as the opening day for a new Imperial Parliament.[3] According to the well-informed Viennese daily, *Der Wanderer,* Minister of Finance Krauss and public opinion in Styria and Moravia wanted an early election for a *Reichstag.*[4] The Liberal Centralists strengthened ministerial power at the expense of the Military. In July, 1850 General Haynau was dismissed and his successor's responsibilities were confined to strictly military affairs.

There were more and more ominous signs which indicated to the Emperor that his Ministers *actually* wanted him to become a constitutional monarch. For Franz Joseph the cup was filling. To prevent the establishment of a constitutional monarchy and to arrest the growing power of the Cabinet, Franz Joseph initiated a "quiet counter-revolution."[5] He contrived to use other political groups' ambition to raise himself to the summit of power. He considered absolute power to be his divine right and essential both for the glory of the Dynasty and the welfare of his peoples.

On 19 November 1850, Carl Frederich von Kübeck, a long-time comrade of Metternich, arrived in Vienna from Frankfurt where he had represented Austria on the German Federal Council. He was soon summoned by the Emperor and instructed to write a draft statute for a *Reichsrat.* Although the formation of an Imperial Council had been prescribed by the March Constitution, Franz Joseph told Kübeck that he wanted the new *Reichsrat* to supersede the Charter. Kübeck, a representative member of the bureaucracy's conservative wing, was a man who from the beginning of the revolutionary era had pressed relentlessly for the reintroduction of Absolutist Centralism to be based on the support of the Army, the Church and the Civil Service.[6]

Nevertheless, Kübeck drafted a cautious document.[7] His proposed Law described the Imperial Council as a purely advisory body, whose president (Kübeck) would rank below the Minister President (Schwarzenberg). Although he condescended to Schwarzenberg's sensitivity, Kübeck created an alternative institution to the Liberal Centralist Cabinet and then filled it with aristocrats and Absolutist Centralist bureaucrats.

The Emperor compelled the Liberal Centralists to share their authority with Kübeck, whom he installed as President of the proposed *Reichsrat*. The Ministers protested the limitation of their power but they were unable to unite in opposition against the Absolutist Centralists once Kübeck had penetrated their political domain. The aristocratic Schwarzenberg's liberalism faded with the passage of time and he now preoccupied himself almost exclusively with foreign affairs. Thun's loyalty to the Liberal Centralist cause was also weakened by his personal alliance with the Catholic Hierarchy. The Liberal Centralists were left to their own devices in a divided and leaderless council. The Cabinet could not yet muster a broader social support than it had earned in 1849 because the second phase of their program, political liberalization, was too timid and was just beginning. Schwarzenberg demonstrated little enthusiasm about the proposed packing of the *Reichsrat* with the enemies of the Constitution, but he shelved his discontent. Schmerling, the Minister of Justice, was the first to resign in protest, but his acceptance of the presidency of the Supreme Court cushioned the political impact of his withdrawal from the Cabinet.[8] In May, Bruck, Minister of Commerce, also resigned.[9]

The other Ministers also fought back. The remaining Cabinet members accused Counts F. Zichy and L. Szögyény-Marich, the two aristocratic members of the new *Reichsrat*, of promoting exclusively their racial, class and family interests. In fact, according to Szögyény-Marich's own admission, they had embarked on a course of obstructionism, attempting to filibuster every proposal from the equality of the Crownlands through the introduction of the Austrian Civil Code in Hungary to the partial maintenance of the institution of entail.[10] There were continuous fruitless debates between the members of the *Reichsrat* and the Cabinet.

In the meantime, Kübeck conceived a bold idea for the overthrow of the March Constitution.[11] In August, 1851 on his advice Franz Joseph broke the deadlock. In a series of letters addressed to the Presidents of the two Councils the Emperor made each Cabinet Minister responsible directly to the ruler thus abolishing the ministerial right of counter-signature. The Imperial Council was converted into a personal advisory body of the Monarch, and Ministers were to submit proposed bills for comment to the Emperor. Both Schwarzenberg and Kübeck were instructed to reconsider the implementation of the March Constitution and submit their proposals to the Emperor who would then decide the fate of the Charter.[12] The Emperor stated candidly: "We have taken a long step forward. We have thrown our constitutional stuff overboard."[13]

Protest still came from Schwarzenberg, Thun and Krauss. On the 17 August 1851 Krauss submitted his resignation to Franz Joseph but the other Liberal Centralists stayed in office to save what little remained of the March Constitution.[14] When Kübeck, following the instructions outlined in the letter of 20 August, established a committee consisting of Liberal Centralist Ministers, Absolutist Centralist bureaucrats and federalist aristocrats to debate ways and means of abolishing the Constitution, Schwarzenberg and Bach attempted to convince their opponents of the values of their old platform. The Minister President spoke in council of foreign policy considerations and the reputation of the regime, while the Minister of Interior insisted on at least some popular participation on advisory bodies. The Liberal Centralists were first rebutted by Magyar aristocrats. Zichy and Szögyény-Marich demanded Hungarian laws for Hungary and the restoration of the pre-1848 Hungarian Constitution. Kübeck opposed both groups and advised unbound absolutism. Once international tension in Europe was lifted, a war between Austria and Prussia avoided and Louis Napoleon's coup had delivered a new blow to what was left of continental European liberalism, the Emperor abruptly terminated discussions. He was ready to issue his Sylvester Patents.[15]

On New Year's Day 1852 the official government daily, the *Wiener Zeitung*, published three documents, each bearing the date of the previous day, St. Sylvester Day in the Catholic calendar. The first patent declared the March Constitution null and void, maintaining only its provisions related to equality before the law and the liberation of the serfs. The second patent re-stated the scrapping of the Constitution, emphasized the unity of the Empire at the expense of Crownland rights, but retained the Constitution's provisions concerning freedom of worship and the rights of Churches. The third document was a note to Schwarzenberg which contained in its appendix a list of Principles for organic laws.

While the first two documents endeavored to reassure the peasantry and the Christian Churches, the Principles emphasized Absolute Centralism by giving minor concessions to nobles and Liberal Centralists and major ones to Absolutist Centralist bureaucrats. Austria's unity was declared perpetual along with its monarchical system. No status was assigned to any Crownland, which meant that Hungary could not enjoy privileges which were not granted to other Crownlands. The Emperor's personal representatives, Viceroys, were to govern the countries or districts. Uniform criminal and civil codes were to be introduced throughout the Empire. Schmerling's liberal judicial reforms were largely obliterated; the Principles destroyed the independence of judges, reunited the executive and judicial powers on the borough level, forbade formation of juries, and proscribed public trials. The Emperor, however, wished to retain the services of the Liberal Centralists.

The bureaucracy's political sphere of influence was broadened on both borough and, more particularly, on the municipal level of administration. Ample room remained for progressive civil servants to proceed with the modernization of the Empire without marked interference from the Army or the dominant local nobles. On Bach's insistence the formation of advisory committees comprising representatives of landowners and industrialists to assist district and viceroyal authorities was projected in the Principles.

Several articles of the third document attempted to appease the traditional ruling class. Large estate owners were removed from under the jurisdiction of village officials and placed under the authority of the boroughs. Former landlords with smaller holdings were authorized to form groups for the same purpose in order to avoid the possible embarrassment of ex-serfs taxing their former masters. Class struggle on the municipal level was tilted in favor of the wealthiest tax payers. The economically retrograde institution, the entail, was partially preserved to provide "special protection" for the landed nobility.

The Sylvester Patents delivered another blow, an almost fatal one, to the Liberal Centralist program. The documents offered new portents of hope for the enemies of the Schwarzenberg-Bach Administration. The death of Schwarzenberg in April, 1852 removed a major opponent of Habsburg absolutism. Franz Joseph did not name a replacement for the position of Minister President but entrusted Field Marshal Kempen, an enemy of Bach, with the management of the recently established Police Authority. Bach was no longer in charge of internal security. Count Carl Grünne, an Absolutist Centralist and spokesman for the military establishment, began to participate in high level discussions following Schwarzenberg's death. The Liberal Centralist Minister of War, Csorics, was now gradually driven towards political oblivion.[16] The pious party at the Court, which supported the Absolutist Centralists was led by the Emperor's former tutor Cardinal Rauscher and had as "members" the Emperor's prestigious mother, Sophia, and Cabinet Minister Thun. Their influence was growing rapidly. The Jesuits returned to Austria after decades of forced absence. Further educational concessions were given to the Catholic Church. To make evident the new relationship between the Church and the state, the Minister of Justice ordered his courts to pronounce judgment not "in the name of His Imperial Majesty," a formula in use since 1849, but "... of His Imperial, Royal and *Apostolic* Majesty."[17] The title "Apostolic" was bestowed on the first Hungarian king, St. Stephen.

In alliance with the Church, compromising continuously but taking advantage of both the Church and the Emperor's fear of international republicanism and communism, Alexander Bach, the last representative of the Liberal Centralist program, remained at his post to continue rejuvenation in the spirit of the March Constitution. He believed that even under the new circumstances the economic and social alteration of the Danubian Empire could progress. Despite all the odds working against him, Bach

> followed the dictates of his ambitions with such admirable tenacity and possessed such boundless skills in adjusting to the changing circumstances and in recovering lost advantages, that during the following years [his] influence in general policy making in fact did not decline, but instead showed signs of increase.[19]

In the newly developed balance of power situation between Liberal and Absolutist Centralists, the interests of the lower and middle classes were protected by the surviving Liberal Centralists. Within the Government they retained their grip on the field of economic and public administration while all other areas were now dominated by aristocratic, military and clerical groups.

The power struggle between Liberals and Absolutists raged from 1850 to 1853. The former group was steadily losing ground while the forces of absolutism continued their rapid ascent. Each party had its own solution to the Hungarian question. The Schwarzenberg-Bach Administration continued its administrative, economic and social rejuvenation of the Empire but abandoned political liberalism. The

March Constitution, nevertheless, remained a source of inspiration for the Liberal Centralists. The process of modernization was modified to pacify the now powerful Absolutist Centralists. In the spring of 1850 the Cabinet initiated an administrative re-organization of Hungary. A sub-committee, whose membership included two Hungarian aristocrats, was established to make recommendations. In June the sub-committee presented its report for Cabinet approval.[20] In conformity with Article Ninety-Two of the March Constitution, the country's administrative unity was to be retained but the viceroy's authority in Hungary was limited in fear of the increased aristocratic influence and a revival of Magyar oppression of minorities as a result of a strengthened central administration at Buda.[21] The country was divided into five districts whose borders were drawn not according to historical but rather with regard to national, geographic and economic considerations. At times, political motivations, such as the weakening of Magyar dominance, became an overriding factor. The predominantly Magyar counties of Tolna and Baranya, for example, were attached to the heavily German populated Sopron District despite the fact that direct transportation to Sopron was impossible without a detour to Pest-Buda, the original district capital for the two counties. Other borders were also adjusted but mainly to facilitate administrative efficiency. By the fall of 1850 the most important territorial changes were completed and within a few months all offices were completely staffed. The reorganized administration began to function in all districts on 1 January 1851.[22]

During the new administrative regime, the *Provisorium*, which lasted from January 1851 to May 1853, Bach and Schmerling realized the constitutional separation of public administration and justice above the borough level. The Patent of 29 November 1851 introduced the modernized Austrian Civil Code of 1811 in Hungary.[23] The criminal laws of the Empire were also codified. Offices for government prosecutors were organized along with a Bar for Hungarian lawyers, whose training, duties and responsibilities towards their clients and before the courts were minutely described.[24] The pre-1848 legal anarchy was replaced by laws in the service of administrative and judicial legality. However, because the members of the legal profession during the *Provisorium* gave little support for the reform program, Bach began to attribute administrative difficulties in Hungary to Magyar gentry officials and aristocratic judges whom he accused of wedging themselves between his Government and the common people. In 1853 he was forced to abandon the constitutional nationality policy and "import" reliable officials from other Crownlands, the so-called Bach hussars. This policy, however, made him indistinguishable from his opponents, the Absolutist Centralists, and overshadowed his later modernization efforts. With the initial forfeiture went the last hope for popular support for the Liberal Centralists in Hungary.

Meanwhile, the reform-minded Ministers, regardless of difficulties, were able to continue the rejuvenation of the Empire. The three principles on which the Liberal Centralist Ministers based their program were the satisfying of the state's desperate hunger for revenue, the fostering of rapid economic expansion and the improving of the population's living standard.[25]

The Liberal Centralists wished to use the power of the state to stimulate the economy and viewed with alarm the Army's enormous share of state revenues. For the Absolutists, domination in Germany and security at home had priority. Both parties agreed, however, on the need for additional state funds to fulfill either party's political program. Eventually, the Cabinet convinced the Emperor that a selective austerity program, especially in the area of military expenses, must be effected without delay. The budget for 1851 assigned 14 million forints less to Csorics, Minister of War, than during the previous year—a reduction of 10 per cent.[26] For additional economy, in October, 1851 an Imperial Rescript ordered a cutback in military personnel and the dissolution of several reserve regiments.[27] Staff reductions in various governmental offices also resulted in some savings.[28]

Revenue from indirect taxes increased rapidly when introduced in Hungary in the midst of growing prosperity. By the middle of 1852 revenues were up 11.6 per cent from the previous year and 24.5 per cent from 1850.[29] This rise was due partially to soaring grain prices in the markets of the Empire and Western Europe and to the measures Liberal Centralist Ministers had undertaken to stimulate the Hungarian economy.[30]

In the early 1850's Hungary produced 80 to 90 million Pozsony bushels of wheat and was marketing it at increased prices.[31] The average cost of four major grains had risen between 116 per cent and 235 per cent from 1850 to 1854.[32] French demands for wool and German orders of livestock, even at inflated prices, further augmented Hungary's national income. Higher agricultural efficiency and boom prices benefited the entire Hungarian population. Tax on farm lands rose only from 53 million in 1850 to 59 million forints in 1851 and remained constant in 1852.[33] Not until the end of the *Provisorium* did the Government demand a larger share of burgeoning Hungarian agricultural profits.

Revenues from indirect taxation, income taxes and the floating of bonds poured in rapidly to government coffers. The new gains eventually made the convertibility of currency possible, whch in turn, stimulated the influx of foreign capital. Subsequent state and foreign capital investments further spurred on Hungary's trade, commerce and agriculture.

State monopoly of the tobacco trade introduced in Hungary for the first time on 1 March 1851, provided the Empire with one of the largest sources of income from excises. In establishing the monopoly

the Schwarzenberg regime employed reasonable compensation rather than outright expropriation of private Hungarian tobacco cultivation and processing.[34]

During the summer of 1851 Geringer issued cash advances to tobacco producers.[35] The following year the transaction was repeated to the extent of one million forints.[36] In addition, the Government raised payments for crops by seven to ten per cent.[37] Once economic incentives were provided, the Hungarian tobacco growers, who had even been relieved of the universal and compulsory corvée, responded by doubling both production and yield. Despite rises in the retail prices of cigars, cigarettes and processed snuff sales increased rapidly[38] and, as a result, the income of the treasury from the tobacco monopoly also rose significantly.[39]

Another indirect tax, the stamp and licence tax, which had brought 7.7 million forints from Cisleithania in 1850, yielded 8.3 million during the first half of 1852, following its introduction in Hungary.[40] The abolition of government distribution centers for state owned salt mines and a rise in the price of salt brought further administrative savings and profits for the treasury.[41]

Indices of growing middle class prosperity were the sharp increases in the field of non-agricultural income tax and state railway profits. Revenues from income taxes tripled from 1850 to 1851.[42] During the *Provisorium* the Vienna-Pest railroad line, for example, was doing a thriving business doubling its earnings for a five month period in 1851/52 from the corresponding time span in 1850/51.[43]

However, since military expenses had approximated 90 per cent of the combined direct and indirect tax revenues, the Government decided to issue state bonds both in 1851 and 1852 with the threefold purpose of reducing the budgetary deficit, lowering the agio and raising capital for railroad and other direct governmental investments.

Vacillating confidence abroad made the first loan only a moderate success. Nevertheless, the Minister of Finance was able now to withdraw some of the inconvertible paper money from circulation.[44] In 1851 bills with a face value of 25 million forints were destroyed and, as a result, the gold and silver agio began to decline.[45] The 1852 bond issue was a complete success as international businessmen judged current conditions ripe for a greater involvement in the economic affairs of Austria. The most successful Viennese financier, Anselm Rothschild, agreed to float the loan in London and he had little difficulty unloading the new issues.[46] A quarter of the total loan raised abroad, mainly in London, was used for further consolidation of the currency.[47] In early 1853 the increased value of the gulden even began to threaten the export trade.[48] As Austrian finances acquired stability, the removal of legal obstacles, which had curtailed the development of industries, could have a major effect on growth.

Once all Hungarian citizens became taxable subjects there was no need for the maintenance of the internal tariff wall between Cisleithania and Transleithania. It was dismantled rapidly after October, 1850.[49] Hungarian agricultural and mining products found ready markets within the Empire, while industrial goods became cheaper for the Hungarian consumer. The Government encouraged industry and commerce to adapt to the existing division of labor among the Crownlands by developing available natural resources and traditional industrial skills.

From an internal economic reorganization Austria proceeded towards an eventual customs union with Germany. A governmental tariff commission, which had been functioning since 1849, made certain recommendations in early 1851 to the Congress of Agriculture, Industry and Trade. Bruck who chaired the meetings was most disappointed at the reception that Austrian and Bohemian businessmen gave to the Commission's proposals for lower tariffs—only the Hungarians expressed their approval.[50] The Commission's strategy was ultimately accepted. The Patent of 6 November reduced import tolls and cancelled most export duties.[51] Finished products now sold cheaper in Hungary and the elimination of the earlier Josephine prohibitive tariff system offered new life to Hungarian agriculture and commerce.

Another economy stimulating measure came with the introduction of Lower Austrian weights and measures throughout the Empire. Industry as a result could interchange parts and purchase tools and raw materials at lower costs, thereby producing finished products more efficiently at competitive prices.[52] New trade regulations restricted the operation of the anti-free trade craft guilds and forbade the formation of new ones.[53] In addition, a provisional trade law disallowed the exclusion of citizens from industrial and commercial practices as well as organizations on the bases of religion, nationality, birth and position of parents.[54] The Ministers sided with the emerging Hungarian middle classes, especially with the commercially most active Jewish merchants and traders, in opposing the guilds.

The Government encouraged the activities of independent businessmen and aided them in establishing chambers of commerce and crafts. The first chamber was initiated in Vienna during the Revolution of 1848. Bach soon introduced the institution throughout the Empire. The chambers became semi-official and semi-autonomous, promoting free trade and representing the interest of their membership towards the Government. They eventually supplied the Cabinet with information, and proposed and commented on bills on which the Ministers could base their measures for the promotion of economic progress.[55] Furthermore, in the process of expanding free trade, the Government passed much of the trade supervisory work to local chambers of commerce and craft, while the royal free cities as commercial corporations were deprived of their customary trading monopolies.[56]

After consultation with the Hungarian chambers several new laws were issued to promote economic growth. A law regulating industrial and commercial patents, blocked by the Hungarian Diet in 1820, gave new impetus to industry through the efforts of enterprising individuals.[57] The Minister of Finance granted tax concessions of up to ten years to encourage the renovation of buildings.[58] At the end of the *Provisorium,* the new Civil Code made a major contribution to the orderly development of trade and commerce. No amount of beneficial legislation could take the place, however, of actual financial investments. Hungary had no experience in internal capital accumulation and the importation of capital was at its infancy. Without active governmental intervention only a snail paced economic progress was possible.

The Government, therefore, decided to explore new avenues in their search for economic success. They entered the transport business in Hungary. Railroads were to offer opportunities for employment, bring producers in closer contact with consumers, increase economic activities and the unity of the Empire. In March 1850 the State purchased the entire Hungarian railroad system at a cost of 21 million forints.[59] In 1850 the Treasury spent 17 million forints on railroad construction, equipment, purchases of old routes and telegraph-lines. By the beginning of 1851, 302 miles of railway were completed and an additional 100 miles were under construction.[60] The Vienna-Pest route which had been recently extended to Szolnok, was hoped to create a major economic impact on the Hungarian Plain.[61] A new line between Marchegg and Pozsony made an extra connection between the Hungarian and Austrian railway networks. In 1851 tracks were laid between Cegléd and Szeged with spurs to Temesvár and Félegyháza.[62] In August 1851, the city of Kecskemét celebrated its linkup with the South-Eastern Lines.[63] The Austrian State Railway Company expanded aggressively in Hungary. It quickly acquired large tracts of land,[64] an interest in iron ore mining and the metallurgical industry.[65] By the end of 1852 over 17,000 workers were employed in railway construction.[66] In Vienna preparations were under way to link Szolnok and Debrecen.[67] Franz Joseph was also urging his Ministers to accelerate railway construction to connect Hungary with Fiume and Galicia.[68]

The increasing number of railroad lines were complemented by the operations of the Danube Steamship Corporation (DSC) which operated as a monopoly. In 1851 the company moved passengers and goods on its 51 ships and 200 barges along the Danube River.[69] In a Northern suburb of Buda a large port was constructed.[70] In 1852 the DSC received a renewed and revised Charter and soon afterwards it cooperated with the Government in connecting the newly opened Pécs coal mines with a dock on the Danube thereby radically reducing the cost of coal—and the Company's fuel costs.[71] The DSC scheduled new routes on the Tisza and Kőrös Rivers while the Government spent 3.43 million forints between 1850 and 1856 on regulating the former and authorized the employment of 5,000 workers for cutting and dyking the latter.[72] With the exception of Venice, most funds for waterways were given to Transleithania, since, in comparison with other Crownlands, transportation had been neglected in Hungary. To raise more funds for waterway construction the Government charged landowners for flood protection and borrowed money from the House of Sina, one of the largest banking houses in Austria.[73] The Rothschilds were majority shareholders in the DSC but French, English, Italian, and South German monies along with the Austrian Treasury were also participating in the development of Hungary's transportation system.[74]

In 1851 Hungary's highways were nationalized. Under the central direction of a governmental engineering bureau and its district officers, local authorities organized road works with corvée and hired labor financed with corvée exemption payments.[75] Besides the numerous local road constructions a few major highways like the Pest-Eperjes or Tétény-Fehérvár routes were started during the *Provisorium*.[76]

Several other measures were brought forth to facilitate the free flow and availability of capital. Hungary was in dire need of money to recover the losses caused by the Revolution, the Civil War and the Russian Intervention. With some direct support from the Government and domestic commercial banks, capital slowly became available for industrial and agricultural investments.

Eventually, in spite of the opposition of Viennese banking circles, the Government fostered the growth of banks. Deposits in saving banks by 1851 were well over the pre-1848 level.[77] The Austrian National Bank opened branches in Prague and Pest providing each with initial assets of 2 million guldens.[78] The Pest Commerce Bank, fearing competition, sent a delegation to Vienna to protest the appearance of a rival, even though the National Bank, at first, had restricted branch activities and only later had extended commercial loans. Nevertheless, in Hungary, capital was available to commerce and industry at a low competitive rate of four to five per cent.[79] The semi-compulsory government bonds temporarily deprived, however, the commercial communities of sizable cash holdings. The Jewish merchants of Pest, for example, were forced to buy bonds for more than 600,000 forints. The five per cent state loan albeit, brought a reasonable return on investment and were good credit collaterals.[80]

Before 1853, in the field of agriculture, uncertain property relations deprived the former landlords of most regular credit facilities. Saving banks, the Pest Commerce and the Austrian National Bank were commercially oriented and abstained from the mortgage field which was a high risk area before the complete elimination of the entail system. To lessen the financial difficulties of the aristocracy and the gentry, the Government imposed a moratorium on non-commercial debts between 1849 and 1854. In 1853 property relations were regulated allowing free sale and mortgaging of most real estates. In addition, the Government forwarded cash to the former landlords in the form of compensation for lost *robot*. By the end of the *Provisorium*, it agreed to bear the full cost of the emancipation of the serfs.[81]

From early 1851 interest payments on future compensations were accelerated. A simple declaration of eligibility on the part of the landowner was required to receive the advance. In cases of condemned or wanted revolutionaries, family members often applied for and received the advances, although this was illegal. Between November 1850 and February 1852, 3.3 million forints was distributed to former

Hungarian landlords.[82] The Church was also paid advances.[83] The governmental district committees concerned with the administration of advances and compensation payments continued to publish monthly lists in the daily press of newly approved recipients of grants. Some compensation was also paid for damages inflicted in 1849 by Russian occupying forces.[84]

The Government extended technical assistance to landowners who continued to cultivate their family estates and to entrepreneurs and peasants who had recently purchased farmlands. Stud farms were supplied with stallions from the royal stables in order to improve the quality of the horse stock in Hungary.[85] Modern tobacco plantations were also organized.[86] The reform Cabinet "launched vigorous programs of agricultural education on all levels."[87] The Minister of Education granted a yearly subsidy to the Magyaróvár Agricultural Institute.[88] The Government also provided financial aid and encouragement for the formation of a forestry association which would promote the scientific development of Hungary's woodlands.[89] Late in 1851 an agricultural exhibition was opened at Pest by the Viceroy to upgrade farming methods.[90] The Cabinet imported agricultural machinery and purchased choice cattle from abroad.[91]

The maintenance and development of the Revolution's land reform was to crown the modernization of Hungarian agriculture. The Liberal Centralist economic rejuvenation efforts remained incomplete without the fulfillment of Bach's social program. The land reform, if it were to be conceived "in the spirit of social justice"[92] could not have been realized with Magyar gentry bureaucracy as the day-by-day Hungarian administrative experiences of the Ministry of Interior indicated. Bach opposed any negotiations on the issue of new land arrangements with the nobles "in the belief that whatever principles were arrived at in that manner would perforce be contrary to the welfare of the rural masses."[93] Consequently, the issuance of a land patent suffered considerable delay. Such law was only published in the closing days of the *Provisorium* and brought to fruition by "Bach hussars" who from 1853 replaced the most hostile Magyar civil servants. If rejuvenation could not be done with the cooperation of the Hungarian ruling class, Vienna was determined to accomplish it without them. On this matter, there was complete agreement between Bach and the Absolutist Centralists.

The Absolutists were not, at first, unfriendly to the Hungarian nobility. The Kübeck inspired Sylvester Patents promised the gentry and aristocracy some political benefits and the lessening of the Liberal

Centralists' influence in Hungary. It was not clear at the start of the period whether the Emperor would utilize his new powers to further Absolute Centralism or instead apply absolutist methods in alliance with the traditional ruling classes in Hungary and elsewhere in the Habsburg realm.

Initially, there were signs that either road might be taken. For the Hungarian aristocracy and gentry there were encouraging developments. In the pre-1848 tradition, the Emperor appointed a senior member of the Habsburg family to govern Hungary. In September, 1851 Archduke Albrecht was named Commander of the Third Army and Viceroy of Hungary.[94] Several magnates accompanied the Archduke on his first tour of the country. At each stopover he was warmly welcomed in the hope that he would act as a mediator between the King and the country.[95] When the Police Directorate was established as a separate entity from the Liberal Ministry of Interior it was placed under the direct supervision of the Emperor and the Archduke. The fact that the director of the new institution, the Absolutist Centralist General J. Kempen, was an old enemy of Bach gave additional reasons for Magyar optimism.[96] But the Emperor and his Absolutist Centralists soon revealed their true intentions.

Before leaving for his new post Albrecht promised Franz Joseph to rule Hungary with an iron hand. Unlimited centralization and the germanization of Hungarian public life were the main features of his program.[97] The new Viceroy, to dispel Hungarian illusions, told Szögyény-Marich that his sole assignment was to inspire obedience to the Imperial will.[98] When Bach inquired of the Archduke about the number of non-Hungarian civil servants needed for the replacement of uncooperative Magyars, the reply was brief: "Many, but only the best."[99] The Viceroy's influence began to exert itself during the second half of the *Provisorium* when he finally decided to settle at Buda and take charge of viceroyalty affairs.[100] Before long Albrecht had forced the reluctant district *Főispán* (formerly Chief Commissioner) of Pest to introduce German as the official language in his predominantly Magyar district.[101] As of 1 January 1853 German legal texts in the governmental gazette, the *Reichsgesetzblatt,* were to be the only official ones although translations were published in provincial *Gesetzblätter* for information purposes.[102] The germanizers hoped that a man who entered the public service and spent his career speaking and writing German would probably end up feeling as a German. It was a very debatable supposition in Hungary where the opposite process had taken place. Most Germans, Jews, Slovaks, and German and French-speaking aristocrats became Magyar patriots.

Another fruitless attempt at germanizing was made by means of the educational system. German was taught from the upper elementary grades. Thun's "enthusiastic school directors proudly declared that even the Lowland herdsmen would study the alphabet in German."[103] In high schools an intensive language program was introduced. Eventually, certain subjects were taught only in German. Newly appointed professors at the Pest Law School were required to have a working knowledge of German since this institute was soon transformed into a bilingual university. By February, 1853 examinations were conducted in German.[104] Professors from Germany or Austria proper began to receive appointments at the Pest Medical School in 1851.[105] During the same year the *Pesti Napló* reported the germanization of the József Technical School at Buda as a "violation of the Constitution" and accused the Imperial Government of systematic germanization of Hungary's officialdom and schools.[106] The charge was unjust. "Systematic germanization" was impossible as long as Liberal Centralists had any political influence in Vienna and the civil service in Hungary remained predominantly Magyar. In 1852 the *Ost-deutsche Post* complained that manpower selection in Hungary was based on the old Liberal language policy.[107] Albrecht and the Absolutist Centralists had to postpone their all out effort at germanization until they could eliminate Bach's influence, or at least his liberalism, at the Court.

Franz Joseph was not willing to dismiss Bach. He needed his astute Minister for the expert containment of international republicanism and communism. Bach's exaggerated reports of European conspiracies made the renegade revolutionary's services indispensable.[108]

When the Emperor visited Transleithania in 1852 Bach's hold temporarily faded; Albrecht, Grünne and Kempen dominated the political scene. The planned royal circuit had been announced at the end of April.[109] Within a week 41 former revolutionaries had been sentenced to death and confiscation of their properties, although the sentences were later reduced to long terms of imprisonment.[110] From the initial period of preparation, the press continued to publish news about sentences of floggings and short prison terms for minor political offences.[111] During the royal journey no general amnesty was issued, although 286 persons were freed in Hungary and Transylvania and many heavier sentences passed since 1849 were reduced.[112]

The refusal to declare a general amnesty was intended to give evidence of strength and it also revealed a desire on the part of the "father" to discipline his rebellious "sons." Provocative military celebrations of Imperial victories at Arad and Pest, the very places where the captured leaders of the Hungarians were hanged in 1849 and who were now considered martyrs by most Magyars were needless.[113] After his visit, the Emperor, convinced that he was following the correct course, confidently declared that the Hungarian nation was content and the nobility was in the process of reconciling itself to the inevitable.[114] The inevitable was undivided power concentrated in the hands of the Emperor and his most trusted Absolutist Centralists who, in turn, had faith only in the Imperial Army, the gendarmerie and the Catholic Hierarchy.

The military courts, under the supervision of Archduke Albrecht, as head of the Third Army, were determined to forestall a new rebellion by intimidation. For current political crimes, the courts sentenced peasants, laborers and intellectuals to flogging and meted out short jail terms to nobles and the well-to-do citizens.[115] Death sentences were pronounced against 36 revolutionary leaders, but since they were in exile the accused were tried *in absentia* and only their names were nailed to the gallows. Several prominent people, like Baron M. Vay and Count L. Csáky, were arrested and condemned to die on the gallows although the sentences were not carried out.[116]

The military actively suppressed all political parties and organizations which might have been a front for oppositional activity. The Patent of 26 November 1852 ordered the re-registration of all associations and the submission of their charters for governmental approval. The law forbade outright the formation of political parties regardless of their sympathies concerning the regime.[117]

The military courts also attempted to keep a close watch on the Hungarian press. Press affairs fell within the jurisdiction of the Army and its military courts. Military prosecutors constantly harassed publishers and editors to counter-balance the press law of the Liberal Ministers.[118] Schmerling, Krauss and Thun, however, took a firm stand on the question of free press. In vain did Albrecht and local government attorneys protest the anti-regime attitude of the semi-official *Magyar Hirlap* and demand the prompt dismissal of its editor. After the Cabinet had discussed the matter repeatedly, the Ministers refused to comply, although some minor concessions were made to the Absolutist Centralists.[119]

A new press law, the Patent of 27 May 1852, reintroduced censorship, forbade the import of foreign publications, forced political newspaper owners to post bonds, and made not only the publishers and editors but also printers, translators, and distributors responsible for seditious writing. Criminal courts were to replace civil courts in trying violators of the Press Patent. In fact, however, this meant the exclusion of military commanders and judges from overseeing the publication field.[120] Hungarian journalists at first became cautious and turned the daily press into "sleepers" while awaiting the results of the clash between the Absolutists and Liberal Centralists. To their delight they soon discovered that the new overseers of the press were the pro-Magyar de la Motte who replaced Geringer, and Protmann, the police chief of Pest-Buda.[121] The earlier prudence of the Hungarian journalists now seemed unwarranted. New periodicals were authorized and a display of oppositionism was once again tolerated.[122]

Towards the end of the *Provisorium* the situation deteriorated. The organizational activity of a dozen Kossuth agents, the riots in Habsburg Italy, and the attempt on the Emperor's life on 18 February 1853 by a Hungarian tailor completely unnerved the Absolutists. Hanging for political crimes resumed.[123] Measures against lawyers, politically active Protestant ministers, and discriminatory edicts against Jews were approved in Vienna from 1852. Lawyers, who had remained passive following the Revolution of 1848/49 were debarred for five years. Local administrators were to determine the maximum number of lawyers who could practice in the area under their jurisdiction. This made further debarrment or, at least, dispersal of revolutionary-suspect lawyers possible.[124] Scottish Protestant missionaries were expelled from Pest and the arrest of ministers and pastors became a frequent event.[125] The Greek Orthodox clergy did not fare much better. Their Church was flatly denied any support and autonomy in Hungary.[126] The introduction of the anti-Semitic sections of the Austrian Civil Code in Hungary concerning Jewish witnesses at civil courts, marriage regulations, and Bach's instructions to prevent the importation of Hebrew prayer books and religious literature foreshadowed the more vital economic sanctions that were to come late in 1853.[127] Whatever social support the Liberal Centralists had gained during the previous three years, the Absolutist Centralists lost for the regime by relying exclusively on the traditional pillars of the Habsburg Empire. Grünne brought the Army and Kübeck the Administration into line. The third pillar, the Roman Catholic Church, was next to regain its former privileged status.

Negotiations with the Holy See for a concordate commenced in October 1852.[128] The Jesuits were allowed to open their first house at Nagyszombat in early 1853.[129] The Government forbade Roman Catholic children to attend Protestant schools.[130] All in all, the increased authority of the Roman Catholic Church finalized the preparations for Franz Joseph's new administrative experiment, the *Definitivum* which was launched in March, 1853.

The progress of the quiet counter-revolution transformed the balance of power situation into a regime of Imperial Neo-Absolutism. The Emperor became alarmed once the Liberal Centralists proceeded to implement the more democratic features of the March Constitution and attempted to replace the traditional pillars of the Monarchy with a wider social base. While the Ministers made a concentrated effort to rejuvenate Hungary administratively, economically and socially, the Absolutist Centralist clique at the Court and the Magyar ruling class in Hungary worked at political cross purposes.

During the *Provisorium* the Liberal Centralists were able to lay the foundations for the industrial revolution in Hungary but they could not resist the forces of absolutism and the Hungarian aristocracy. The second phase of the Liberal program, the political involvement of the Hungarians in rejuvenation, which could have gained support for the Ministers from the many beneficiaries of the reforms and the economic boom, was not given a chance to materialize. Division within the Cabinet also contributed to the downfall of the Liberal Centralists.

The Absolutist Centralists' platform of germanization, revived terror and the return of privileges to the Catholic Church served no useful purpose but instead antagonized the majority of the people. Initially, the Sylvester Patents revived the political hopes of the Hungarian ruling class. By 1853 the Absolutists had so frustrated the aspirations of the nobility that their sluggish opposition turned into outright rejection of all forms of Viennese centralism.

III

The Impact of Government Policies on the Aristocracy

Until 1848 the most influential group in Austrian government, business and society was the uppermost layer of the nobility, the aristocracy. In each Crownland they stood at the apex of a pyramid-type social system. Their members achieved prominence at the Court, in the diplomatic corps, in the Army and the hierarchies of the Churches. Generally, their loyalty belonged to the Habsburgs rather than to the country where their estates were located.

In Hungary, according to the country's Constitution, only the lay lords, the highest officials of the state, the *magnates regni* and the head of the counties, the *foispans*, belonged to the aristocracy.[1] The Habsburgs had combined the granting of titles with the endowment of larger estates and also conferred titles on most pre-Habsburgian aristocrats. Thus, by the middle of the nineteenth century there was in Hungary a socio-economically homogeneous social group of about six hundred families who each owned at least 5,000 holds of land.[2] "In Hungary fifty-eight per cent of the cultivated land in Transdanubia, forty-one per cent of that in North Hungary, thirty-four per cent of the Great Plain consisted of *latifundia*."[3] Wealth, education, political influence in Vienna and traditional leadership made the aristocracy the most prestigious group in Hungary. As few as two or three families could wield politically decisive influence in any Hungarian county.

The aristocracy became cosmopolitan in their outlook as a result of Maria Theresa's effort to demagyarize and attach them to the Court in Vienna. The process was reversed in the Reform Era, although, even in the 1850's, many of the aristocrats still could not speak Hungarian. Their partial alienation from their country created a rift between them and the lower echelons of the Hungarian nobility. By the early 1840's the two groups split into opposing political forces.

Most of the politically active magnates, 105 of them to be exact, joined Count Ferenc Zichy's political club, the Great Casino. An official Conservative Party under the leadership of Counts György

Apponyi, Emil Dessewffy and Baron Sámuel Jósika was founded in 1847 by the members of this pro-government reform association.[4] While accepting a substantial part of the platform of Lajos Kossuth, the leader of the liberal gentry opposition, the Conservatives rejected Kossuth's hostile attitude towards Vienna. The aristocrats realized that separation from Austria was an economically unsound proposition and also that it would not be tolerated under any condition by the Habsburgs. They saw the fate of Magyardom safest within the Monarchy because they considered the nation too weak to stand alone in the midst of the numerically superior, often hostile nationalities.

Their ideas, however, did not prevail. The Revolution of 1848 and the Hungarian War of Independence which followed *Vormärz* temporarily swept the Conservative Party from the political arena and Kossuth and his followers took charge in Hungary's destiny. In Dessewffy's words, "after March 13 (1848), the influence of the Conservative Party as a determining factor ceased to exist."[5] However, Conservative ranks remained intact particularly after Prince Pál Esterházy resigned from the Hungarian Government which, at that time, had taken a direction towards national independence. The Prince, along with other aristocrats, left Hungary. The Conservatives transferred their base of operation to Austria proper.

The Conservative Party became a political club again. The aristocrats' unquestionable loyalty to the Emperor, their rejection of revolution and separatism, their willingness to offer once again their political experience, connections and even financial resources to support a Crown besieged from all sides made possible renewed cooperation between the House of Habsburg and the Conservatives of Hungary.

Baron Sámuel Jósika and Count György Apponyi, both former chancellors, who had left the turmoil of Buda for the tranquility of Salzburg, were secretly invited early in September, 1848 to Vienna by the Empress. Negotiations commenced about the future of a Hungary without Kossuthites. The only achievement of these preliminary talks was a promise that "reliable men" would be consulted about the fate of Hungary following her pacification.[6] A few weeks later at the Imperial military headquarters other Conservatives like Counts Emil Dessewffy, Antal Széchen, József Ürményi and Ede Zsedényi were advising the sympathetic Prince Windischgrätz, Commander-in-Chief, on state affairs. They induced Humelauer, a councillor of the Foreign Ministry who was attached to the Prince, to compose a memorandum warning the Cabinet not to wedge themselves between Magyardom and the Emperor since the Cabinet's jurisdiction did not extend to Hungary.[7] From September, 1848 several other Conservative proposals were forwarded to the Court.[8] The more significant ones were debated later by the Schwarzenberg Cabinet. The plan of the former chancellor and Conservative leader Mailáth[9] was discussed at the December 16 Cabinet meeting.[10] The memoranda of other Old Conservatives, primarily those of Dessewffy,[11] Andrássy,[12] Széchen,[13] Pázmándy and Ghyczy[14] were also considered.[15]

They proposed the pacification of Hungary through the establishment of a provisional military dictatorship and the severe punishment of Kossuth and other separatists. The plans attempted to accommodate the Liberal Centralist program without relinquishing Hungary's integrity and limited autonomy within a unified Empire. The memoranda presented various ideas for social and economic progress. The authors wished to retain the traditional aristocratic political leadership in cooperation with other classes, especially the well-to-do peasantry. The sharing of power between Magyars and Germans, dualism, as the idea was later identified, was also mentioned.

To receive proposals more in conformity with governmental ideals than the submitted memoranda, Prince Schwarzenberg, the new Minister President, invited Jósika and Apponyi to submit proposals about the future reorganization of Hungary. Neither Conservative leader, however, was willing to comply. Dessewffy also considered clarification of Austro-Hungarian relations untimely. The Old Conservative leaders procrastinated since they thought that at the conclusion of the Civil War they would be in a stronger bargaining position.[16] Negotiations, nevertheless, proceeded. Jósika and Széchen lobbied in Schönbrunn, but left in a huff to protest the imminent threat of the Court's adoption of Liberal Centralist policies.[17] Count György Andrássy's negotiations with Hübner, Schwarzenberg's secretary, also proved futile in spite of the fact that they both disapproved Stadion's constitutional plans, particularly the intended effacement of Hungary's ancient rights and privileges.[18] Regardless of the numerous setbacks, the Old Conservatives continued to demand their share of power in a post-revolutionary Hungary.

Powerful forces soon came to their aid. Windischgrätz, an ultra-conservative federalist, with influence at the Court and a large army behind him, pressured the Liberal Centralist Government to work in conjunction with the Old Conservatives in Hungary. The uncertain situation in the Hungarian and Italian theatres of war and the anti-Liberal Centralist stance of the Imperial Parliament, were additional factors whch inadvertently supported the Old Conservative cause.

At its meeting of 6 January 1849 the Cabinet reluctantly authorized negotiations with the most active loyal aristocrats for the purpose of forming an unofficial council to advise the Government on the reorganization of Hungary. To entice the Old Conservatives the Ministers promised to respect the territorial integrity of Inner Hungary, to eliminate the revolutionary April Laws and to grant Hungarians identical civil rights with the citizens of Austria proper.[19] Schwarzenberg sanctioned the formation of an unofficial advisory body of Old Conservatives.[20] The Cabinet, to confine the Council's activities to the application of governmental policies, appointed a senior civil servant, Pipitz, to sit on the Committee. Kübeck, a confidential advisor of both the Court and the Cabinet, was requested to formulate their operating procedures.[21] The Committee had barely commenced its task when their work became superfluous by the issuance of the March Constitution. In Chairman Apponyi's eyes this was a "perfidious act," a personal affront to him and his colleagues.[22] Primarily, the Conservatives resented the centralization of government in Vienna and the detachment of Transylvania, the Serbian Bánát, Voivodina, Fiume and the Military Frontier from Hungary.[23] In protest, Dessewffy relinquished his membership in the Vienna Academy of Sciences— but remained with the Committee which also planned to remonstrate vigorously, by resigning *en bloc*.[24] Before attempting to disband, however, the Committee presented the Government with detailed plans for a new Hungary.

The Old Conservatives suggested the relegation of absolute power to the king and the appointment of a Hungarian minister to advise him on matters concerning Hungary. The preservation of the country's historical rights, tradition and institutions figured prominently in their draft. They considered as essential the immediate establishment of a provisional military dictatorship and a central civil government at Buda, the punishment of rebels, the purging of Church and governmental offices and the introduction of press censorship. The Conservative language policy aimed at the maintenance of Magyar as the official language except for communication with the Cabinet. In response to the demand of non-Magyar nationalities the primary schools were also exempted. Old Conservative economic proposals were not different from the Government's projected reforms: the abolishing of the tariff wall, the introduction of the tobacco monopoly to Hungary and the development of a modern transport system.[25] In conclusion, Apponyi expressed in writing his colleagues' reservations regarding the March Constitution, which they believed would only serve the rebel cause.[26] He stated that the elimination of the ancient Hungarian Constitution would provoke the rejection of even the most progressive reforms of the Imperial Government. The unpleasant impact of the March Constitution could be lessened, however, by a manifesto which would indicate the non-applicability of the Charter during the present state of siege.[27] Apponyi insisted that the Committee could not continue its work under the new circumstances. But it did.

By the end of March the Committee produced a new document on taxation. The members proposed that three-fifths of the tax burden should be borne by the nobility. They requested temporary tax relief for Hungary in general and the nobility in particular to facilitate a post-Civil War economic recovery. They pointedly suggested the levying of new taxes on the liberated peasant landowners to increase governmental revenues for a land compensation fund. Most of these proposals were approved in principle by both Kübeck and Windischgrätz.[28]

Without waiting for instructions from the Liberal Centralists, the Prince began to pursue his own political ideals by the reorganization of Hungary quite independently of the Viennese Cabinet but with the support of the Old Conservatives and other Royalist Hungarians. As his forces entered Hungary in January 1849, Windischgrätz appointed provisional royal commissioners to assist the military in pacifying and administering Hungary. The commissioners were, without exception, Hungarian Conservatives.[29] The Prince concerned himself mainly with the conduct of the campaign against Kossuth and his generals and left the coordination of the reconquered land's political administration to General Rousseau, who, following the occupation of Buda, organized, in close consultation with the Old Conservatives, a Central Military and Civil Commission.[30]

On 15 January 1849 László Szögyény-Marich, former Vice-Chancellor of Hungary and now a leading Old Conservative, received Windischgrätz's invitation to take immediate charge of Hungary's political administration. According to Szögyény-Marich the offer was accepted at their 17 January meeting on the condition that Hungary's integrity along with the country's constitutional institutions would be preserved. Magyar hegemony was to be safeguarded and, as a consequence, the official language of public administration was to remain Magyar.[31] On 20 January Szögyény-Marich occupied his post at Buda and began organizing various governmental offices.[32] The civil administration's leading personnel was recruited exclusively from the

Old Conservatives, who were determined to shape Hungary as they had recently proposed in their memoranda. In Pest County, Commissioner Antal Babarczy obtained authorization from the Military for the parallel display of both the Imperial and Hungarian colors. Similar concessions were granted in Fejér and Veszprém counties.[33] Szögyény-Marich protested every step the Liberal Centralists had taken towards the separation of Croatia from the Kingdom of Hungary. On the publication of the March Constitution, Szögyény-Marich, just as the Unofficial Advisory Council, submitted his resignation in protest. Count Felix Zichy-Ferraris, one of the Old Conservative royal commissioners, also threatened to resign his post when General Baron Johan Burits ordered a *Te Deum* in celebration of the March Constitution.[34] None of the resignations materialized when Windischgrätz reassured the Old Conservatives of his continuous support.

The Prince disapproved his son-in-law Minister President's policies towards Hungary. Windischgrätz condoned the exclusive use of Magyar as the language of public administration in spite of the Government's explicit instructions to the contrary and even in contrast with his own personal preference for the German language. Pre-1848 institutions were restored at Buda and several officials were told outright not to maintain direct communication with the Liberal Ministers without the Commander-in-Chief's authorization—in distinct contravention of earlier instructions to Windischgrätz by Bach.[35]

The Liberal Centralist Ministers understandably prepared for the moment when they could convince the Emperor about the absurdity of the situation, the incompatibility of Aristocratic Federalism and Liberal Centralism. It was Kossuth who unintentionally came to their rescue. His army mounted a successful spring campaign, shattering Windischgrätz's military reputation, and his Parliament dethroned the Habsburg Dynasty on 14 April 1849, infuriating young Franz Joseph who "viewed his deposition as a personal affront for which he held the Hungarian magnates primarily responsible."[36] Windischgrätz was promptly dismissed.[37] The Old Conservative Administration collapsed as Kossuth's *Honvéd* Army swept most of Western Hungary clean of Imperial forces. When Windischgrätz's replacement, Lieutenant-General Baron Ludwig Welden, misunderstanding the existing political situation, invited Szögyény-Marich, Szécsen, Edmund Zichy and other Old Conservatives to assist him in establishing a military dictatorship in Hungary, he soon met the fate of his predecessor.[38]

On 25 May the Cabinet convened to reconsider the Hungarian leadership question. Old Conservatives were accused of intriguing and attempting to alienate Welden from the Ministers.[39] The Baron, after repeated military misfortunes at the hands of the *Honvéd* Army was finally forced to resign on the last day of May. Negotiations with the Old Conservatives were terminated but individual aristocrats were invited to underwrite the Government's reform program and political methods.

In response, a few Old Conservatives retired to their estates while others congregated at Baden. Several aristocratic royal commissioners resigned. Most of the Hungarian aristocrats, however, decided to cooperate with the Liberal Centralist regime and, in the process, undermine it from within.[40] Old Conservative civil commissioners remained attached to Austrian and Russian army units. They volunteered to assist the Emperor and his allies in defeating the Kossuthites, the common political enemy.[41] The Cabinet could not yet disburden the Hungarian Administration of the only indigenous experienced royalist administrators at their disposal. Vince Szentiványi remained commissioner of Pest; Ignác Rohonczy of Pozsony and István Szirmay of Kassa.[42] Count György Andrássy and Sándor Andreansky received appointments.[43] The new civil service leadership was dominated once again by loyal Magyar Conservative aristocrats, who now as individuals began to oppose the Liberal Centralist political program.

In May, Imperial Commissioner Count Felix Zichy-Ferraris warned the Minister President that although it was possible to conquer Hungary without the participation of Hungarians, the retention of the country would be impossible without them.[44] Zichy-Ferraris and other Conservatives hoped for a Hungarian at the helm of their kingdom.[45] Baron Jósika, who for a while was allowed to attend Cabinet meetings, proposed a new office to handle Hungarian affairs. When even this was rejected, he requested that a few reliable Hungarian advisors be unofficially permitted to assist the Ministers on matters of concern to Hungary. Jósika's second plan was accepted and, as a result, Bach invited Count Emil Dessewffy to become one of his unofficial counsellors.[46]

Chief Commissioner at the Russian headquarters, Count Ferenc Zichy, pressured the Government to provide amnesty for his rebel compatriots.[47] At the same time he convinced Tsar Nicholas I's favorite general, Paskevich, to join the camp of Old Conservative sympathizers led by Windischgrätz and Metternich.[48] But, as the fighting in Hungary ended, the Liberal Centralists had less reason to reopen discussions about leadership in Hungary. They decided to deliver a "final" blow against the Old Conservatives.

The Cabinet and the Court planned the court martialing on trumped up charges of the aristocrat former Hungarian Prime Minister, Count Lajos Batthyány.[49] Neither the appearance of the most prominent magnates in the witness box for the defence nor the appeals of Tsar Nicholas I for clemency could alter the Austrian Emperor's determination to provide an object lesson for Hungary. Batthyány was executed by a firing squad on 6 October 1849. A few aristocrats who had supported Kossuth shared Batthyány's fate or were imprisoned. A handful went into exile. Franz Joseph's obstinacy "did more to awaken a feeling of nationalism in the magnates than the flaming oratory of Lajos Kossuth or the desperate battles of their countrymen against foreign invaders during 1849."[50]

When Haynau's executioners were teaching Hungary the necessity of loyalty to the House of Habsburg during the trying October days of 1849, Old Conservative influence in Vienna was at its lowest ebb.[51] Illness overtook Apponyi and Jósika was no longer consulted about Hungarian affairs.[52] Baron Jósika "confessed to me," wrote the British journalist Paton, "that he was now without the slightest influence with the cabinet of Vienna and the party of uncompromising centralisation."[53] The liberal Viennese press was prompted to initiate a vitriolic smear campaign against the nonexistent Conservative Party and its alleged grand strategy.[54] Count Antal Szécsen departed reluctantly for London to justify Batthyány's execution to the British public and counter Hungarian revolutionary propaganda in general.[55]

The availability of a free press permitted several of the surviving Old Conservatives to turn to the newspapers. Count Emil Dessewffy fired the opening salvos in October, 1849. His anti-centralist Conservative program was published in the *Pester Zeitung*.[56] He continued to write critical articles from early February, 1850 for the *Lloyd* and the *Augsburger Allgemeine Zeitung*.[57] Jósika, however, considered Dessewffy's attacks premature. When the *Presse* offered its services to him, Jósika declined in the conviction that open opposition to the Government was not as yet a necessity.[58] His view was not widely shared. With influential backers, such as the new primate, Scitovszky and Pest Commissioner Vince Szentiványi, the pro-Old Conservative journalist Károly Vida transformed the first post-revolutionary daily, the *Figyelmező*, into a mouthpiece of the opposition.[59] The paper asserted that there was only one party in Hungary, the coalition of Old Conservatives and other oppositionists.[60] The editors demanded local control of internal affairs and attacked Bach and his "paper system."[61] The public was gleeful. Local political clubs, the casinos, as well as the literary circles willingly supported the *Figyelmező* whose circulation by 1850 had reached 2,000—a respectable number by contemporary standards.[62] Another daily, the *Magyar Hirlap*, which began publication on 15 November 1849, was initially also a pro-Old Conservative paper. The Catholic Hierarchy's forum, the *Religio*, followed the oppositionist platform too.[63] But by the end of 1850 the *Magyar Hirlap* and a new daily, the *Pesti Napló*, were in the hands of an isolated group of Magyar intellectual nationalists who endorsed the March Constitution.

A number of aristocrats together with a group of writers, who all met regularly at the home of Old Conservative József Ürményi, decided to do something about the *Pesti Napló's* pro-Bach anti-Conservative line. Through varied intrigues and manipulations, Simon Bánffy, a confidant of the Ürményi circle, captured the editorship of the *Pesti Napló*. Bánffy gradually replaced the staff with pro-Conservative journalists and writers.[64] During the *Provisorium* Zsigmond Kemény, Antal Csengery, Mór Jókai, Pál Gyulai, Károly Bérczy, János Pompéry, György Úrházy, János Erdélyi, Imre Vahot, Miksa Falk and Gusztáv Wenzel, all outstanding writers and publicists of the time, contributed to the *Pesti Napló*.[65] In light of the close correlation between the Old Conservative platform and the content of the articles which appeared in the *Pesti Napló* from the end of 1850, Medgyesi's claim that the Conservatives misunderstood and alienated the intelligentsia cannot be accepted.[66] Throughout 1851 the paper openly advocated the Old Conservative program and attacked the regime at the slightest excuse. They emphasized the leading role of the Magyars within Hungary[67] and the need for aristocrats at the helm of the state[68] to safeguard the 800 years-old Hungarian Constitution,[69] national unity[70] and culture.[71] The editors declared the *Provisorium* a dismal failure which "could not live up to expectations" and therefore must be terminated in the interest of Magyardom.[72] Under the heading "Self-Government" the *Pesti Napló* stated provocatively: "In principle, the present regime is a good one, but it is not to our liking."[73]

Conservative propaganda also found its expression in pamphleteering. In 1850 Pál Somssich's *Das legitime Recht Ungarns und seines Königs*[74] aroused the ire of the Hungarian Liberal Centralist press for branding the Austrian Government as illegal, absolutist and as dismemberers of the Kingdom of Hungary.[75] The pamphlet, however, was welcomed by the public.[76] The Conservative Mailáth's attack on

Bach[77] or the works of Ede Zsedényi did not provoke much journalistic retort.[78]

A greater boost was given to the Old Conservative cause when the Catholic Hierarchy entered their political camp. During the first half of 1849 the Hungarian Roman Catholic Church had attempted to cooperate with Vienna. Towards the end of the Revolution of 1848, as the Kossuth regime became more radical, the Catholic Hierarchy, led by Primate János Hám, believed that their influence, privileges, properties and the Catholic system of education was in danger. Consequently, as General Windischgrätz reconquered Hungary, he was welcomed by most members of the Hierarchy as a liberator.[79] The Magyar patriotism of the lower clergy and a few bishops, however, induced the wrath of first, General Windischgrätz and later Bach, Minister of Interior. The General fined the clergy one million forints; the Minister jailed the compromised bishops. Churchmen were subjected to similar retribution as lay Hungarian Kossuthites. The leaders of the Hungarian Catholic Church also feared that one of the results of centralization would be their subordination to the Viennese Archbishop. They had little inclination to relinquish the direction of their Church.[80] Furthermore, the Church could not ignore its members' national consciousness by refusing to recognize Hungary's special role within the Empire. The Hierarchy, in response to the complex situation, at first chose cautious cooperation with the new regime. The fine was never paid, but smaller gifts were forwarded to Prince Windischgrätz's headquarters.[81] During the autumn of 1849 the Church went on the defensive.

The new primate, Scitovszky, appealed to Haynau, Bach and Franz Joseph on behalf of imprisoned churchmen but his pleas were usually disregarded. Viale Prela, papal nuncio at Vienna, intervened for the imprisoned Bishop Rudnyanszky for whose release the clergy had collected 20,000 signatures. Rudnyanszky was freed but exiled from Hungary and confined at an Austrian monastery.[82] In most bishoprics the documents which concerned compromised priests were destroyed to prevent arrests.[83] Nevertheless, several bishops were temporarily incarcerated and maltreated.[84] As a result, the Government's conciliatory gestures proved insufficient to counter its original punitive approach. The Catholic Hierarchy could not be deterred from joining the loyal opposition, the Old Conservatives.

Towards the end of 1849 the Catholic weekly, *Religio*, began publishing reports about current persecutions in addition to their earlier articles about the tribulations of the clergy during the Revolution.

Hostile outbursts against other government policies also appeared on the pages of the clerical paper.[85] On 6 January 1850, the Liberal Centralists were defied in another way. During the inauguration of Primate Scitovszky at Esztergom, 440 invited clerical, aristocratic and official guests witnessed the celebration, listened to patriotic speeches and toasts, Scitovszky's hailing of the Emperor and Szentiványi's lionization of the Primate. Only the Cabinet's direct intervention prevented Scitovszky from leading a delegation to Franz Joseph to express the country's loyalty, beg the Emperor's pardon for the clergy's part in the Revolution and petition "for the nation's just rights."[86]

The Hierarchy demanded concession after concession for only nominal support of the Government. The high clergy, courted by both Liberal Centralists and Old Conservatives, strove for financial independence from the state by gaining a clear title to the Catholic Church's 400,000 holds of land, by getting returned its properties which had been partly nationalized during the Revolution and by receiving compensation for lost tithes in the form of subsidies.[87] In 1850, the Esztergom Conference of Bishops demanded 50 per cent of the incomes of vacant sees and emphasized the autonomy of bishops within the Church and in relation to the state. They insisted on immunity from state prosecution for the clergy. At the same time, the Hierarchy tightened their grip on the entire educational system and also opposed the introduction of civil marriages.[88] Even their intolerance of Protestants and Jews, appreciated by neither the Government nor the aristocrats, was occasionally evident.[89] Nevertheless, the Roman Catholic Church received the requested concessions. The gains emboldened their allies, the Old Conservatives, to intensify their anti-Liberal Centralist campaign.

Although attacking the aristocrats, the *Pesti Napló* reluctantly admitted that "the Old Conservatives temporarily appear to the public as representative of Magyar interest."[90] A well informed police agent at Pest advised his superiors about the increased agitation amongst the magnates for Magyar leadership in Hungary.[91] In the first days of spring, 1850, Counts Apponyi, Dessewffy and Baron Jósika drew up a memorandum during a series of secret meetings. The document was circulated among fellow aristocrats for their signatures and was then in April forwarded to the Emperor.[92] To the original 24 signatories the names of Count Szécsen and Pál Somssich were later added.[93] Szögyény-Marich personally conveyed his approval of the April Memorandum to Minister President Schwarzenberg.[94]

The authors reassured the Emperor of their own and the Country's unflinching loyalty and branded the Revolution as a rebellion which had been carried out under the pretext of political reforms. They recognized the need for a unified Empire, lauded the elimination of privileges and the emancipation of the serfs, but condemned current administrative practices which, in their view, were unconstitutional and bureaucratic and, consequently, most provocative. They claimed that Austria's role as a Great Power could only be maintained through the lasting pacification of Hungary with Magyar cooperation. This would be forthcoming once the Country's integrity, traditional institutions, including her diet, and her 800 year-old Constitution were restored and Hungarian internal affairs directed by Hungarians from the nation's capital once all retribution ceased.

This program was acceptable to most Hungarians with the exception of the Kossuthite republicans, who enjoyed a limited popularity and the Liberal Centralist intellectuals who had never managed to attract followers during the period. The signatories of the April Memorandum were labelled by the official world as conspirators and revolutionaries and defamed

> through the medium of a docile press, as bigoted conservatives and aristocrats, who, irritated at the paternal Liberalism of the Austrian Government, were agitating for the recovery of their class privileges and exclusive national rights.[95]

For months the *Pesti Napló*, the *Magyar Hirlap*, the *Pester Morgenblatt* and the *Pester Zeitung* attacked the Memorandum and its authors. Schwarzenberg and Bach personally derided the Conservatives as greedy, irresponsible landlords who had largely imaginary grievances.[96] Most historians of the Era, from Berzeviczy to Medgyesi, accepted the official interpretation of the April Memorandum and belittled its impact on both the Government and the Hungarian society.[97]

Archduke Albrecht, shortly after his appointment, consulted Count Apponyi. Franz Joseph conferred with other loyal aristocrats. At the time of Albrecht's departure for Hungary, the Emperor considered employing Magyar legal experts to advise the Archduke on Hungarian affairs. According to Medgyesi the Old Conservatives had a major role in prompting the Emperor to visit Hungary.[98]

A few weeks after the delivery of the April Memorandum, Baron Lajos Wirkner informed the Minister President that the Old Conservatives were more powerful and better organized than ever before since the best of the former opposition had joined them.[99] Old Conservative activities were coordinated at first from Vienna and Pozsony and later from Pest-Buda and various country places but the extent to which their endeavors were organized is not easily verifiable. Some evidence is, however, available. Count Lónyai wrote in his diary:

> From Pozsony where he [Emil Dessewffy] transferred his residence for the winter, he journeyed to Vienna on numerous occasions. Jósika, Apponyi, Sennyei, Ürményi, Barkóczy, György Andrássy and others were encouraged by Dessewffy not to sink into ultimate despondency. They met at Jósika's during forenoons; in the evenings, after theatre, at Szögyény's place. I often went to Vienna with Dessewffy on matters related to the Tisza loan, and I was present a few times at the friendly gatherings of the Magyar *fronde*; now and then during a pleasant conversation the curtain was slightly raised over their unceasing covert activities during these years.[100]

Conservative gatherings sanctioned participation in the Government on a selective basis. Two Old Conservatives accepted posts in the Imperial Council after receiving written approval from Jósika and Ferenc Deák, the only prominent member of Kossuth's Cabinet who had avoided exile and arrest after 1849.[101] Five Hungarian aristocrats accepted ambassadorial appointments,[102] others sat on ministerial committees in charge of advising the Government on the land question[103] or the administrative reorganization of Hungary in view of the *Definitivum*.[104] Dessewffy outlined the rationale of such participation in a letter to Jósika.

> We live in disgraceful times, and it is imperative that right, honor and honesty be personified in at least a few men in order that these qualities should not disappear completely. This task is ours in Hungary and no one can, or will resolve it, if not we.[105]

According to an army report concerning public opinion, the Old Conservatives had their representatives at all levels of government, including the Viceroyal Council.[106] A Kassa senior army officer's statement confirmed the veracity of the report:

> Everybody knows, that this party is really alive in this district, works diligently and maintains far reaching connections.[107]

The Police Chief of Pest-Buda noted bitterly in 1852:

> It is surprising what advances are made in favor of Magyarism. The Old Conservative Party gains more terrain daily.[108]

Similar reports about the magnates' growing influence over the gentry and the intellectuals reached Archduke Albrecht and Alexander Bach from all five Hungarian districts.[109]

Having members and sympathizers in the civil service and possessing a wide social base amongst the Magyar gentry and the intellectuals, the Old Conservatives decided not only to present the nation with a program but also to lead the Country to the ultimate realization of their own platform. They publicly demonstrated their loyalty to the House of Habsburg albeit they demanded concessions. Hungarian patriots were flattered in order to ensure their support against the Liberal Centralist political regime which the magnates wanted to discredit in the eyes of the Emperor; in short, the Old Conservatives attempted to prove that they were the only viable political group capable of providing alternate leadership in Hungary.

The first loyalty demonstrations materialized when Archduke Albrecht was appointed Viceroy and Head of the Third Army. The Hungarians awaited the arrival of one of their wealthiest landowners, the Archduke, with great expectations. In October, 1851 Albrecht toured many parts of his new dominion and was well received by the aristocracy. During one of his public appearances at the National Theatre in Pest, the walls echoed the loud *vivats* for the new Viceroy.[110] Although Emil Dessewffy and several of his political associates had their reservations about counting their chickens before they were hatched, Pál Sennyey along with other Old Conservatives heralded Albrecht as the forerunner of changing times.[111]

At the Vác town reception on 14 October the Primate Scitovszky and other members of the high clergy paid their respects to the Archduke.[112] The most patriotic demonstration developed at Székesfehérvar where magnates and clergymen addressed Albrecht in Hungarian and entertained him with Magyar music while the Hungarian tricolor flew above the crowd.[113] It was all in vain. The Archduke was, unlike Windischgrätz, closer to Kübeck's Absolutist Centralist views than to Aristocratic Federalism. He rejected the role of a go-between who would forward to Franz Joseph grievances of loyal subjects for remedy.[114]

When the Emperor himself went to Hungary, a renewed effort was made to demonstrate the loyalty of the Hungarians to a king who was "misled" by his "evil" Liberal Centralist Ministers.[115] The Old Conservatives wanted to re-emphasize Magyar loyalty and, in turn, receive further concessions.[116] The Primate issued a circular ordering his bishops to attend the June 5 Buda reception for the Emperor.[117] Prince Pál Esterházy's suit, which he had ordered especially for the royal visit, involved a personal expenditure of 20,000 forints.[118] The Emperor was feasted at Eger by Count Gyula Szapáry[119] and at Balatonfüred by Count Fesztetics.[120] Other active Old Conservatives, amongst them Ferenc Zichy, György Mailáth and Vince Szentiványi participated in these loyalty demonstrations.[121]

Habsburg inflexibility, abetted by Absolutist Centralists and Alexander Bach, led Franz Joseph to refuse the granting of major concessions. The Emperor was now

> more firmly convinced, that the Conservative Party [sic!] was exaggerating the dangerous sentiment supposedly prevailing in Hungary, and he became less inclined to listen to their complaints.[122]

The Old Conservatives were disappointed but not discouraged.[123] Even minor compromises were greatly magnified; the Trencsén County aristocrats hailed the Sylvester Patents as a first step towards self-government.[124] In the Kassa District the introduction of a Hungarian-type civil service uniform was regarded as a preliminary measure towards the re-introduction of the exclusive use of Magyar in the administration.[125] The Old Conservatives of the same district felt complimented when Franz Joseph revived the usage of the term "Apostolic" and "royal."[126] The Conservative influenced Hungarian press was overjoyed when the March Constitution was eliminated. The Kassa District Commissioner became a celebrity during his introductory circuit when he promised to respect the ancient laws and customs of Hungary.[127]

In the countryside the Old Conservatives conducted a rumor campaign against the Government. They agitated for a loose personal union between Austria and Hungary, and for a special status for Hungary within the Empire.[128] They opposed any change that smacked of centralism. According to a confidential military report from Vas County, Count Herman Zichy had spoken disparagingly to lower officials about Liberal Centralist reform legislation.[129] In the Kassa District every new law was branded anti-national.[130] In the Pest and Pozsony Districts the aristocrats challenged the introduction of the *Definitivum* and declared it unrealizable.[131] The metamorphosis of a social class was in the making.

To gain public support the magnates built new palaces in Pest and actively participated in the social and cultural life of Hungary.[132] Prominent Conservatives left Vienna for their estates in Hungary.[133] Others moved from country estates to the Hungarian capital.[134] Here the National Casino opened its doors during the first month of 1853, with a predominantly Old Conservative membership—and with a sprinkling of Magyar patriots from other classes.[135] During the 1853 Pest social season the high nobility began to attend the public balls.[136]

The gossip columns of the *Magyar Hirlap* proudly described a grand party at Count György Károlyi's palace where everybody spoke and sang in Hungarian and danced the *csárdás*.[137] National costumes were worn when Franz Joseph visited the country.[138] In April, 1850 when Mihály Torkos, a member of the Imperial Supreme Court who had previously been a commissioner of the aristocratic Windischgrätz-Szögyény Administration, visited the Emperor, he donned his Magyar costume and addressed the Emperor in Hungarian.[139] The Academy of Sciences declared in its 1852 report that the Academy's aim was to cultivate the Magyar language and to develop sciences—in Hungarian.[140] Aristocrats presided over the Academy, the National Theatre, the National Fine Arts Club, various casinos and economic as well as philanthropic associations.[141] A financial campaign for the National Library was sponsored by the well-known Old Conservatives Ürményi, Zsedényi and Somssich.[142] Eventually, conservative nationalism became a rallying point for national unity and

> ... the aristocratic Magyar nationalism of the "Old Conservatives," who alone had access to those in power in the period of neo-absolutism, contributed greatly to the changes that ultimately led to the acceptance of Hungary's home rule.[143]

A major attribute of their nationalism was the drive to modernize the Hungarian economy, its agricultural sector in particular. The modernization of Hungary concerned both *Vormärz* Liberals and Conservatives and now in the 1850's again all active vectors, Magyar gentry, aristocratic and Austrian bourgeois, converged on the point called rejuvenation. There is not much substance to Szekfű's assertions that the Government manufactured a crisis situation in post-revolutionary Hungary[144] or that the Viennese Cabinet encouraged the fragmentation of the large estates in order to create more medium-sized farms.[145] A contrary view, put forward mostly by Marxist historians, was that Vienna favored the loyal aristocracy in dispensing economic benefits in the form of higher classification for compensation purposes related to the emancipation of the bonded peasants.[146] The moratorium on debts applied to all landowners. The highest compensation was paid to landlords in Fejér, Sopron, Moson, Pozsony, Vas and Tolna counties where land productivity was greatest. In these counties there were many small Magyar, Serbian, Croatian, German and Slovak farms in addition to the mammoth estates. In several other counties, like Bereg and Árva, each owned almost in their entirety by a single aristocratic family, minimum compensation per acre was paid due to the low yield of arable holdings.[147] Little did it matter that Alexander Bach and his fellow Ministers disliked and distrusted the Magyar magnates;[148] they had no other option but to accommodate the entire Hungarian agricultural interest of the only Crownland that was capable of supplying the industrial and urban parts of the Empire with agricultural produce at a reasonable price.[149]

The Hungarian *latifundia* had already benefited from the economic boom which accompanied the Napoleonic Wars. The aristocrats reinvested most of their profits. The estates were modernized and expanded often at the expense of the common. From the turn of the century machinery was imported, expert managers were hired and bonded labor was gradually replaced by contractual workers and landless cottagers. The economic upsurge was followed by hard times but the aristocrats weathered the depression quite well because of rising wool prices on the world market. Due to over-expansion and scandalous financial dealings in Vienna during the 1830's and 1840's aristocratic indebtedness increased and credit worthiness decreased but not to the extent of weakening their economic preponderance.[150]

By the 1850's, the largest estates had reached European standards. Agricultural implements were purchased from England.[151] Threshing-machines and iron plows were common sights on the aristocratic holdings. A farm machinery association was formed at Pest-Buda mainly by aristocrats to provide a domestic source of equipment for their large farms.[152] Most owners of *latifundium* employed agronomists and educated their own agriculturalists, whom they then paid well and even provided with pension. Fertilization, drainage operation and the elimination of the three-field system were the prime concerns of estate managers. Scientific forestry, which had been initiated by Count István Széchenyi, was eagerly taken up by the aristocracy when the price of lumber quadrupled between 1832 and 1852. Jews were engaged to market estate-products. As urbanization progressed, the estate owners whose lands were located near towns imported Swiss and Tyrolian milk cows for their expanding dairy farms.[153]

Alcohol manufacturing was pursued on the estates of Counts Móric Sándor, György Károlyi, László Czindery and Prince Pál Esterházy. There were many modern flour and sugar mills owned by Mihály Zichy, Prince Coburg and other large agricultural producers.[154] Magnates had major interests in industries from iron smelters to bridge building.[155]

Economic modernization of Hungary had been initiated by them decades before the appearance of the Viennese Liberal Centralists. Notwithstanding, together with the new peasant proprietors and Jewish businessmen, the aristocracy were, indeed, the true beneficiaries of Liberal Centralist reforms. In the early 1850's the aristocrats, Jews and the Liberal Centralists became the chief driving forces behind the growing Hungarian economy. From the aristocracy's unappreciative attitude towards the Government for the substantial economic achievements attained during the military rule and the *Provisorium* one must draw the conclusion that the Old Conservatives felt that progress was inevitable—under any government. What they really desired was

> lawful constitutional freedom within a firmly established Monarchy; progress without revolution; a more powerful and united Austria, as well as a noticeable development of their own Fatherland; and strong guarantees for the above conditions as well as for the opportunity for peaceful legislative development.[156]

A clean loyalist slate, wealth, common ideology, optimism, a sense of manifest destiny, traditional leadership and a loose political association enabled the Old Conservatives "to take on" the Liberal Centralists and in conjunction with the Absolutist Centralists dislodge them from power.

Early successes in 1849 under Windischgrätz had electrified the aristocracy and the Magyar Catholic High Clergy. Their devotion to the Dynasty was undiminished and in concert with their patriotism. Once the Liberal Centralists came to power the Old Conservatives' loyalty was called into question. To counter, the aristocracy made use of personal contacts to influence the Habsburgs towards a federalist policy. Some of the magnates demonstratively withdrew from politics while others unsuccessfully attempted to reach a compromise with the Liberal Centralists. The Old Conservatives then modified their program again to attain a wider social base for a more aggressive political campaign against the Liberal Centralists. In harmony with the Catholic Church and the gentry, conservative nationalism was adopted to secure national unity.

From 1851, the aristocrats' legal opposition to the Liberal Centralists effectively weakened the regime. The overthrow of the Viennese Centralists was achieved through the efforts of a determined united Hungarian ruling class. The defeat of the Liberal Cabinet by 1853, however, did not bring victory to the Old Conservatives but rather to the Absolutist Centralists in Vienna. Nevertheless, the Magyar victory that did come in 1860 and ultimately in 1867 was hatched during the *Provisorium* when the Old Conservatives confronted the Liberal and Absolutist Centralists.

The Gentry in Opposition

The surrender at Világos in 1849 was a national tragedy for the Hungarian nobility. They lost their political leadership which they had wrested from the aristocracy during the bitter political struggles of the *Vormärz*. In 1848 they had even sacrificed their economic privileges and relinquished the *robot* of the serfs in fear of class war and in return for peasant support against Viennese centralism, Absolutist or Liberal. The leaders of the nobility had been lost to emigration, their bravest members on the battlefields and their intellectual spokesmen to the barren fields of self-pity or scapegoat hunting. As the world of the noblemen was falling apart, the class itself drifted towards an accelerated decline. The nobility of the *Provisorium*, except for the aristocracy, was only identical in name and in origin with the ruling class of the 1840's.[1] A social metamorphosis was apparent. Differentiation in social structure intensified after 1848 when the combined impact of economic and political losses became apparent.[2]

The upper layer of the untitled nobility was the *nobiles bene possessionati*, gentry or middle nobles, constituting about 20 per cent of the privileged class. In Hungary, out of 136,000 noble families 20,000 to 30,000 belonged to the gentry. Their wealthiest segment owned approximately 4,000 estates and earned at least 3,000 forints yearly on their 1,000 to 5,000 *holds* of land while the rest cultivated 200 to 1,000 *holds* of land per family and enjoyed a yearly income ranging from 500 to 3,000 forints.[3]

> The *bene possessionati* were country gentlemen who lived on their estates most of the year and supervised them according to the methods of their forefathers. Unlike the magnates, they lived unpretentiously and usually managed to save some money.[4]

They were Hungarian in culture and adhered mainly to the Protestant faith.[5] Frequently men of learning, some became renowned constitutional experts and men-of-letters. The gentry were relatively well-educated and before 1848 susceptible to Western ideas of romanticism, liberalism and nationalism.[6] Tradition, class consciousness, life-style and economic interest made the gentry a separate social entity from both the aristocracy and the lesser nobility.[7]

Even before 1848 the majority of the lesser nobility of about 35,000 to 40,000 families belonged to the privileged class only by law but not *de facto*. Their wealthiest segment held one or two hundred acres of land and several families of serfs. Others rented a single section from the aristocracy or the gentry or owned a small lot of about the same size. In either case they lived at a level of subsistence economy, only slightly better than their poorest cousins, the *armalists*, whose only possession was the dogskin parchment on which their origin was certified.

In the past the lesser nobility could participate in the political life of Hungary, but because their vote was not equal to that of the gentry and their limited means often prevented them from bearing honorary offices, or even travel to the county meetings, their political influence remained minimal. At times, however, the *armalists* and the *possessionati* became pawns of Viennese politicians or the *bene possessionati* and as was the case in 1849, of the radical intelligentsia. Following the War of Independence many remained hirelings of the gentry, together with the majority of the intelligentsia whether of common (honoratior) or noble origin.[8] Few of the lesser nobles attempted to promote republicanism or lead the odd social movements of the peasantry. In sum, the lower echelon of the nobility remained outside the ranks of the Hungarian ruling class, the aristocracy and the gentry.

While the early sixteenth century was the age of the gentry, the following two centuries were eras of continuous general economic and political decline for the group. From 1815 the medium landowners' position underwent the dual process of political renaissance and further economic deterioration. The landowners who during the French Revolution and the Napoleonic Wars failed to exploit the economic boom and modernize their estates remained heavily indebted and soon were ruined financially. Only those who abandoned the obsolete agrarian methods and acquired both capital and technical expertise were able to counter the forces which weakened the impact of the boom.[9]

To supply the healthy grain market and later the flourishing wool trade, enterprising middle nobles borrowed more and more money for investment purposes.[10] The easing of entail regulations allowed the landlords to raise more cash than they could have previously secured.[11] Due to fluctuating market conditions, poor transportation facilities and distances from major markets, extravagant life styles and, in particular, Vienna's partisan policies, even the successful members of the gentry faced certain financial difficulties.

The pre-1848 Viennese Government placed unusually high duties on Hungarian grains destined for export and for Austria proper. When the gentry began to cultivate new staples, notably tobacco and wool, the Austrian agricultural producers were protected again by the raising of the already high internal tariff wall between Hungary and Cisleithania.

> The policy of the Vienna Government was to weaken the Magyar gentry economically, lessen their resistance to Austrian rule, and prevent them from assuming the leadership of the nation.[12]

Consequently, on the eve of the Revolution of 1848 the nobility was indebted to the amount of 300 million forints for which the creditors collected 18 million forints in interest—an amount approximating Hungary's annual tax revenue. The gentry, to extricate itself from the increasingly oppressive economic circumstances intensified its exploitation of the serfs or increased the domain at the expense of rustic holdings. More *robot* was demanded of the serfs who were deprived of pay for overtime *robot*. However, the middle nobility soon became disturbed by the low productivity of statutory labor. During the *Vormärz* prosperous nobles had already started to consider the use of wage labor to replace *robot*. Those members of the gentry who for the benefit of the wool trade illegally increased their share of the common clearings and pastures were in no great need of *robot*, but their circumvention of the law resulted in the alienation of large segments of the peasantry.[13]

In 1848 the Hungarian War of Independence and Revolution attempted to solve the economic problems of the gentry via autarky and emancipation. After Világos autarky was shelved for its proven economic unfeasibility. The gentry was also having second thoughts over the giving up of their right to *robot* and other privileges. They certainly had no desire to go beyond the social and economic reforms of 1848. Some considered the social legislation of the Revolution against the interest of the gentry, which indeed it was in so far as its immediate impact was concerned. Korizmics, a most reputable gentry economist, suggested heavier taxes on those who had received free land, that is, the liberated serfs.[14] On the pages of the *Pesti Napló* several ex-lords proposed the levying of redemption dues on the free peasants much to the dismay of the Liberal editors.[15] In the view of the *Magyar Hirlap* the emancipation was a "rush job." The editors recommended that the remainder lands[16] should stay with the lords and the gentry should be excused from paying taxes until the question of redemption was settled.[17] More and more gentry came to conclude that the Emancipation had brought few economic advantages.[18]

In the counties of Bihar, Nógrád and Szabolcs there were frequent illegal demands for various services abolished during the Revolution.[19] The gentry of Bihar tried to claim *robot* retroactively for the Civil War years.[20] In Baranya County the local gentry petitioned the courts for compensation from their ex-serfs for unfulfilled past *robot* obligations.[21] In addition, the gentry fought for the retention of the privileges which Kossuth and Bach had left untouched. Many remnants of former landlord-serf legal relations were preserved.[22] Furthermore, until 1853 ambiguity prevailed concerning the separation of meadow and forest lands, the legal status of vineyards and minor royal usufructs which had been retained by the lords in 1848.

Gentry rights were challenged by the Hungarian lower classes rather than the Government.[23] There were reported forest and meadow land occupations by peasants in Vas, Zemplén, Arad, Heves, Bihar and Tolna counties, some of whom had also sold wine illegally in 1849.[24] In 1850 lesser nobles and peasant renters in Zala, Somogy, Szabolcs, Szepes and Gömör counties often refused to pay vineyard tithe.[25] The intensity of the class struggle, however, declined as more and more appeals were channeled in the direction of the courts or directly to the Emperor rather than to local gentry authorities, who preferred "simpler" solutions—the employment of the army or the gendarmerie. Although they might have not always agreed on methods, both the Liberal Centralists and the gentry wanted to consolidate the new agricultural ownership regime. The ex-landlords retained most arable land; there remained only the question of how they would adjust to the new situation of greater economic opportunities but diminished supplies of free labor and capital. A series of crop failures in Western Europe and Cisleithania began to have a stimulating effect on the Hungarian economy. Prices of most agricultural products and of arable lands rose steadily despite several good harvests in Hungary during the early 1850's. The expanding domestic market also provided the gentry with possibilities. Hungarians, for example, consumed 800,000 hundredweights of tobacco in 1850 but of this amount the local market supplied only 430,000 hundredweights.[26] Government measures contributed to the general prosperity, especially to the welfare of those agricultural producers who successfully solved the problems of capital and labor shortages, and who introduced modern methods of cultivation to increase the productivity of their lands. The *bene possessionati* belonged to that group.

The post-revolutionary cash position of the gentry was seemingly worse than that of the aristocracy. The middle nobles had donated or been pressured into giving financial support to the Kossuth regime. In 1849 when the Hungarian Kossuth currency was declared illegal by Windischgrätz, savings were wiped out. Hardest hit were areas where the revolutionaries had made their last stand.[27] Warring armies destroyed buildings and equipment. The newly introduced direct taxes weighed heavily on the gentry class which was unaccustomed to paying taxes. Contemporaries spoke of economic disaster, the disappearance of the gentry as a class because of the *bene possessionati*'s increasing indebtedness and inability to hire workers and pay taxes.[28] Nationalist Magyar historians later offered a seemingly logical explanation for the gentry's tax problems; the middle nobles had demonstrated their disapproval of the Government via passive resistance, one manifestation of which was non- or late-payment of taxes.[29] Many Western historians accepted this explanation at face value.[30] In fact, the gentry had difficulty raising capital, which they needed for machinery, labor and taxes.

Money was expensive because of the moratorium on old debts, the traditional distrust of gentry credibility and shortage of modern financial institutions in Hungary. Nevertheless, the gentry continued to borrow at high interest rate from saving banks and local merchants and traders. From 1850 a limited amount of advance cash compensation in the form of annuities eased somewhat the capital need of the middle nobility. The cost of rent which rose along with the land prices also benefited the gentry[31] in spite of the rising rental fees; there was a scramble for new land leases.[32] Some of the old tenants, particularly the lesser noble renters of demesne, protested the increased rents and the occasional cancellation of leases.[33] Nevertheless, the gentry was not anxious to allow the benefits of the agricultural boom to remain with renters.

> [In] most cases, landowners did not let all of their property but only a part of it in order to use the rent they collected for the economic development of the land farmed by themselves... In all, slightly less than one-fifth of the total of Hungarian landed property was farmed by leaseholders.[34]

The proportion of lessors was higher among the gentry landowners whose principal source of labor in the past had been the *robot*. They either sold their patrimony outright or experimented with sharecropping.[35] One former landlord who parcelled out his demesne confided to a sympathetic English traveller: "I have been in this way freed from the annoyance of finding labor, at this time, for my field."[36]

For the gentry, who insisted on managing most parts of their estate, the elimination of the *robot*, and the unavailability of bonded workers precipitated a rise in wages. Employers were further aggravated by the reluctance of ex-serfs to hire themselves out to landlords who had formerly mistreated them. Sagacious peasants refused labor in a deliberate attempt to drive their new competitors into bankruptcy.[37] In any case, the liberated peasants, what with newly acquired lands and additional employment on government projects, had sufficient work. According to the calculations of György Szabad there was need for 291 million labor-days in the Hungarian agricultural sector in the 1850's and male workers could provide 423 million days of work in addition to the available labor force of peasant women.[38] Regrettably, these figures did not take into consideration psychological and geographical factors. Surplus labor did not necessarily mean available labor. Distance from markets, the size of estates in a given county and the seasonable distribution of labor need accounted more for the employment situation than did national averages. For example, in Baranya County the peasants refused to cut wood for the ex-lords for any amount of money.[39] In contrast, the Jewish renters in Zemplén County had little difficulty hiring harvesters.[40] In the Rábaköz the "good" gentry was also preferred by the discriminating laborer.[41]

The relative shortage of labor was coupled with a relative increase in labor cost.[42] Relative cost of labor, that is, the proportion of average labor cost to the gross income per hold of the employers, was depressed despite its rise in absolute terms. This opinion is shared by Berzeviczy[43] and contemporary observers who considered labor cheap but the gentry tight fisted.[44] Bernát, however, emphasized the gentry's economic difficulties and produced a ratio of 1/6 for relative cost.[45] If one uses Bernát's own data as they appear throughout his book, a greater variation becomes evident.

The average labor cost per cadastral *hold* was six forints and the average wheat cost four forints per Pozsony bushel. A cadastral *hold* yielded five to 22 Pozsony bushels or 30 to 132 forints. The average labor cost per cadastral *hold* over gross income per cadastral *hold* varied from 1/5 to 1/22. Therefore, regardless of the 100 to 400 per cent increase in wages, the relative cost of labor remained between five to 20 per cent.

The low value of the daily earnings of peasants can also be demonstrated by an examination of the cost of basic commodities in Hungary in the early 1850's.[46] Nevertheless, even the low cost of labor caused difficulties to over 40 per cent of the gentry, although the problem of paying it was satisfactorily solved by most of them as their tax returns demonstrated.[47] Some of the gentry even made advance payments.

Tax collectors only encountered difficulties because of certain ill-conceived governmental regulations or natural calamities. In Hungary the time between notification of arrearages and seizure of the tax-payer's assets was reduced to a mere eight days, the total process comprising only one month. Nevertheless, 75 to 90 per cent of all arrears were collected without recourse to auction.[49] Demands to pay taxes in full after the poor harvest of 1852 in the Kassa and Pozsony districts and unjust levying of taxes due to faulty cadastral surveys rather than defiance of the Government brought some of the gentry into conflict with the authorities.[50] The post-revolutionary economic boom took care of many wounds of the middle nobility.

Not even the lack of agricultural expertise could stand between prosperity and the *bene possessionati*. In the past they had been both politicians and farmers and many maintained their dual roles after the Revolution but few understood ranching, marketing, and crop diversification sufficiently to safeguard their income from the fluctuations of the international commodity market. Nevertheless, none of these factors influenced them adversely since no great amount of knowledge was necessary to grow wheat or other cereals, the most extensively cultivated crops of the 1850's, and tobacco required little attention in the virgin soils which were being brought under cultivation from 1849.[51]

The future was not promising because neither the moratorium on debts nor the high wheat prices could last forever, but between 1849 and 1853 there was prosperity for the gentry.[52] According to a Hungarian historian "the position of the agricultural producer in the last century was best under absolutism."[53] Even György Szabad, a hostile critic of the nobility, admitted, although reluctantly, that at least a thin layer of the gentry who had a well organized demesne before 1848 reaped the benefits of post-revolutionary prosperity.[54]

The Hungarian gentry lived in relative comfort. Its increasing income was spent on the mainstays of good living: plentiful food, wine, fancy dresses for the ladies and four-horsed carriages to visit neighbors or the local gentry club, the casino.[55] This was the golden age of the family and social life in Hungary. From Világos to the mid-1850's rather than being an era of national mourning, it was, for the children of the beneficiaries of the economic boom, a period of indolence, cosmopolitan nonchalance, and at places, slavish imitation of Viennese modes.[56] The cynical gentry youth spurned politics in place of epicureanism. The first ball season after the Revolution proved so successful that it continued into the solemn Lent period.[57] During the following years the social events were equally well-attended.[58] This boisterous behavior of the young scions was frowned upon by many Magyar patriots.[59] Of course, the senior members of *bene possessionati* families viewed life with a broader perspective.

The pattern of the past was reversed, now interest in agriculture preceded politics. After 1849 the majority devoted all their energies to the development of their estates.[60] Buildings had to be restored, labor recruited, machinery purchased, burnt or stolen seeds replaced and conflicts concerning past obligations of ex-serfs and disputes over land boundaries settled. Gentlemen farmers began to spend their winters as well as other seasons overseeing their estates.[61] There was however, another reason for the gentry to stay at home. It was fear.

During the Revolution the middle nobility had provided the leading cadres for Kossuth's Army and his administration. By 1849 the *bene possessionati* began to disassociate themselves through the Peace Party from the radical intelligentsia and the lesser nobles. They rejected the separatist and democratic tendencies of the Kossuthites but their opposition was not significant enough for Vienna to dissociate them from Kossuth's radical supporters and, consequently, spare them from punishment and persecution.[62] Fear of arrest now haunted those who had had any connection with the Kossuth regime.[63] Neighbors harassed each other—denunciators mushroomed throughout the country.[64] The message of no more rebellion against the Habsburgs, delivered through summary military courts, was understood by the middle nobility. Any provocative act of individual or conspiratorial nature magnified the gentry's fears because of expectations of increased oppressive measures.[65]

The gentry were also apprehensive that the Liberal Centralists in Vienna were only making false promises and would avoid instituting actual reforms. They were dissatisfied over legal uncertainties, delayed compensation payments for *robot,* the snail-pace separation and consolidation of land holdings and irregular governmental enforcement of retained privileges.[66] In the Sopron District the new modern Civil Code was viewed as an attempt to wipe out the gentry as a class.[67] In the midst of economic prosperity a sense of security and permanence was absent.

For the *bene possessionati* the most frightening prospect was the possibility of *jacqueries*. The countryside remained in a state of turmoil until 1852. Peasant violence, often instigated by the lesser nobility, was directed against the former lords rather than the Habsburgs. Many cottagers firmly believed that Kossuth would soon return and distribute the lords' estates amongst the landless.[68] Those who had received land in 1848 put their faith first in Ferdinand and then in Franz Joseph. By 1853 some peasants handed over anti-Habsburg agitators to authorities.[69] They credited reforms to Vienna and "distrusted city-bred lawyer literati and country squires."[70] Geringer advised Bach about the weak political position of the gentry whose influence over the lower classes had "almost completely" disappeared.[71] The Kassa District gendarmerie, for example, maintained that in the case of a general upheaval the peasants would attack the nobility.

For the gentry the most deplorable aspect of the situation was the position taken by certain senior civil servants who often welcomed this alienation of gentry and peasantry except for its anarchistic aspects.[73] The experience of 1848 and 1849, the memory of past atrocities, awakening national consciousness and the Government's policy of national equality weighed heavily on the minds of those gentry who lived in areas where the majority of the population consisted of hostile Slovak, Ukrainian, Rumanian or Serbian peasants. A tense situation existed in both northern and southern Hungary.[74] The gentry feared Slavic intellectuals who together with some germanizing Austrian bureaucrats seemed to threaten their Magyar culture, which they claimed to have safeguarded since the late eighteenth century.[75] In the opinion of Geringer, fear for Magyardom reached neurotic stages in 1850.[76]

Fear and prosperity helped to ensure continuous opposition to Kossuthite republicanism, and to further social reforms. The gentry's unwanted dependence on Vienna produced only moderate resistance to the Government, whose politics the gentry abhorred but on whom they ultimately relied for security which was now threatened from many directions.

The general mood was one of regret and bitterness. The gentry congratulated themselves on their supposed generosity to their serfs, regarded themselves as the vanquished but ever determined bearers of Magyar national consciousness. They cursed Kossuth and his chief general, Artur Görgey. They blamed them along with others, such as "lazy" peasants, "greedy" Jews and "proud" aristocrats for the gentry's plight and for the catastrophe of Világos. Zsigmond Kemény's widely read treatises, *After the Revolution* and *One More Word After the Revolution,* branded Kossuth as a dreamer who embodied all excesses of virtue without facing geopolitical realities of an Austrian Empire.[78] The author considered the Revolution a political mistake of the Magyar gentry but neither did he accept Viennese centralism as a viable alternative.

In addition to rejection of the Revolution, complaints against the Government became the most common conversation topics in gentry households and clubs.[79] A member of the middle nobility remarked bitterly to his British guest in 1851:

> They have taxed everything, my house, garden, crops, my wine and the tobacco in my fields; and even my wife and my servants must pay their poll tax.[80]

Mór Jókai's literary hero, Adam Garamvölgyi, promised his neighbor not to smoke, to avoid the tax and improve his appetite; not to drink wine, to escape the tax and sleep better; not to hunt, to evade applying for a permit and not to catch a cold; and, finally, not to sue in order to refrain from paying court fees and to have more friends.[81] The fictional Garamvölgyi actually attempted to follow Kossuth's advice but his counterpart in real life never became much of an oppositionist between 1849 and 1853.[82]

Some gentlemen promised to cease smoking as a form of protest against the state tobacco monopoly. After a week or so the Magyars kept their pipes continuously stuffed as before. Tobacco production and consumption rose steadily in Hungary.[83] Hunting was abandoned by necessity and not by choice since the military government confiscated all firearms. The courts were kept busy settling quarrels between ex-lords and liberated serfs. Opposition to the Government nevertheless, did exist, although it was only symbolic on the social level.

During the Easter holidays in 1850 patriots visited the grave of a Russian colonel who had attempted to join the Hungarian *Honvéd* Army with his regiment and was subsequently executed by Paskevich, the head of the interventionary forces in Hungary in 1849.[84] At social events the nobility wore national costumes and endlessly ordered the gypsies to play the *csárdás,* the Magyar national dance.[85] Ladies demonstratively avoided dancing with imperial officers, wore jewelry engraved with the initials of executed Magyar generals and a patriotic slogan—written in German.[86] Noblemen made it a mark of honor to deceive customs officials and deliberately made a show of leaving restaurants or railway carriages whenever Slavic or Austrian officials or officers appeared on the scene.[87]

In the spring of 1852 gentry circles, while eagerly following foreign news in the hope that events in France might bring beneficial changes to Hungary,[88] began debating how to receive the Emperor during his maiden visit.[89] However, when the Emperor Franz Joseph did not grant a much expected general amnesty or return constitutional privileges to the gentry, the Hungarian royal tour lost its initial chance for success.[90] In a few areas of the Pozsony District the gentry would not participate in the Emperor's reception. At Ungvár only a fraction of the local aristocracy and gentry appeared at public ceremonies. Others left town without attending to the customary decoration of their houses.[91]

In the Szepes area authorities were unable to raise a *banderium,* a cavalry escort for guarding Franz Joseph.[92] At the Eperjes reception most gentry families were represented, but not by their most distinguished members.[93] The Nagyvárad gendarmerie's depiction of the gentry attitude towards the Emperor as "lukewarm" was most apt.[94]

By early 1853, however, at the time of the attempted assassination of Franz Joseph, the gentry's sentiments towards their ruler became more affectionate. In the Districts of Pozsony, Nagyvárad and Pest the attempted regicide was abhorred.[95] Only the gendarmeries of Szatmár, Heves and Borsod counties reported "mixed reaction" to the event.[96] Suddenly, the gentry's differentiation between government and sovereign became obvious. It was the initial step towards conciliation between the king and the country at the expense of the Liberal Centralists and the nationalities. Resistance to government, especially its nationality policies was much more uncompromising.

Children were removed from school if the headmaster or mother superior could not speak Hungarian. University students insisted on ostracizing those who would not converse in Magyar.[97] Germans, Slavs and Jews were pressured to assimilate so that during the census of 1850 many of them registered as Magyars. They had to send their children to Magyar schools because the knowledge of Magyar was an important step towards acceptance by the ruling class.[98] Those who resisted magyarization were denounced as pan-Slavs. Csengery, a prominent gentry-publicist wrote in 1851 to his father: "We shall sustain the superiority of our race."[99]

Csengery's assertion reflected the views of the gentry-ridden middle level administrators. Fears of the nationalities and a need for a strong state apparatus weighed heavily on their minds. To relieve the gentry of their anxieties the Magyar civil servants excluded, when possible, other nationalities from holding public office and deprived them from recourse to sympathetic administrators. Furthermore, they actively mistreated the lower classes, abused their pro-governmental colleagues and sabotaged Liberal Centralist reforms willfully or through neglect. The opposition of the gentry bureaucrats was not symbolic but paralyzing and destructive albeit not revolutionary.

In principle, the *bene possessionati* opposed collaboration with the Government.[100] The generalization in Macartney and Szabad's statements that the entire Hungarian gentry refused to bear public office is not acceptable in the light of available evidence.[101] Only in a few areas did the gentry stay in the background leaving all offices to honoratiors and poorer landlords.[102] In fact, during the autumn of 1850, when competitions were opened for numerous administrative posts at the viceroyalty, district, county and borough offices, the authorities received far more applications than required.[103] At Makó, for example, before the administrative reorganization of Hungary over 25 qualified individuals competed for four senior positions.[104] When one considers the average gentry income and their initial financial difficulties after the Revolution, it is unlikely that they would have frowned upon the possibility of doubling their income. In addition to their income from farming, they could receive a yearly salary of between 1,000 and 3,000 forints but the gentry had to compete with the aristocracy for positions in the judiciary.[105] There were only a few gentry families which had no immediate members in government service between 1849 and 1853.[106] The honoratiors, whose opinions and political views differed little from the gentry, could still less afford to decline governmental positions because of their complete lack of financial independence.[107] Once in office, gentry and honoratiors combined their efforts against non-Magyar competitors.

Slovak intellectuals wanted representatives in the civil service, their language accepted at par with German and Magyar, the formation of Slovak boroughs with Slovak administrators, trilingual schools and Slovak village councils. These nationalists were frustrated by hostile Magyar civil servants who ignored their constitutional rights and, in addition, accused them of pan-Slavic leanings and tried to provoke them into anti-governmental manifestations.[108] Slovak leaders complained of extraordinarily heavy fines imposed on their co-national peasants in Nyitra and Trencsény counties. Ukrainians of the Kassa District also demanded, unsuccessfully, respect for their language from an "alien" administration.[109] Serbs in the neighborhood of Világosvár and Germans from Soroksár protested the uneven hand of justice in their respective districts.[110] The Magyar civil servants equally oppressed both the ethnic and the Magyar peasantry.

Gentry officials thought of themselves as masters of the people whom they often treated, in the opinion of better educated German bureaucrats, in a most uncivilized manner.[111] In a Transdanubian village all male inhabitants were flogged for tax evasion and "stubbornness." [112] Lawyers, who attempted to assist peasants from the Kassa district with their court cases, were harassed. The judges, who were with few exceptions former landlords, attempted to frighten away the peasants from using regular and special courts and when the tactic failed they applied the laws inequitably.[113] Class and ethnic discrimination was not practised against those who cooperated—peasants who preoccupied themselves with work, wine and religion. To gain their support, some civil servants tried to take credit for Viennese reforms while blaming the Liberal Centralists and their own non-magyar colleagues for all difficulties.[114] A compaign was conducted against both non-Magyar officials and conscientious Magyar civil servants.

If, at any place, the nationalities managed to enforce the Liberal Centralist nationality program, a public outcry ensued. The presence of a Croatian judge at Zala, Serbian administrators at Kanizsa, Zenta and Szabadka was vehemently denounced on the pages of the *Pesti Napló*.[115] District officials, who had recently been transferred to Hungary from other Crownlands, were constantly criticized for their real and alleged mistakes. They were mocked as "Bach Hussars" and regarded, unjustifiably, as remnants of the Imperial bureaucracy.[116] Protmann, Pest-Buda's police chief, grumbled bitterly to Archduke Albrecht about the success which Magyar civil servants had in discrediting loyal officials.[117]

Some of the administrators, however, took the Government's reform program seriously. They did not just exhaust themselves in fabricating cases and making childish observations on the people's mood as Szekfű has claimed.[118] Some urged their superiors not to adopt a strict tax collecting method until the population adjusted to the new laws. Protest came from one of the county chiefs against the excesses of the Military and against confiscation of firearms at a time when farmers were threatened by roving wolves and foxes.[119] The City of Debrecen speedily modernized its administrative procedures and set up an independent police force.[120] Local officials often proposed the equal distribution among counties of the burden of feeding and quartering Imperial armed forces.[121] These administrators and the population often combined their resources to overcome cholera, rinderpest, floods, famine and inflation.

In addition to the reform administrators, another target, the gendarmerie, was selected by the gentry and pro-gentry honoratior officials. They feared and hated this internal security force because it kept a watchful eye on the bureaucracy and protected peasants from arbitrary ex-landlords and local officials.[122] There was only token cooperation between the Hungarian courts and the gendarmerie. The county chiefs bombarded their superiors with remonstrances about the gendarmes with whom they refused to correlate their security work. Neither did middle level officials execute directives from Vienna with any haste or enthusiasm. Orders from the central government which were considered contrary to the interest of the nobility were ignored. New laws, including the civil and criminal codes, went unexplained. Many officials practised nepotism, accepted bribes and spent more time attending to private business than their official duties.[123]

The civil servants in Hungary worked actively for the preservation of social order and for the maintenance of their hegemony over the nationalities. As individuals they may have served the regime for a better income, career, power or at times for the true benefit of their charges, but as a group they demonstrated a high degree of class consciousness.[124] Their opposition to the Government was colored by their awareness of gentry economic and social interest. In the absence of a leader and a clear political program, the gentry, those who stayed at home as well as those who collaborated, gave support to the national unity group, the Old Conservatives.

When the Old Conservatives made their major move against the Liberal Centralists, they received the backing of the gentry. Three of the signatories of the April Memorandum who had their estates in Zemplén County began to feed the flames of Hungarian constitutionalism. Together with other leaders of the County they convinced a good part of the administrators to resign in support of the Memorandum.[125] The Tolna County Chief reported to his superior that the writings of the Old Conservatives adversely affected public opinion.[126] Following modern liberal journalistic trends, the *Pesti Napló* published an attack on itself from the pen of a North Bihar County correspondent. The writer, in the name of local pre-1848 Liberals, declared that they were determined to join the Old Conservatives and criticized the editor for constantly attacking the party which was laboring for the entire nation.[127] Similar reports came from Arad,[128] Békés,[129] Csongrád[130] and Szepes[131] counties. A Csanád county correspondent of the *Pesti Napló* chided an aristocrat who had agitated for the support of the "stinking Memorandum," but reluctantly acknowledged the Old Conservative gentleman's effectiveness in convincing the local civil servants to resign *en masse*.[132] There were also major resignations in Debrecen and Pozsony.[133] Anti-Old Conservative voices were rare, restricted mainly to editorials.[134] The editors of the *Pesti Napló* admitted that during the first part of 1850, the Old Conservatives had acquired "some" popularity because people believed that, under the circumstances, only this party could remain active.[135]

Another institutional stronghold of the gentry, the Protestant Churches, espoused the policies of the Old Conservatives. In the past, leadership of these Churches had been provided by the middle nobility, but a concentrated Governmental drive to depoliticize the Churches by the expulsion of lay leaders threw the Protestants into disarray. The Government's policy was put into effect with comparative ease. In the spirit of anti-Habsburg, anti-Catholic tradition, many Calvinists and Lutherans had been in the forefront of the revolutionary struggle in 1849 and, as a result, were purged by the Schwarzenberg-Bach Administration. The continuous conflict between Catholics and Protestants, and between the Magyars and non-Magyars of the Lutheran Church further weakened the Protestant cause in Hungary after the Revolution.[136] Protestant leaders consequently restricted their activities to the freeing of the Church from Haynau's tight control, so that they might regain self-government and the independence of their schools. It was not martyrdom, as church historians later claimed, but a compromise for which Protestant bishops, pastors and ministers prepared their congregations.[137] They offered their loyalty to Vienna for Church autonomy.[138] Imitating the strategy of the Old Conservatives, they appealed to Franz Joseph over the heads of the Liberal Centralist Ministers.

On the pages of the *Pesti Napló* the Protestant plan to struggle for autonomy by delegations and pamphlets, was openly declared.[139] On 9 December 1850 the first deputation presented itself to the Emperor.[140] Next spring the Eperjes Conference of Protestant Pastors sent the Conservative Ede Zsedényi to Vienna. At his heels followed other groups from Miskolcs, Kecskemét and Szentes, often encouraged by Old Conservatives.[142] Closer to home, Thun's educational reforms threatened the legitimacy of Protestant gymnasia which lacked adequate funds and qualified teachers to comply with the new regulations. Notwithstanding, the plight of the two Churches attracted the sympathy of Catholics and Jews.[143] The gentry leadership managed to keep Protestant discontent temporarily within limits and in line with the Old Conservative policies. The Protestant Churches would not allow the discontent of their members to surface in fear of retaliation. They put their faith in national unity because they associated the autonomy of the Protestant Churches with the autonomy of Hungary.[144]

The idea of national unity and Conservative leadership was also promoted by the few writers who correctly interpreted the mood of the gentry in the early 1850's. For a year after the Revolution the intellectual wing of the middle nobility remained silent because of fear and the shock of Világos. But once most publicists, novelists and poets abandoned their state of literary stupor, they advanced claims of ideological leadership. They failed, however, to provide their class with an independent political program acceptable to all. They could only mirror gentry sentiments. In the absence of recognized and willing political leaders, they welcomed the aristocracy as their spokesmen just as the middle level bureaucracy and the Protestant Churches had done.

Agonizing over the defeat of Hungary, the intellectuals agreed without much dissension to condemn Kossuthite adventurism. They rejected Kossuth and advocated national unity and sober opposition to germanization, annexation and Austrian civilization. In the midst of economic prosperity their advocacy of consolidation, a certain amount of accommodation with Vienna, social peace and Magyar racial supremacy in the guise of national unity was music to the ears of the Hungarian gentry. Hungarian supporters of the Liberal Centralists like the original editorial guard of the *Pesti Napló* or József Eötvös, cabinet minister in 1848 and philosopher, failed to gain popularity with their ideas of progress and Imperial patriotism.[145] The reading public preferred Jókai, the self-professed bard of national unity and aristocratic leadership,[146] Kemény's pamphlets which urged the nation to protect the future from adventurers and the nationalities and the plays of Ede Szigligeti[147] which were populated with harmless peasants and disarming young nobles. Similarly, *Bánk Bán,* a new patriotic opera, composed by Ferenc Erkel and the *Rákóczi March (Fifteenth Rhapsody)* by Franz Liszt were instant successes.[148] Gentry patriotism gradually deteriorated into Magyar chauvinism. Its adherents oppressed the national minorities but seldom confronted the Habsburgs with equal determination. A cursory survey of the contemporary press may well illustrate this point. The *Magyar Hirlap* constantly spoke of Magyar spiritual superiority over all ethnic groups in Hungary whose cruelty and barbarity was emphasized.[149] The *Pesti Napló* wrote about "centuries of racial superiority" and declared the equality of nationalities a practical impossibility.[150] During the *Provisorium* chauvinism, a poison which Hungary could not overcome for a century, was adopted first by the gentry and then by almost all Magyars.[151] Consequently, all attempts by Kossuth and the émigré gentry leadership to mobilize Hungary through conspiracies were from the outset condemned to failure.

In June, 1851 the butler of the American painter, Walter Gould, visited the exiled Kossuth at a small town in the Ottoman Empire. The butler, alias József Makk, former artillery officer of the Hungarian *Honvéd* Army, convinced Kossuth that the time was ripe to organize a national uprising in Hungary and Transylvania. The ex-governor authorized the formation of a Central Committee, an Invisible Government, and a general plan for the rekindling of the Revolution.[152] Makk was instructed to conduct propaganda and win the support of Magyars in the armed forces, civil service and the priesthood for the establishment of an independent Hungarian republic. The peasants were to resist passively or join guerrilla leaders, like the famous highwayman Sándor Rózsa.[153] Free land was to be the reward for all those who would enlist in the new revolutionary army. Makk, in his own Manifesto, vowed to exterminate traitors and their families. He threatened hostile civil servants with the same and went so far as to depict the barbarities their children would undergo. These nonsensical statements were crowned by the offer of a Magyar pope for the Catholic clergy.[154]

Makk, whose sanity and military honor was questioned by many who knew him even before the issuance of the Manifesto, established his headquarters at Bucharest under the watchful eyes of the local police and the Austrian consul.[155] Nevertheless, he still managed to send agents to Transylvania. There a popular teacher, János Török, organized a small band of dissatisfied intellectuals, priests and landlords. Török was, however, already under police observation. Total failure occurred when a gentry member of the group, Mihály Bíró, handed over the membership list to authorities.

Makk's emissaries contacted the Kossuth family at Pest whose house was also being watched by Protmann's police agents. Kossuth's sister, Mrs. Meszlényi, however, had her own ideas about the leadership of the conspiracy. She selected her children's tutor, Károly Jubál, to head the organization and urged her brother to put his trust with this old friend of the family. Jubál, who led the Pest Committee of revolutionaries, was more than willing to replace Makk. His group had some successes in organizing a network of activists in Transdanubia, but their ranks had also been infiltrated by the police.[157]

Kossuth was perturbed by Makk's inefficiency, his secret dealings with a rival émigré revolutionary group and his disregard of an earlier promise to avoid contact with the Kossuth sisters. Neither did he tolerate Mrs. Meszlényi's interference with his plans. He now commissioned the former General Sándor Gál to organize a Transylvania army and head the Invisible Government in Hungary, which so far had Makk as its sole member. Gál, in turn, sent his agents to Transylvania from his new headquarters in Constantinople.[158] Meanwhile, Kossuth was chasing his mirages to London, hoping to coordinate his plans with Mazzini and the French radicals—who refused to give him financial aid for arms purchases. When Kossuth ordered his agents to arouse the armies near Hamburg and organize an uprising of the Viennese, Bach decided that it was time to wind up the plot.[159] Most of the arrested conspirators were sent to the gallows.

The Conservative *Pesti Napló's* jibe at Kossuth as "the Magyar Don Quixote" was not without merit at that time.[160] He had turned deaf ears to the warnings of his own agents who complained against aristocrats, gentry, civil servants and ordinary clergymen for not sympathizing with the cause. He would not comprehend the general lack of a revolutionary mood in Hungary. Of the approximately 200 persons who were involved in the Hungarian and Transylvania conspiracy, the majority were ex-*honvéds*, purged civil servants and intellectuals.[161] The gentry had abandoned Kossuth's sinking ship months before Világos and were now dismayed when they saw how enthusiastic patriots were again senselessly sacrificed for a revolution few people had ever wanted. There were not many illusions left about Kossuth's ability to solve the gentry's real social and economic problems. Berzeviczy stated this most succinctly:

> It is beyond doubt that the majority of the nation did not agree with the aims of the émigrés and that it wished to achieve success through other means. It is also beyond doubt that the friends of the émigrés at home often misled their associates concerning the mood of the people and the possibilities for a new revolution.[162]

The other potential leader of the *bene possessionati*, Ferenc Deák, despite claims by generations of admiring historians, failed to give guidance to his people between 1849 and 1853.[163] In the spring of 1850, after a military court failed to indict him for any wrong doing during the Revolution, Deák retired to his estate in Transdanubia. He rejected Schmerling's invitation to assist in creating a civil code for Hungary and allowed the Viennese liberal paper, the *Ostdeutsche Post* to print his reply to the Minister of Justice.[164] In this way he publicly demonstrated his dislike of the Liberal Centralists, but suggested no alternative direction for the future. His home was opened to aristocratic and gentry politicians alike.[165] His reply to Szögyény-Marich, who asked his views on Magyar participation on the Imperial Council, was non-committal but sympathetic.[166] The policy of Deák until the mid-1850's remained unclear and in Lukács's opinion, Deák, just like the whole gentry, indubitably approved the actions of the Old Conservatives.[167] Some of Deák's friends also remained politically inactive like Ákos Trefort, Gábor Klauzál and Mór Lukács, or without influence as was the case of Eötvös and Kemény, who overestimated the gentry's willingness to sacrifice its political leadership permanently for progress, prosperity and national hegemony.[168]

The *bene possessionati* had no other option but to back the only legitimate oppositionist group, the Old Conservatives. Gentry officials, Protestant clergymen and intellectuals safeguarded their social dominance and cultural hegemony within the legal framework of the post-revolutionary regime. Without acceptable leaders and mass support the gentry could not reach for the reins of power unless they risked all that had been gained or maintained. They were determined to ride out the storm in the shadow of the Old Conservatives whose campaign against the Liberal Centralists they had actively supported. The gentry was anxious to differentiate between the Liberal Centralists, whose views they found too democratic and liberal, and the Habsburg edifice. The former they helped to destroy, the latter to rebuild as a protective umbrella against rebellious peasants and non-Magyar nationalists.

Conclusion

The failure of the Revolutions of 1848 brought about the defeat of the Hungarian independence movement but not of liberalism, the ideology of the middle classes. The House of Habsburg employed a group of right wing liberals, the Liberal Centralists, to rejuvenate the Empire economically, socially and culturally and to bring new glories for the House and more business for the Austrian bourgeoisie in Germany. The Liberal Centralists, contrary to the *Reichstag,* offered to tackle the nationality question before liberalizing the Imperial institutions. They suspected that modernization was impossible with the social-reactionary dominant classes in Transleithania and, therefore, wished to introduce the March Constitution gradually in the whole Empire after they had broadened their mass base to include other classes besides the Cisleithanian bourgeoisie.

In Hungary, in light of these considerations, Haynau's terror in 1849, tightly controlled by the Cabinet, became essential in the scheme of things to avoid any interruption, a new uprising, in the interest of rejuvenation. During the Terror many martyrs were created, whom the Magyars have revered ever since, but in whose name national rising did not occur for more than a hundred years.

Once Hungary was pacified, the Liberal Centralists quickly wound up the military rule in order to commence their program within the framework of the March Constitution. The Cabinet attempted to provide justice, security and prosperity for all classes and nationalities. Hungary was to be rejuvenated, her schools upgraded, the public administration and legal system de-bureaucratized and her laws modernized. The pacified country was to be neither exploited nor colonized. Hungary was to participate on equal terms in the division of labor within the Empire and eventually in the common market of a united Germany dominated by Austria.

Favorable international economic developments gave an unexpected boost to rejuvenation. The economic boom and a lack of significant foreign competition magnified the impact of the Liberal Centralist financial and other reforms on the Hungarian economy. Agriculture flourished, railways and waterways were constructed, domestic capital was accumulated and foreign capital imported. Hungary soon arrived at the brink of an industrial revolution. The Schwarzenberg-Bach Administration next intended to introduce, albeit very gradually, the more liberal-democratic features of the March Constitution. The Press was already free, proposed bills were publicly debated but the state of siege still existed and there were no parliamentary or notable local elections. Major changes were only in the offing for 1851.

As the March Constitution was becoming more and more of a reality, Franz Joseph decided to intervene before his power would be seriously curtailed by a *de facto* constitutional monarchy. Taking advantage of the defeat of the Left in France, Schwarzenberg's settling of the conflict with Prussia without recourse to war and of the Liberal Centralists' inability to widen their social base, the Emperor gradually reverted to political absolutism. He used the Absolutist Centralists at the Court to halt the progress of Liberal Centralism. Since the Absolutists were even less flexible than their opponents in Vienna, they also failed to gain the support of the Hungarian ruling class. As a matter of fact, they inadvertently stimulated the rise of a united opposition in Hungary.

Hostilities between Vienna and the Magyar ruling class grew despite the efforts of the Hungarian aristocracy. Their political leaders, the Old Conservatives, were the only segments of the Hungarian ruling class which from the outbreak of the Revolution remained at the side of the Habsburgs. In 1849 they tried, together with Windischgrätz, to establish a new Imperial order. The aristocrats could afford and were willing to cooperate with the Liberal Centralists in rejuvenating Hungary and in preserving some of the social and political achievements of the Revolution of 1848. The Liberal Centralists, however, decided to cast aside the aristocracy because they considered them reactionary, selfish and a priori enemies of progress and not just of centralism à la Vienna. The Schwarzenberg-Bach Administration failed to see the enormous power, influence and economic dynamism of the Magyar aristocrats and that they needed the cooperation of the ruling class more than *vice versa*. Furthermore, Viennese politicians of the 1850's could not differentiate between the interest of the Austrian and the Hungarian Catholic Hierarchies. They failed to see that concessions to Catholicism in general might not be construed as desirable *per se* by the Primate of Hungary and other clerics at Esztergom. When finally the Government began to widen the application of the March

Constitution, it was too late. The appearance of the Absolutist Centralists as a new potential ally at the Court eliminated the need of a compromise between the Viennese Liberals and the Old Conservatives in Hungary. Aristocrats in the civil service, the Catholic Hierarchy and the media undermined the authority of the Ministers, pressured the Emperor to make concessions and devised a platform which enabled the *bene possessionati,* the pro-gentry honoratiors and the Protestant Churches to support the Old Conservatives against the Schwarzenberg-Bach Administration.

After overcoming post-Revolutionary economic setbacks, the gentry too took advantage of free trade and other Liberal Centralist economic policies. However, due to their dominant role in the Revolution of 1848, they bore the brunt of Haynau's military dictatorship. They were also intimidated by class-conscious peasants and hostile nationalities. The simultaneous presence of fear and prosperity weakened their ability to reach out for exclusive political dominance of a Magyar state. The *bene possessionati* utilized and participated in the state apparatus and paid their taxes. In the absence of effective leaders of their own—Kossuth was uninspiring and irresponsible and Deák was hesitant and non-committal—the gentry accepted the leadership and resistance methods of the Old Conservatives whom they served faithfully from their posts in the civil service and the Protestant Churches.

By 1853 the Magyar ruling class with the aid of the Emperor and the Absolutist Centralists had defeated the Liberal Centralists and, in particular, their political designs for Hungary. During the struggle the economic, social and cultural reforms of the Liberal Centralists and the political hostility of both Liberal and Absolutist Centralists in Vienna gave renewed strength and stimulus to the Old Conservatives and their allies. The metamorphosed aristocracy and the gentry stood united in opposition until in 1860 the Emperor finally abandoned the policy of centralism and initiated negotiations in the interest of a new settlement. Habsburg rule was maintained in exchange for Magyar dominance in an autonomous Hungary.

Appendix

TABLE NO. 1
Hungary's Tobacco Production in 1852 and 1853

Year	1852	1853
No. of Planters	44,694	54,429
No. of Joch* Planted	29,154	31,522
Tobacco Grown in Centner**	179,822	365,519
Yield Centner / Joch	6.16	11.59

* 1 Joch = 1.4223 acres

** 1 Zollcentner = 50 kilograms

Source: Anon. [B. von Meyer], *Rückblick auf die jüngste Entwicklungs-Periode Ungarns,* Vienna, 1857, pp. 72–73.

TABLE NO. 2
Currency, Weights and Measures

Currency

Austria		Hungary
Gulden		Forint
1 Gulden = 60 Kreuzer	=	1 forint = 60 krajcár (kr.)
1 Kreuzer = 4 Groschen	=	1 krajcár = 4 garas

Square Measures

1 Joch (yoke) =

.76 hectares = 1.43 acres = 1 cadastral hold

Weights and Dry Measures

1 Zentner = 1 mázsa = 123.48 lb.

1 Pfund = 1 font = 1.235 lb.

1 Pozsony mérő (bushel) = 62.5 liter

1 Pest mérő (bushel) = 94 liter

TABLE NO. 3

Population Distribution in Máramaros County by Nationality — 1850

Magyar	15,940	Jewish	13,850
Rumanian	47,681	Armenian	2,970
Ukrainian	97,585		

Civil Servants in Máramaros County by Nationality — 1850

Magyar	20	Ukrainian	3
German	9	Polish	3
Rumanian	1	Slovak	1

Court Officials, Including Judges, in Máramaros County by Nationality — 1850

Magyar	26	Ukrainian	5
German	2	Armenian	3
Rumanian	6	Slovak	2

Source: *Pesti Napló*, 15 November 1851.

CHART NO. 1,

Exchange rates

Pound sterling quotations at the Viennese

stock exchange during the Provisorium.

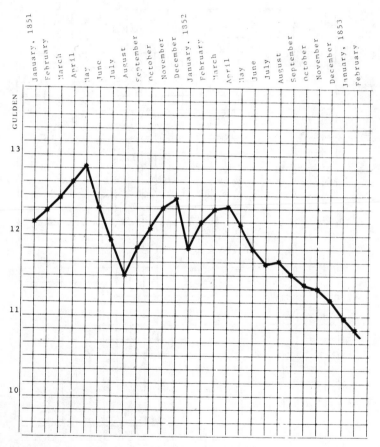

Source: <u>Pesti Napló</u>, 1851-1853, first quotation of
each month

CHART NO. 2.

Agio

Quoted rates at the Vienna Stock Exchange immediately
before and after the London floating of Austria's
state loan of 1852

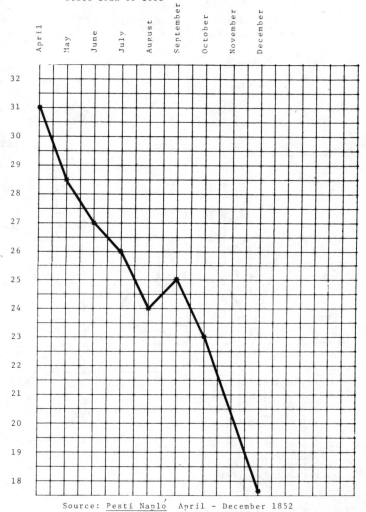

Source: Pesti Napló April - December 1852

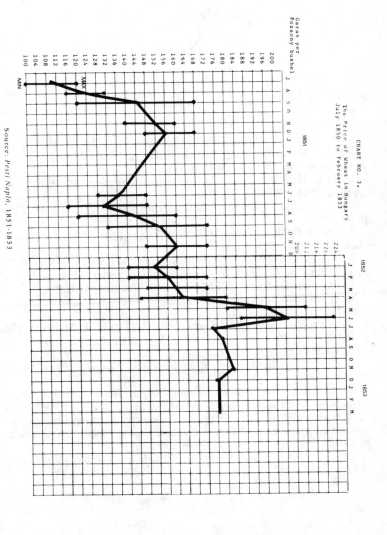

CHART NO. 3.

The Price of Wheat in Hungary
July 1850 to February 1853

Garas per
Pozsony bushel

1851   1852   1853

Source: *Pesti Napló*, 1851-1853

Notes

INTRODUCTION

1. Péter Hanák, "Recent Hungarian Literature on the History of the Austro-Hungarian Monarchy, 1849–1918. A Historiographical Survey," *Austrian History Yearbook,* Vol. 1 (1965), p. 158.

2. Oscar Jaszi, *The Dissolution of the Habsburg Monarchy,* Chicago and London, 1964 (1929), pp. 100 ff.

3. Erik Molnár et al. (ed.), *Magyarország története,* II, Budapest, 1967, p. 9.

4. Joseph Redlich, *Emperor Francis Joseph of Austria, A Biography,* Hamden, Conn., 1965, p. 76.

5. William E. Lingelbach, *Austria-Hungary,* New York, 1971, p. 378.

6. Viktor Bibl, *Von Revolution zu Revolution,* Vienna, 1924, pp. 228–232.

7. Eva Priester, *Kurze Geschichte Österreichs,* Vienna, 1949, pp. 401 ff.

8. *Az absolutismus kora Magyarországon, 1849–1865,* I, p. 70.

9. Molnár, *op. cit.,* p. 11.

10. Heinrich Friedjung, *Österreich von 1848–1860,* I, Stuttgart, 1908, p. 100.

11. Redlich, *op. cit.,* p. 76.

12. Louis Eisenmann, *Le Compromis Austro-Hongrois de 1867,* Paris, 1904, p. 135.

13. Robert A. Kann, *The Multinational Empire: Nationalism and National Reform in the Habsburg Monarchy 1848–1918,* II, New York, 1970, p. 65.

14. Stanley Z. Pech, "The Czechs and the Imperial Parliament in 1848–1849" in *The Czech Renascence of the Nineteenth Century,* (eds.) Peter Brock and H. Gordon Skilling, Toronto, 1970, p. 211.

15. Bálint Hóman and Gyula Szekfű, *Magyar történet,* V, Budapest, 1936, p. 441.

16. Kann, *op. cit.,* II, pp. 52 f.

17. Péter Hanák (ed.), *Magyarország története az abszolutizmus korában,* (Manuscript), Budapest, 1969, p. 11.

18. Redlich, *op. cit.,* p. 80.

19. *Szögyény-Marich László országbíró emlékiratai,* II, Budapest, 1903–1917, p. 40.

20. Lingelbach, *op. cit.,* p. 381.

21. C. A. Macartney, *The Habsburg Empire 1790–1918,* London, 1968, p. 391.

22. Hóman, *op. cit.,* p. 441.

23. Imre Révész, *Fejezetek a Bach-korszak egyházpolitikájából,* Budapest, 1957, p. 77.

24. Kenneth W. Rock, "Rejuvenation by Edict: The Habsburg Example after 1848," Paper read before the meeting of the Rocky Mountain Social Science Association, Salt Lake City, Utah, 29 April 1972 (p. 18).

25. Friedjung, *op. cit.,* I, p. 351.

26. Andrew H. Brenman, "Economic Reform in Neuzeit Austria, 1825–1859," unpublished doctoral dissertation, Department of History, Princeton University, Princeton, 1965, p. 41.

27. A.J.P. Taylor, *The Habsburg Monarchy 1809–1918. A History of the Austrian Empire and Austria-Hungary,* London, 1964, pp. 93 ff.

28. K. Tschuppik, *The Reign of the Emperor Francis Joseph,* London, 1930, p. 31.

29. László Révész, "Die Bedeutung des Neoabsolutismus für Ungarn," *Der Donauraum,* Vol. XIV (1969), p. 146.

30. Eisenmann, *op. cit.,* p. 187.

31. Kann, *op. cit.,* II, p. 84.

32. Taylor, *op. cit.,* p. 93.

33. Péter Hanák, Tibor Erényi and György Szabad, *Magyarország története 1849–1918, Az abszolutizmus és a dualizmus kora,* Budapest, 1972 (1973), pp. 21 ff.

34. Hóman, *op. cit.,* p. 444.

35. Berzeviczy, *op. cit.,* I, pp. 234 ff.

36. Oszkár Sashegyi, *Az abszolutizmuskori levéltár,* Budapest, 1965, pp. 284 ff.

37. R. Charmatz, *Minister Freiherr von Bruck,* Leipzig, 1916.

38. H. Fournier, *Österreich-Ungarns Neubau,* Vienna, 1917.

39. Péter Hanák, "Hungary in the Austro-Hungarian Monarchy: Preponderancy or Dependency? " *Austrian History Yearbook,* Vol. III, Pt. 1 (1967), pp. 260–302.

40. George Barany, "Hungary: The Uncompromising Compromise," *ibid.,* pp. 234–259.

41. Ivan Zolger, *Der staatsrechtliche Ausgleich zwischen Österreich und Ungarn,* Leipzig, 1911.

42. Henrik Marczali, *Hungary in the Eighteenth Century,* Cambridge, 1910.

43. Redlich, *op. cit.,* p. 61.

44. Gábor G. Kemény, *A balavásári szüret,* Budapest, 1945, p. 260.

45. Zoltán Kramar, "The Road to Compromise, 1849–1867; a Study of the Habsburg-Hungarian Constitutional Struggle in Its Terminal Phase," unpublished doctoral dissertation, Department of History, University of Nebraska, 1967, pp. 31 f.

46. J. Miskolczy, *Ungarn in der Habsburger-Monarchie,* Vienna and Munich, 1959, p. 117.

47. Gusztáv Beksics and Sándor Márki, *I Ferenc József és kora,* in Vol. X of *A magyar nemzet története,* (ed.) Sándor Szilágyi, Budapest, 1898, pp. 406 ff.; Redlich, *op. cit.,* p. 64; Kramar, *op. cit.,* p. 32.

48. Macartney, *op. cit.,* p. 410.

49. *Ibid.,* p. 432.

50. Aladár Mód, *400 év küzdelem az önálló Magyarországért*, Budapest, 1951, pp. 228 f.

51. Vilmos Sándor, *A tőkés gazdaság kibontakozása Magyarországon 1849–1900*, Budapest, 1958, *passim*.

52. Iván T. Berend and György Ránki, *A monopolkapitalizmus kialakulása és uralma Magyarországon 1900–1944*, Budapest, 1958, *passim*.

53. György Szabad, *A tatai és gesztesi Eszterházy-uradalom áttérése a robotrendszerről a tőkés gazdálkodásra*, Budapest, 1957, p. 326.

54. Bartholomew de Szemere, *Hungary from 1848 to 1860*, London, 1860, p. 73.

55. Jaszi, *op. cit.*, p. 195.

56. Gyula Szekfű, *Három nemzedék és ami utána következik*, Budapest, 1934 (1920), p. 188.

57. Menyhért Lónyay, *Közügyekről. Nemzetgazdászati újabb dolgozatok*, Pest, 1863, p. 162.

58. Károly Keleti, *Visszapillantás Magyarország közgazdaságának egynegyed századára*, Budapest, 1875, pp. 4 ff.

59. Ferenc Erdei, "A szabad parasztság kialakulása," *Sorsunk*, Vol. III, No. 7 (1943), pp. 691 ff.

60. Hanák, *Hungary. . . ,* p. 284.

61. Victor-L. Tapié, *The Rise and Fall of the Habsburg Monarchy*, New York, 1971, p. 284.

62. Lingelbach, *op. cit.*, p. 383.

63. See footnotes 64, 65, 69, 70 and 71.

64. Erzsébet Andics, (ed.), *A nagybirtokos arisztokrácia ellenforradalmi szerepe 1848–49–ben*, 3 volumes, Budapest, 1965.

65. Lajos Lukács, *Magyar függetlenségi és alkotmányos mozgalmak 1849–1867*, Budapest, 1955, p. 16.

66. Dominic C. Kosary, *A History of Hungary*, New York, 1971 (1941), p. 256.

67. Szekfű, *Három nemzedék. . . ,* p. 170.

68. Jaszi, *op. cit.*, p. 195.

69. Emil Niederhauser, *A jobbágyfelszabadítás Kelet-Európában*, Budapest, 1962, pp. 148 f.

70. Pál S. Sándor *et al., Parasztságunk a Habsburg önkényuralom korszakában 1849–1867*, Budapest, 1951, p. 27.

71. Molnár, *op. cit.*, p. 23.

72. Rudolf Springer [Karl Renner], *Grundlagen und Entwicklungsziele der österreichisch-ungarischen Monarchie*, Vienna, 1906, pp. 9 ff and 95 ff.

73. Redlich, *op. cit.*, p. 470.

74. Kann, *op. cit.*, p. 128.

75. Redlich, *op. cit.*, p. 97.

76. Tschuppik, *op. cit.*, p. 75.

77. W. Rogge, *Österreich von Vilagos bis zur Gegenwart*, I, Leipzig, 1872, p. 60.

78. Macartney, *op. cit.*, p. 378.

79. Sylvia Medgyesi-Mitschang, "The Influence of the Hungarian Aristocracy upon Franz Joseph from 1851 to 1861," unpublished doctoral dis-

sertation, Department of History, University of St. Louis, St. Louis, Mo.,
1971, p. 94.
80. Kramar, *op. cit.*, p. 54.
81. Brenman, *op. cit.*, p. 14.
82. Taylor, *op. cit.*, p. 105.
83. Sashegyi, *op. cit.*, pp. 38 ff.
84. *Toldy Ferenc összegyűjtött munkái*, VI, Pest, 1868–74, *passim*.
85. Gusztáv Wenzel, "Endlicher István emlékezete," *Új Magyar Múzeum*,
Book IV (1851), pp. 197 ff.
86. György Gracza, *Az 1848–49–iki magyar szabadságharcz története*, V,
Budapest, 1898, p. 1312.
87. Florence A. Foster, *Francis Deak, Hungarian Statesman: A Memoir*,
London, 1880, p. 117.
88. Zoltán Ferenczi, *Deák élete*, II, p. 240.
89. Szekfű, *Három nemzedék*, p. 182.
90. Ferenc Pölöskei and Kálmán Szakács (eds.), *Földmunkás és szegényparasztmozgalmak Magyarországon, 1848–1948*, Budapest, 1962, I, p. 48;
Lukács, *op. cit.*, p. 33; Oszkár Sashegyi (ed.), *Munkások és parasztok mozgalmai Magyarországon 1849–1867. Iratok*, Budapest, 1959, *passim*.
91. Kann, *op. cit.*, I, p. 131.
92. Medgyesi, *op. cit.*, p. 107.
93. Sashegyi, *Az abszolutizmuskori* . . . .
94. Friederich Walter, *Die österreichische Zentralverwaltung*, 6 volumes,
Graz, 1950–1964.
95. Dávid Angyal (ed.), *Falk Miksa és Kecskeméthy Aurél levelezése*,
Budapest, 1925.

CHAPTER ONE:
THE LIBERAL CENTRALISTS AND THEIR HUNGARIAN POLICIES

1. Péter Hanák (ed.), *Magyarország története az abszolutizmus és dualizmus korában*, (Manuscript), Budapest, 1969, p. 7.
2. This is a geographical identification of the area west of the Leitha River,
which included all Austrian lands except the ones under the Hungarian Crown.
Lands east of the Leitha were generally known as Transleithania.
3. Victor-L. Tapié, *The Rise and Fall of the Habsburg Monarchy*, New
York, 1971, p. 289.
4. Robert A. Kann, *The Multinational Empire: Nationalism and National
Reform in the Habsburg Monarchy 1848–1918*, II, New York, 1970, pp.
68–72.
5. C. A. Macartney, *The Habsburg Empire 1790–1918*, London, 1968,
p. 406.
6. Hans Schlitter, *Versäumte Gelegenheiten: Die oktroyirte Verfassung
vom 4. März 1849, Ein Beitrag zu ihrer Geschichte*, Zurich, Leipzig and
Vienna, 1920, p. 45.
7. Oszkár Sashegyi, *Az abszolutizmuskori levéltár*, Budapest, 1965, pp.
28 f.

8. Kenneth W. Rock, "Reply," *Austrian History Yearbook*, Vols. VI–VII (1971), p. 165.

9. Stanley Z. Pech, "The Czechs and the Imperial Parliament in 1848–1849," *The Czech Renascence of the Nineteenth Century*, (eds.) Peter Brock and H. Gordon Skilling, Toronto, 1970, pp. 203 f.

10. Benjamin Rigberg, "The Federal Movement in the Habsburg Domain: 1840–1871," unpublished doctoral dissertation, Department of History, University of Pennsylvania, Philadelphia, 1946, pp. 138 ff.

11. Pech, *op. cit.*, p. 204.

12. Kann, *op. cit.*, p. 204.

13. For the complete and official Hungarian text see *Gyűjteményét a' Magyarország számára kibocsátott legfelsőbb Manifestumok és Szózatoknak, valamint a' cs. kir. hadsereg főparancsnokai által Magyarországban kiadott hirdetményeknek*, Buda, 1849, pp. 47 ff., cited hereafter as *Collection*.

14. Inner Hungary was the Kingdom of Hungary proper, that is Hungary without Transylvania, Croatia, etc.

15. Eva Priester, *Kurze Geschichte Österreichs: Aufstieg und Untergang des Habsburgerreiches*, Vienna, 1949, pp. 403–405.

16. Bach temporarily replaced Stadion from April, 1849. It soon became clear that Stadion was not going to recover from his illness and, consequently, he was replaced by Bach on July 28 (Macartney, *op. cit.*, p. 439; Sashegyi, *op. cit.*, p. 138).

17. Kann, *op. cit.*, pp. 83 f.

18. A.J.P. Taylor, *The Habsburg Monarchy 1809–1918: A History of the Austrian Empire and Austrian Hungary*, London, 1964, pp. 93 ff.

19. Gyula Bernát, *Az abszolutizmus földtehermentesítése Magyarországon*, Budapest, 1935, p. 87 f.

20. A. A. Paton, *The Goth and the Hun; or Transylvania, Debreczin, Pesth, and Vienna in 1850*, London, 1851, pp. 194 and 368 ff.

21. Miksa Falk, *Kor-és jellemrajzok*, Budapest, 1903, p. 31.

22. Sashegyi, *op. cit.*, p. 30.

23. On the intervention see Erzsébet Andics, *A Habsburgok és Romanovok szövetsége: az 1849 évi magyarországi cári intervenció diplomáciai előtörténete*, Budapest, 1961; Kenneth W. Rock, "Schwarzenberg versus Nicholas I, Round One; the Negotiation of the Habsburg-Romanov Alliance against Hungary in 1849," *Austrian History Yearbook*, Vols. VI–VII (1970–1971), pp. 109 ff; and my "The Russian Intervention in Hungary," *War and Society in the Nineteenth Century Russian Empire*, (eds.) J. G. Purves and D. A. West, Toronto, 1971, pp. 73 ff.

24. Joseph Redlich, *Emperor Francis Joseph of Austria, A Biography*, Hamden, Conn., 1965, p. 62.

25. Joseph Karl Mayr (ed.), *Das Tagebuch des Polizeiministers Kempen von 1848 bis 1859*, Vienna and Leipzig, 1931, pp. 145 f.

26. *Collection*, pp. 96 ff.

27. *Ibid.*, pp. 108 ff.

28. György Gracza, *Az 1848–49-iki magyar szabadságharcz története*, V, Budapest, 1898, p. 1256.

29. Palmerston to Possonby, 2 August 1849, Jenő Horváth (ed.), *Origins*

of the Crimean War; Documents relative to the Russian Intervention in Hungary and Transylvania 1848-1849, Budapest, 1937, p. 238.

30. Nesselrode to Medem, 30 May 1849, Andics, *op. cit.,* p. 400.

31. Árpád Károlyi (ed.), *Németujvári Gróf Batthyány Lajos első magyar miniszterelnök főbenjáró pöre,* I, Budapest, 1932, p. 547.

32. Document 200, Cabinet meeting, Vienna, 31 August 1849, in *ibid.,* p. 579.

33. Haynau to Schönhals, 24 August 1849, Lajos Steier, *Haynau és Paskievics,* II, Budapest, 1928, p. 417.

34. Péter Gunst (ed.), *Magyar történelmi kronológia, Az őstörténettől 1966-ig, Segédkönyv a magyar történelem tanulmányozásához,* Budapest, 1968, p. 241; Macartney, *op. cit.,* p. 432; Redlich, *op. cit.,* p. 61.

35. Gunst, *op. cit.,* p. 241.

36. Redlich, *op. cit.,* p. 62, D 36/1850/312.

37. Magyar Országos Levéltár (Hungarian National Archives) MOL, Abszolutizmuskori Levéltár (Archives of the Age of Absolutism) AB, K.K. (III) Armee Commando für Ungarn und Siebenbürgen, Polizei Section, D 36–38, D 36–1850/312. Cited hereafter as MOLAL, D . . .

38. Kenneth Willett Rock, "Reaction Triumphant: The Diplomacy of Felix Schwarzenberg and Nicholas I in Mastering the Hungarian Insurrection, 1848-1850, A Study in Dynastic Power Principles and Politics in Revolutionary Times," unpublished doctoral dissertation, Department of History, Stanford University, 1968, p. 301.

39. For a complete list of the executed and murdered and related data see MOLAL, Általános Iratok (General Papers), D 37/1850/8207 and unnumbered booklet.

40. Heinrich Friedjung, *Österreich von 1848-1860,* I, Stuttgart, 1908, p. 230.

41. 24 July 1850.

42. *Collection,* p. 138.

43. MOLAL, Jósa Péter Nagyváradi Ker. Főbiztos (Péter Jósa, Chief Commissioner of the Nagyvárad District), D 81/1850/6252.

44. Friedjung, I, *op. cit.,* p. 218 f; Gunst, *op. cit.,* p. 241.

45. *Pesti Napló,* 3 and 15 March 1850.

46. *Az ausztriai birodalmat illető birodalmi törvény- és kormánylap,* 1850, p. 1913, cited hereafter as *Official Gazette.*

47. *Pesti Napló,* 9 April 1850.

48. Gunther E. Rothenberg, "The Habsburg Army and the Nationality Problem in the Nineteenth Century, 1815-1914," *Austrian History Yearbook,* Vol. III, Pt. 1 (1967), p. 74.

49. *Collection,* p. 110.

50. MOLAL, Szentiványi Vince Pesti Ker. Főbiztos (Vince Szentiványi, Chief Commissioner of the Pest District), D 77/1850/5874 and 10,055.

51. MOLAL, D 81/1850/5189 and 5866; S. Biró *et al., A magyar református egyház története,* Budapest, 1949, p. 329.

52. *Collection,* p. 206 f.

53. *Ibid.,* p. 206.

54. Erzsébet Andics, (ed.), *Iratok 1849 március-1850 április,* Volume III

of *A nagybirtokos arisztokrácia ellenforradalmi szerepe 1848–49-ben,* Budapest, 1965, pp. 40–42.

55. *Infra,* p. 34 and pp. 39 f.

56. Gusztáv Beksics and Sándor Márki, *I Ferencz József és kora,* Vol. X of *A magyar nemzet története,* (ed.) Sándor Szilágyi, Budapest, 1898, p. 1320; Albert Berzeviczy, *Az absolutismus kora Magyarországon 1849–1865,* I, Budapest, 1922, p. 176.

57. Oscar Jaszi, *The Dissolution of the Habsburg Monarchy,* Chicago and London, 1964, p. 97.

58. Paton, *op. cit.,* p. 310.

59. *Collection,* p. 143.

60. Alfréd Lengyel, *Győr megye történetének írásos emlékei (1001–1918),* Győr, 1965, pp. 81 ff.

61. *Alleruntertänigster Vortrag des treugehorsamsten provisorischen Ministers des Innern Alexander Bach, betreffend die allerhöchste Genehmigung der Grundzüge für die Organisation der politischen Verwaltungsbehörden,* Vienna, 1849.

62. MOLAL, Der Bevollmächtigte Kais. Commissar für die Civilangelegenheiten in Ungarn Karl Freiherr von Geringer, (from 1851) K.K. Statthalterei für Ungarn, D 51–55, Elnöki Iratok (Presidential Papers), D 51/1849/103.

63. *Ibid.,* Általános Iratok (General Papers), D 55/1849/4195.

64. *Pesti Napló,* 27 March 1850, Nagyszombat; 12 April 1850, Zalaegerszeg; 29 April 1850, Eperjes; 13 April 1850, Székesfehérvár; 3 May 1850, Győr; 29 May 1850, Debrecen; 31 May 1850, Nagyvárad.

65. *Ibid.,* 2 August 1850.

66. MOLAL, K.K. Disciplinar Comité D 59/1849.

67. MOLAL, Pester K.K. Staatsprüfungs-Commission, Staatsrechtlich-Administrative Abtheilung D 62/1850.

68. *Pesti Napló,* 9 and 11 September 1850.

69. Erik Molnár (ed.), *Magyarország története,* II, Budapest, 1964, p. 26.

70. *Hölgyfutár,* 20 December 1849.

71. *Pesti Napló,* 9 March 1850.

72. Pál Török, *Pest-Buda 1850-ben,* Budapest, 1944, p. 51.

73. F. Szabó, "Betyárvilág Orosháza környékén a szabadságharc után," *A Szántó Kovács Múzeum évkönyve,* I, Orosháza, 1959, p. 49.

74. MOLAL, D 77/1849/2730.

75. Berzeviczy, *op. cit.,* I, pp. 168–170.

76. Karl Schadelbauer, *Amtliche Stimmungsberichte 1850/51 und 1859/60,* Innsbruck, 1960, p. 42.

77. MOLAL, Rohonczy Ignác Soproni Ker. Főbiztos (Ignác Rohonczy, Chief Commissioner of the Sopron District), D 64/1849/1403.

78. *Pester Zeitung,* 16 December 1849.

79. *Pesti Napló,* 30 April 1850; György Vadnay, "Az első zsandár tisztek Zemplénben," *Adalékok Zemplén vármegye történetéhez,* Vol. VII, No. 2 (February 1901), p. 59 f.

80. K. Rock, "Rejuvenation by Edict: The Habsburg Example after 1848," Paper read before the meeting of the Rocky Mountain Social Science Association, Salt Lake City, Utah, 29 April 1972.

81. Berzeviczy, *op. cit.*, I, pp. 169 f.
82. MOLAL, D 36/1850/301 and D 77/1850/1678.
83. *Pesti Napló*, 10 February 1851.
84. *Ibid.*, 17 April 1851.
85. *Collection*, p. 19.
86. *Ibid.*, pp. 113 f; *Official Gazette*, 1849, pp. 110 f; *ibid.*, 1850, pp. 1694 ff.
87. Mária Lóránth, *Adatok az úrbéri kárpótlás történetéhez 1849-1853*, Budapest, 1927, p. 14; *Pesti Napló*, 13 April 1850.
88. The Kossuth regime intended to deduct the advances from the capital and not from the interest (See Gyula Szekfű in Bálint Hóman and Gyula Szekfű, *Magyar történet*, V, Budapest, 1936, p. 446).
89. Gyula Bernát, *op. cit.*, pp. 26 and 30.
90. MOLAL, Uray Bálint Debreceni Ker. Főbiztos (Bálint Uray, District Chief Commissioner of the Debrecen District) D 79–80, D 79/1850/97; Pál S. Sándor et al., *Parasztságunk a Habsburg önkényuralom korszakában 1849-1867*, Budapest, 1951, p. 28; *Pesti Hirlap*, 12 September 1850.
91. Lóránth, *op. cit.*, p. 17.
92. Hanák, *op. cit.*, p. 17.
93. Miksa Faragó, *A Kossuth-bankók kora, a szabadságharc pénzügyei*, Budapest, n.d. [1912?], pp. 173 f.
94. Haynau to Radetzky, 6 July 1849, Steier, *op. cit.*, I, pp. 164 f.
95. Krauss to Windischgrätz, 9 March 1849, Andics (ed.), *op. cit.*, pp. 34 ff.
96. Sándor Jirkovsky, *A magyarországi pénzintézetek története az első világháború végéig*, Budapest, 1945, p. 82.
97. *Collection*, p. 115; Ottó Lakatos, *Arad története*, I, Arad, 1881, p. 219.
98. Faragó, *op. cit.*, p. 275.
99. 24 February 1849.
100. *Collection*, p. 112; Faragó, *op. cit.*, pp. 316 f.
101. *Ibid.*, p. 298.
102. *Pesti Napló*, 11 April 1850.
103. Török, *op. cit.*, p. 7.
104. *Official Gazette*, 1850, p. 971; *Pesti Napló*, 22 April 1850, Menyhért Lónyay, *Közügyekről, nemzetgazdászati újabb dolgozatok*, Pest, 1863, pp. 133 ff.
105. Sándor (ed.), *op. cit.*, pp. 44 ff.
106. *Wiener Zeitung*, 20 June 1850.
107. Bernát, *op. cit.*, p. 26.
108. *Official Gazette*, 1850, pp. 861 ff.
109. Hanák, *op. cit.*, pp. 54–56.
110. *Ibid.*
111. MOLAL, Általános Iratok (General Papers), D 55/1849/2663.
112. *Tanrendszerterv a gymnasiumokat és realiskolákat illetőleg Közzététéve a bécsi cultus- és oktatásministerium által tömött kivonatban fogalmazva*, Buda, 1850.
113. János Hajdú, "Felsőbb oktatásügy és tömegnevelés," *Magyar Művelődéstörténet*, V: *Az új Magyarország*, (ed.) Sándor Domanovsky et al., Budapest, n.d., pp. 327 ff.
114. Tibor Győry, *Az orvostudományi kar története 1770-1935*, Budapest, 1936, pp. 500–502.

115. *Pesti Napló,* 1, 5 and 8 August 1850.

116. Hajdú, *op. cit.,* p. 346.

117. MOLAL, K.K. Ministerium des Cultus und Unterrichtes, Akten Ungarn, Woiwodina und Siebenburgen, D 4/1848–1860; *Pester Zeitung,* 8 November 1849; *Pesti Napló,* 4, 22 and 23 October 1850; Sashegyi, *op. cit.,* pp. 148 ff and 284 ff.

118. *Pesti Napló,* 26 November 1850; Erik Molnár, *op. cit.,* p. 19; Lakatos, *op. cit.,* p. 226.

119. Julius Kornis, *Education in Hungary,* New York, 1932, p. 26.

120. "A lay state which determined for itself the kind of religious life which it will employ and a governing activity according to the principles of his [Joseph II] philosophy for the welfare of the great masses with the purpose that the Emperor should have the greatest weight and authority both inside and outside: that was the essence of his system called after his name Josephinism" (Jaszi, *op. cit.,* p. 67).

121. Ferenc Eckhart, *A püspöki székek és a káptalani javadalmak betöltése Mária Terézia korától 1918-ig,* Budapest, 1935, pp. 304–307.

122. Antal Meszlényi, *A magyar katolikus egyház és az állam 1848/49-ben,* Budapest, 1928, p. 231 ff; János Földy, *Világostól Josephstadtig 1849–1856,* Budapest, 1928, p. 21; Eckhart, *op. cit.,* p. 306; Gracza, *op. cit.,* p. 1252.

123. *Hám János szatmári püspök és kinevezett prímás emlékiratai 1848/49-ből,* (ed.) János Scheffler, Budapest, 1928, pp. 16–22.

124. Török, *op. cit.,* p. 80.

125. Zsigmond Grossman, *A magyar zsidók a XIX. század közepén, 1849–1870,* Budapest, 1917, p. 7; Bíró, *op. cit.,* p. 329.

126. MOLAL, D 77/1850/17578.

127. Dávid Angyal (ed.), *Falk Miksa és Kecskeméthy Aurél elkobzott levelezése,* Budapest, 1925, p. 22.

128. 8 May 1850 and 20 September 1850.

129. Macartney, *op. cit.,* p. 443.

130. Tapié, *op. cit.,* p. 295.

131. *Pesti Napló,* 3 May 1850.

132. Imre Révész, *Fejezetek a Bach-korszak egyházpolitikájából,* Budapest, 1957, p. 17.

133. Macartney, *op. cit.,* pp. 410 and 444.

134. 25 and 26 July 1849.

135. Hám, *op. cit.,* pp. 14 ff; Révész, *op. cit.,* pp. 16 f; Eckhart, *op. cit.,* p. 309.

136. Erzsébet Andics, *Az egyházi reakció 1848–49-ben,* Budapest, 1949, pp. 85 and 96.

137. Ferenc Eckhart, "Egy nagy magyar főpap életéből," *A Bécsi Magyar Történeti Intézet Évkönyve,* II, Vienna, 1932, p. 273.

138. Lóránth, *op. cit.,* p. 22.

139. MOLAL, D 77/1850/4321.

140. W. Rogge, *Österreich von Vilagos bis zur Gegenwart,* Leipzig, 1872, p. 358.

141. Révész, *op. cit.,* pp. 33 ff.

142. Franz Zimmermann, *Das Ministerium für die Evangelischen Gesamtstaate Österreich 1849 bis 1860,* Vienna, 1926, p. 87.

143. János Hajdú, *Eötvös József br. első minisztersége,* Budapest, 1933, *passim.*

144. Mihály Zsilinszky, *A magyarhoni protestáns egyház története,* Budapest, 1925, p. 682.

145. *Pesti Napló,* 18 December 1850.

146. *Ibid.,* 27 July 1850.

147. Lajos Venetianer, *A magyar zsidóság története a honfoglalástól a világháború kitöréséig,* Budapest, 1922, pp. 205-207.

148. Grossmann, *op. cit.,* p. 8.

149. *Pester Zeitung,* 6 July 1850.

150. Győry, *op. cit.,* p. 499.

151. Distribution of students by religion during the academic year 1851/ 1852:

Roman Catholic	265
Protestant	79
Orthodox	16
Jewish	160

(*Pesti Napló,* 28 October 1852)

152. Angyal, *op. cit.,* p. 19 ff; MOLAL, K.K. Armee-Ober-Commando Feldmarschall Alfred Fürst zu Windischgrätz: Politische und Administrative Section, Általános Iratok (General Papers), D 8/1849/223.

153. István Kereszty, *A magyar és magyarországi időszaki sajtó időrendi áttekintése: 1705-1867,* Budapest, 1916, pp. 75-76; Angyal, *op. cit.,* pp. 30 ff and 56 ff.

154. P. Gyulai to K. Szász, 11 May 1850, *Gyulai Pál levelezése 1843-tól 1867-ig,* (ed.) Sándor Somogyi, Budapest, p. 49; *Pesti Napló,* 3 September 1850.

155. 4 May 1850.

156. 18 April 1850.

157. 21 February 1850.

158. 30 August 1850.

159. Pál Gyulai to K. Szász, 11 May 1850, Gyulai, *op. cit.,* p. 45.

160. Berzeviczy, *op. cit.,* I, p. 142.

CHAPTER TWO:
THE DEFEAT OF THE LIBERAL CENTRALISTS

1. *Pesti Napló,* 20 November 1850.

2. *Ibid.,* 25 September 1850.

3. *Ibid.,* 23 August 1850.

4. *Der Wanderer,* 4 December 1850.

5. Berzeviczy, *op. cit.,* I, p. 253.

6. Joseph Redlich, *Das österreichische Staats- und Reichsproblem: Geschichtliche Darstellung der inneren Politik der Habsburgischen Monarchie von 1848 bis zum Untergang des Reiches,* Leipzig, 1924-1926, I, pp. 109 and 401; Friederich Walter (ed.), *Aus dem Nachlass des Freiherrn Carl Friederich*

Kübeck, von Kübau: Tagebücher, Briefe, Aktenstücke (1841–1855), Graz, 1960.

7. Complete text in *Pesti Napló,* 23 and 24 April 1851.

8. *Ibid.,* 22 and 24 January, 1851; Hanák, *op. cit.,* p. 9; Berzeviczy, *op. cit.,* I, pp. 254 f.

9. Rudolf Kiszling, *Fürst Felix zu Schwarzenberg, der Erzieher Kaiser Franz Josefs,* Graz, 1952, p. 187.

10. László Szögyény-Marich, *Szögyény-Marich László országbíró emlékiratai,* II, Budapest, 1903–1917, pp. 37 and 53–66.

11. Max von Kübeck (ed.), *Tagebücher des Karl Friedrich Freiherr von Kübeck von Kübau,* II, Vienna, 1906, pp. 55–58.

12. *Pesti Napló,* 28 August 1851.

13. F. Schnurer, *Briefe Kaiser Franz Josephs an seine Mutter,* Salzburg, 1930, p. 160, cited by Macartney, *op. cit.,* p. 453.

14. Redlich, *Emperor . . . ,* p. 87.

15. Berzeviczy, *op. cit.,* I, pp. 261–275.

16. Kübeck (ed.), *op. cit.,* p. 65; Rock, *Rejuvenation . . . ,* p. 25.

17. My emphasis. The word "Royal" was, of course, added in consideration of the Hungarians who thought of the Habsburgs as their kings and not their emperors (*Pesti Napló,* 12 March 1852).

18. Christoph Stölzl, *Die Ära Bach in Böhmen: Sozial geschichtliche Studien zum Neoabsolutismus 1849–1859,* Munich and Vienna, 1971, pp. 257–267.

19. Berzeviczy, *op. cit.,* I, p. 284.

20. Sashegyi, *op. cit.,* p. 39.

21. Schlitter, *op. cit.,* p. 55.

22. *Pesti Napló,* 17 and 18 September 1850.

23. *Official Gazette,* 1852, p. 24.

24. Text of Patent of 24 July 1852, in *Pesti Napló,* 13, 14 and 15 September 1852.

25. *Pesti Napló,* 10 February 1851.

26. *Ibid.,* 23 July 1852.

27. *Ibid.,* 30 October 1851.

28. *Ibid.,* 12 June 1852.

29. *Ibid.,* 16 September 1852.

30. No American or Canadian wheat was available in quantity. Russian grain was expensive because of the high cost of transportation. In 1848/49 U.S. exports totalled 1.5 million bushels and Russia sent abroad 1.3 million *chetverka* wheat. By 1861 these amounts rose to 36.2 million and 9.6 million respectively (Bernát, *op. cit.,* p. 285).

31. *Pesti Napló,* 3 December 1852.

32. Andrew H. Brenman, "Economic Reform in Neuzeit Austria, 1825–1859," unpublished doctoral dissertation, Department of History, Princeton University, 1964, p. 270.

33. *Pesti Napló,* 22 July 1852.

34. Brenman, *op. cit.,* p. 280.

35. *Pesti Napló,* 17 July 1851.

36. *Ibid.,* 6 July 1852.

37. *Ibid.,* 13 May 1852.

38. *Die indirecten Abgaben Österreichs in den Jahren 1847, 1850 bis 1859,* (ed.) K.K. Finanzministerium, Vienna, 1860, pp. 189–193, 208.

39. See Chart 1; also *Pesti Napló,* 12 February 1852.

40. *Pesti Napló,* 16 September 1852; Brenman, *op. cit.,* p. 287.

41. *Pesti Napló,* 15 September 1851.

42. *Ibid.,* 22 July 1852.

43. *Ibid.,* 29 April 1852; Károly Keleti, *Visszapillantás Magyarország közgazdaságának egynegyed századára,* Budapest, 1875, p. 12.

44. *Pesti Napló,* 27 November 1851.

45. *Ibid.,* 20 May 1852; see also Chart II.

46. A. Corti, *The Reign of the House of Rothschild,* New York, 1928, p. 322.

47. *Pesti Napló,* 10 September 1852.

48. *Ibid.,* 26 January 1853. See also Charts I and II.

49. *Official Gazette,* 1850, pp. 925–927.

50. Alexander Matlekovits, *Die Zollpolitik der Österreichisch-Ungarischen Monarchie von 1850 bis zur Gegenwart,* Budapest, 1877, pp. 10–12.

51. *Pesti Napló,* 28 November 1851.

52. *Ibid.,* 13 October 1851; Brenman, *op. cit.,* p. 168.

53. Géza Eperjessy, "A Pest megyei céhesipar 1686–1872," *Pest megye múltjából. Tanulmányok,* (eds.) F. Keleti — E. Lakatos — J. Makkai, Budapest, 1965, p. 274; Gyula Szávay, *A magyar kamarai intézmény és a budapesti kamara története, 1850–1925,* Budapest, 1927, pp. 203–206.

54. *Pesti Napló,* 11 March 1851.

55. Zoltán Sárközi, "A Budapesti Kereskedelmi és Iparkamara hivataltörténete, *Levéltári Szemle,* Vol. XVII, No. 1 (January–April 1967), pp. 61–62; Tapié, *op. cit.,* p. 290.

56. Hanák, *op. cit.,* p. 51.

57. *Pesti Napló,* 2 December 1852.

58. *Ibid.,* 11 July 1851.

59. Carl Czörnig, *Österreich's Neugestaltung, 1848–1858,* Stuttgart and Augsburg, 1858, p. 382; *Mitteilungen aus dem Gebiete der Statistik,* Vol. VI, Book 3, (ed.) Direktion der Admin. Statistik, Vienna, 1855, p. 18.

60. *Pesti Napló,* 29 September 1851.

61. *Ibid.,* 14 December 1850.

62. *Magyar Hirlap,* 22 August 1851; Czörnig, *op. cit.,* pp. 377–378 and 382.

63. *Pesti Napló,* 28 August 1851.

64. Inexpensive land came from the state and also from municipalities. The latter offered their land in an effort to be linked to the network. See article on the Nagyvárad railroad lobby in *Pesti Napló,* 19 October 1852.

65. Hanák, *op. cit.,* p. 70.

66. *Pesti Napló,* 9 November 1852.

67. *Ibid.,* 3 March 1851.

68. *Ibid.,* 4 September 1852.

69. Hanák, *op. cit.,* p. 67.

70. *Pesti Napló,* 19 July 1852.

71. Brenman, *op. cit.,* p. 237.

72. *Pesti Napló,* 2 August 1851; Szávay, *op. cit.,* p. 240.

73. Brenman, *op. cit.,* p. 236.

74. Hanák, *op. cit.,* p. 67.
75. MOLAL, K.K. Landes-Baudirection für Ungarn, D 231;
	K.K. Ministerial Commissär Ritter F. v. Mitis, D 232;
	K.K. Districtual Bauamt zu Pressburg, D 233;
	K.K. Districtual Bauamt zu Oedenburg, D 234;
	K.K. Districtual Bauamt zu Kaschau, D 279 and D 235;
	K.K. Districtual Bauamt zu Grosswardein, D 236;
	K.K. Bezirksbauamt zu Grosswardein, D 237.
76. *Pesti Napló,* 3 July 1851 and 7 October 1852.
77. István Nagy, *A mezőgazdaság Magyarországon az abszolutizmus korában (1849–1867),* Budapest, 1944, p. 25.
78. Szávay, *op. cit.,* p. 208.
79. *Pesti Napló,* 18 October 1851.
80. *Ibid.,* 18 September 1851.
81. Bernát, *op. cit.,* p. 265; Lóránth, *op. cit.,* p. 26.
82. *Ibid.,* pp. 17–18.
83. The priests of Szepes, for example, received 61,000 forints for their losses of feudal dues (*Pesti Napló,* 20 October 1852).
84. *Ibid.;* Albert Berzeviczy, *Régi emlékek 1853–1870,* Budapest, 1907, p. 64.
85. *Pesti Napló,* 29 and 30 October 1851.
86. Anonymus [Bernhard Fischer von Meyer], *Rückblick auf die jüngste Entwicklungs-Periode Ungarns,* Vienna, 1857, pp. 73–74.
87. Brenman, *op. cit.,* p. 106.
88. *Pesti Napló,* 18 August 1851.
89. *Ibid.,* 9 July 1851.
90. *Ibid.,* 3 November 1851.
91. Jirkovszky, *op. cit.,* p. 44.
92. Friedjung, *op. cit.,* I, p. 349.
93. Johann Kalchberg, *Mein politisches Glaubensbekenntnis,* Leipzig, 1881, p. 308.
94. *Pesti Napló,* 17 September 1851.
95. Lajos Lukács, *Magyar függetlenségi és alkotmányos mozgalmak 1849–1861,* Budapest, 1955, p. 40; Szögyény-Marich, *op. cit.,* p. 49; Sashegyi, *Az abszolutizmuskori . . . ,* p. 42.
96. *Pesti Napló,* 10 May 1852; Rock, *Rejuvenation . . . ,* p. 25.
97. Archduke Albrecht to Franz Joseph, 31 October 1851, cited in Lukács, *op. cit.,* p. 40.
98. Szögyény-Marich, *op. cit.,* II, p. 49.
99. MOLAL, K.K. Militär- und Civil-Government für Ungarn, Civil Section D 46/1853/1697.
100. Sashegyi, *op. cit.,* p. 42.
101. *Ibid.,* p. 293.
102. *Pesti Napló,* 1 and 4 January 1853.
103. Kornis, *op. cit.,* p. 23.
104. F. Eckhart, *A jog- és államtudományi kar története 1667–1935,* Budapest, 1936, pp. 398 and 437.
105. Győry, *op. cit.,* p. 518.
106. 1 February 1851.

107. 4 February 1852.

108. Friedrich Walter, *Die österreichische Zentralverwaltung*, Pt. 3: *Von der Märzrevolution 1848 bis zur Dezemberverfassung 1867,* Vienna, 1964, p. 568; Stölzl, *op. cit.,* Chapter 6. A special section of the Ministry of Interior handled émigré activities. Police agents, some of whom were former revolutionaries as was the case of the actor Gábor Egressy, were sent to Europe's capital cities and major ports. During the first year of the *Provisorium* they had sent 4,000 often fictitious reports to Vienna. The Emperor received news about Kossuth's appeal to the military border regiments to rise against the germanizing policies of his regime and also reports of a planned uprising in Hungary. Kossuth's propaganda tour of England and the United States made Schwarzenberg needlessly concerned to the extent that he asked Bach to place the security forces on alert (Dénes Jánossy, *A Kossuth emigráció Angliában és Amerikában 1851–1852,* Budapest, 1948, I, pp. 462–466; Gunther E. Rothenberg, *The Military Border in Croatia 1740–1881, A Study of an Imperial Institution,* Chicago and London, 1966, p. 163).

109. *Pesti Napló,* 30 April 1852.

110. *Ibid.,* 6 and 7 May 1852.

111. *Ibid.,* 19 and 20 May, 4 June, 3, 7 and 19 July, 21 and 26 August, 3 September, 14 October, 2 November and 4 December 1852.

112. *Ibid.,* 24 June, 10 and 16 July, 13 and 18 August 1852.

113. *Ibid.,* 21 June, 14 July, 11 August 1852.

114. Friedjung, *op. cit.,* I, p. 434.

115. *Pesti Napló,* 7 October 1851; 19 May, 4 June, 7 July, 19 July, 21 August, 3 September, 19 October and 7 November 1852; 6 January 1853.

116. *Ibid.,* 15 July and 25 August 1852. Vay was jailed for eight months.

117. *Pesti Napló,* 12 and 14 January 1853.

118. *Ibid.,* 22 July and 8 August 1851.

119. MOLAL, D 55, Zeitungsakten/1852/group 52; Béla Dezsényi, *Az időszaki sajtó története a Dunatáj országaiban,* Budapest, 1947, p. 32; Angyal, *op. cit.,* pp. 53 and 78 ff.

120. *Pesti Napló,* 4 and 5 June and 30 August 1852.

121. Angyal, *op. cit.,* pp. 48 and 83–85.

122. Newspapers published for the first time in 1852 were the *Budapesti Visszhang, Családi Lapok, Délibáb, Szépirodalmi Lapok.* With them the number of newspapers increased to eighteen (Kereszty, *op. cit.,* pp. 75–78; *Pesti Napló,* 3 January 1853).

123. Members of the Noszlopi group were hanged on 31 December 1852 (*Ibid.,* 4 January 1853).

124. *Ibid.,* 6 November 1852.

125. MOLAL, K.K. Militär- und Civil-Gouvernement für Ungarn, D 39–48, Polizei Section D 44/1852/210, 222 and 483.

126. Zoltán Tóth, *Magyarok és románok. Történelmi tanulmányok,* 1966, p. 391.

127. Venetianer, *op. cit.,* pp. 11–12.

128. *Pesti Napló,* 31 October 1852; Stölzl, *op. cit.,* p. 224.

129. *Ibid.,* 25 January 1853.

130. Zsilinszky, *op. cit.,* p. 683.

CHAPTER THREE:
THE IMPACT OF GOVERNMENT POLICIES ON THE ARISTOCRACY

1. Béla K. Király, *Hungary in the Late Eighteenth Century. The Decline of Enlightened Despotism,* New York, 1969, pp. 21–25; Jaszi, *op. cit.,* p. 161.
2. Károly Galgóczy, *Magyarország-, a Szerbvajdaság s Temesi Bánság mezőgazdasági statisticája,* Pest, 1855, p. 94; Hanák, *op. cit.,* p. 76.
3. Macartney, *op. cit.,* p. 53.
4. A small group of aristocrats supported Kossuth. They formed another political club, the Small Casino. The membership was less than a quarter that of the Great Casino. Their influence at the Court was negligible (László Révész, *Die Änfange des ungarischen Parlamentarismus,* Munich, 1968, pp. 67 f; Sylvia Medgyesi-Mitschang, "The Influence of the Hungarian Aristocracy upon Franz Joseph from 1851 to 1861," unpublished Ph.D. Dissertation, Department of History, University of St. Louis, Mo., 1971, p. 40).
5. *Ibid.,* p. 49. Ms. Medgyesi throughout her doctoral dissertation constantly refers to a formal party. While a Conservative Party did, indeed, exist in Hungary between 1847 and 1848, it ceased to function as an institution during the Revolution and the years following. Neither can one accept Brenman's statement that between 1849 and 1867 no "more than half a dozen [aristocrats] could be considered as politically active at any given time" (Brenman, *op. cit.,* p. 46).
6. Jósika to Metternich, 2 July 1849, Vienna, Andics, *A nagybirtokos...,* III, p. 324.
7. Károlyi, *op. cit.,* I, pp. 12 f.
8. Four of these proposals were published by Károlyi (*Ibid.,* II, pp. 634–639).
9. Text in Lajos Steier, *A tót nemzetiségi kérdés 1848/49-ben,* II, Budapest, 1934, p. 232.
10. Minutes in Daniel Rapant, *Slovenské povstanie roku 1848/49,* III/2, Bratislava, 1954, pp. 162 f.
11. Text in Andics, *A nagybirtokos...,* II, pp. 160 ff and 172 ff.
12. *Ibid.,* pp. 353 ff.
13. Kiszling, *op. cit.,* p. 75; Károlyi, *op. cit.,* I, p. 13.
14. Andics, *A nagybirtokos...,* II, pp. 412 f.
15. Oszkár Sashegyi, "Magyarország beolvasztása az ausztriai császárságba," *Levéltári Közlemények,* Vol. XXXIX, No. 1 (1968), p. 74.
16. *Ibid.,* p. 71.
17. Berzeviczy, *Az absolutismus...,* I, p. 56.
18. Rock, *Rejuvenation...,* p. 24.
19. Sashegyi, *Magyarország...,* p. 68.
20. Members: G. Apponyi, J. Barkóczy, E. Dessewffy, S. Jósika, J. Ürményi, V. Szentiványi, L. Wirkner, and J. Szarka (Berzeviczy, *Az absolutismus...,* I, p. 60; Rock, *Rejuvenation...,* p. 23).
21. Berzeviczy, *Az absolutismus...,* I, p. 60.
22. Szögyény-Marich, *op. cit.,* II, p. 591.
23. Medgyesi, *op. cit.,* pp. 79 f.

24. Károlyi, *op. cit.*, I, p. 591.
25. Schlitter, *op. cit.*, pp. 92 ff.
26. Apponyi to Schwarzenberg, 8 March 1849, Vienna, Andics, *A nagybirtokos* . . . , III, pp. 23–26.
27. Schlitter, *op. cit.*, pp. 87 f.
28. Kübeck to Windischgrätz, 10 April 1849, Buda, Andics, *A nagybirtokos* . . . , III, pp. 168 f; Kübeck to Schwarzenberg, 28 March 1849, Buda, *ibid.*, pp. 119 f; Windischgrätz to Franz Joseph, 19 April 1849, Buda, *ibid.*, pp. 184 ff.
29. Count Emil Dessewffy to Bach, 6 June 1849, Vienna, *ibid.*, pp. 291 ff; Berzeviczy, *Az absolutismus* . . . , I, p. 82; Sashegyi, *Az abszolutizmuskori* . . . , p. 181.
30. *Ibid.*, p. 24.
31. Szögyény-Marich, *op. cit.*, II, p. 5. There is no evidence that Windischgrätz ever accepted these "conditions," although he never tried to interfere with Szögyény's organization which operated in the spirit of the "conditions" (Imre Halász, "A magyar konzervativek az abszolut korszakban," *Nyugat,* Vol. X, No. 21 (1917), pp. 662 f.).
32. Szögyény-Marich, *op. cit.*, II, p. 6.
33. Sashegyi, *Az abszolutizmuskori* . . . , p. 169; Berzeviczy, *Az absolutismus* . . . , I, pp. 83 f.
34. Zichy to Schwarzenberg, 18 March 1849, Győr, Andics, *A nagybirtokos* . . . , III, pp. 71 ff.
35. Kübeck to Schwarzenberg, 28 March 1849, Pest, *ibid.*, pp. 119 ff; Windischgrätz to Schwarzenberg, 12 April 1849, Buda, *ibid.*, pp. 184 ff.
36. Medgyesi, *op. cit.*, p. 3.
37. 6 April 1849.
38. Welden to Szécsen, 25 May 1849, Pozsony and Welden to Edmund Zichy, 25 May 1849, Pozsony, Andics, *A nagybirtokos* . . . , III, pp. 257 ff; Welden to Szögyény, 1 May 1849, Oroszvár, *ibid.*, p. 214; Szögyény-Marich, *op. cit.*, II, p. 19; Friedrich Walter, "Von Windischgrätz über Welden zu Haynau, Wiener Regierung und Armee-Oberkommando in Ungarn 1849/50," *Die Nationalitätenfrage im alten Ungarn und die Südostpolitik Wiens,* (eds.) Friedrich Walter and Harold Steinacker, Munich, 1959, pp. 110 f.
39. Minutes of the Cabinet, 25 May 1849, Vienna, Andics, *A nagybirtokos* . . . , III, pp. 257 ff.
40. Szögyény-Marich, *op. cit.*, II, pp. 20–24.
41. György Spira, *A magyar forradalom 1848–49-ben,* Budapest, 1959, p. 532; Gracza, *op. cit.*, V, p. 936.
42. Berzeviczy, *Az absolutismus* . . . , I, p. 112.
43. Minutes of the Cabinet, 2 July 1849, Vienna, Andics, *A nagybirtokos* . . . , III, pp. 362 f.
44. Felix Zichy to Schwarzenberg [probably May, 1849], *ibid.*, pp. 219 f.
45. MOLAL, D 36/1850/310.
46. Bach to Dessewffy, 26 May 1849, Vienna, Andics, *A nagybirtokos* . . . , III, pp. 262 f; Jósika to Metternich, 2 July 1849, Vienna, *ibid.*, pp. 323 ff.
47. Rock, *Reaction Triumphant* . . . , p. 266.
48. The official translation of Count Zichy's notes for Paskevics is in Andics, *A nagybirtokos* . . . , III, pp. 451 ff.

49. Károlyi, *op. cit.*, I, II, *passim*.

50. *Medgyesi, op. cit.*, p. 183.

51. MOLAL, D 36/1849/304.

52. Jósika to Metternich, 25 February 1850, Vienna, Andics, *A nagybirtokos* . . . , III, pp. 466 f.

53. Paton, *op. cit.*, p. 393; on Paton see Metternich to Schwarzenberg, 24 August 1849, Richmond, Andics, *A nagybirtokos* . . . , III, pp. 399 f.

54. Jósika to Metternich, 25 February 1850, *ibid.*, pp. 466 f.

55. On the Szécsen mission see the correspondence of Szécsen and Schwarzenberg in *ibid.*, pp. 423 f, 430 f, 434 f and 445 f.

56. 3 October 1849.

57. Berzeviczy, *op. cit.*, I, p. 102.

58. Jósika to Metternich, 25 February 1850, Vienna, Andics, *A nagybirtokos* . . . , III, pp. 466 ff.

59. Angyal, *op. cit.*, p. 9.

60. Pál Somssich's article, 29 December 1849.

61. *Figyelmező*, 30 November 1849.

62. In November 1848 the most popular papers had the following number of subscribers: *Kossuth Hirlapja*, 4,977; *Pesti Hirlap*, 2,554; *Magyar Népbarát*, 2,710; *Katolikus Néplap*, 1,399; *Nemzeti Ujság*, 765 (*Pesti Napló*, 4 April 1850).

63. Egyed Hermann, *A magyar katolikus papság az osztrák katonai diktatúra és az abszolutizmus idejében*, Gödöllő, 1932, p. 89.

64. Angyal, *op. cit.*, pp. 37 f; Pál Gyulai to Károly Szász, Gyömrő, 14 September 1850, Gyulai, *op. cit.*, p. 56.

65. Gusztáv Beksics, *Kemény Zsigmond, a forradalom és a kiegyezés*, Budapest, 1883, p. 166.

66. Medgyesi, *op. cit.*, p. 94.

67. *Pesti Napló*, 14 January, 24 January, 24 June, 25 June, 29 July and 16 October 1851; 10 March 1852.

68. *Ibid.*, 3 May, 6 May, 27 May, 15 May, 30 May, 3 June, 5 June, 6 June, 10 June, 7 July and 29 October 1851; 10 December and 29 January 1852.

69. *Ibid.*, 25 January, 6, 7 and 13 May, 14 June, 11 and 15 July and 6 October; 3 and 10 February 1852.

70. *Ibid.*, 1 May and 5 May 1851.

71. *Ibid.*, 17 February, 27, 28 and 20 March 1851; 5 December 1852.

72. *Ibid.*, 4 September 1850.

73. 24 November 1851.

74. Vienna, 1850.

75. *Magyar Hirlap*, 7, 9, 17, 20, 21 August 1850; *Pesti Napló*, 6 and 13 August 1850; *Pester Morgenblatt*, 13, 14 and 19 August 1850; *Pester Zeitung*, 7, 8, 14 and 17 August 1850.

76. *Pesti Napló*, 22 August 1850.

77. *Ibid.*, 4 July 1850.

78. *Verfassung von 4. März, und die erbliche Pairie*, Vienna, 1850; *Über die Verantwortlichkeit des Ministeriums*, Vienna, 1850, which was confiscated by the Viennese police (*Pesti Napló*, 26 April 1851).

79. Primate János Hám to Windischgrätz, 6 March 1849, Andics, *A nagybirtokos* . . . , III, pp. 20 f.

80. Révész, *Fejezetek* . . . , p. 141; Lukács, *op. cit.*, p. 19; Hanák, *op. cit.*, p. 21.

81. János Simor to Lajos Hajnald, 19 August and 29 August 1849, Kézirattári Növendéknapló, 35, 38, 1924, Manuscript Collection in the National Széchenyi Library, Budapest; cited hereafter as *Simor Collection;* Windischgrätz to Franz Joseph, 19 March 1849, Buda, Andics, *A nagybirtokos* . . . , III, pp. 79 f; Hám to Windischgrätz, 31 March, 1849, Pest, *ibid.*, pp. 129 f; József Lonovics, Archbishop of Eger, to Windischgrätz, 29 March 1849, Pest, *ibid.*, p. 133; Hám, *op. cit.*, p. 16.

82. Hermann, *op. cit.*, p. 36 f.

83. Simor to Hajnald, 30 October 1849, *Simor Collection;* MOLAL, D 44/1852/1,261.

84. Meszlényi, *op. cit.*, p. 250.

85. Editorial, Vol. I, No. 1 (1849); Mark Kovács, "Az egyháziak személyes mentessége ügyében," Vol. II, No. 8 (1850); S. Szepessy, "Politikai hirdetmények az egyházi szószéken," Vol. I, No. 39 (1849).

86. Berzeviczy, *Az absolutismus* . . . , I, p. 159.

87. Hanák, *op. cit.*, p. 21.

88. G. J., "Papi mentesség," *Religio,* Vol. III, No. 39 (1851).

89. MOLAL, D 44/1852/1871 res. and D 36/1850/306.

90. 20 March 1850.

91. MOLAL, D 36/1850/310.

92. Medgyesi, *op. cit.*, p. 91.

93. János Asbóth, "A conservativek a forradalom után," in János Asbóth, *Jellemrajzok és tanulmányok korunk történetéhez,* Budapest, 1892, p. 122.

94. Szögyény-Marich, *op. cit.*, II, p. 27. The Memorandum was sent to the Emperor three days later. The complete text was then leaked, presumably by the authors, to the *Pester Morgenblatt,* then translated and reprinted in the *Pesti Napló* and the *Magyar Hirlap* on 19 April 1850.

95. Florence A. Forster, *Francis Deak, Hungarian Statesman; a Memoir,* London, 1880, p. 130.

96. Szögyény-Marich, *op. cit.*, II, p. 28.

97. Berzeviczy, *Az absolutismus* . . . , I, p. 160; Redlich, *Das Österreichische* . . . , p. 470; Rudolf Springer [Karl Renner], *Grundlagen und Entwicklungsziele der österreichisch-ungarische Monarchie,* Vienna, 1906, pp. 95 f; Kann, *op. cit.*, I, p. 128; Medgyesi, *op. cit.*, p. 94.

98. Szögyény-Marich, *op. cit.*, II, p. 47; Medgyesi, *op. cit.*, pp. 56, 95–96.

99. Baron Lajos Wirkner to Schwarzenberg, 22 April 1850, Andics, *A nagybirtokos* . . . , III, pp. 475 ff.

100. Beksics, *A modern* . . . , pp. 462 f. The date of the entry is not indicated by Beksics.

101. *Deák Ferencz beszédei: 1842–1861,* II, (ed.) Manó Kónyi, Budapest, 1903, pp. 383 f; Szögyény-Marich, *op. cit.*, II, pp. 33 and 227 f; Halász, *op. cit.*, p. 665; *Pesti Napló,* 23–24 April 1851. The Székesfehérvár correspondent of the *Pesti Napló* also expressed its satisfaction over Szögyény-Marich's appointment (3 May 1851).

102. *Ibid.*, 29 October 1851.

103. Baron Lajos Ambróczy headed the Committee (*ibid.*, 4 October 1851).

104. Members: Dessewffy, Apponyi, Cziráky, Stephan Hauer, István Nagy and Ferenc Vághy (*ibid.,* 19 and 22 January 1852).
105. Cited in Medgyesi, *op. cit.,* p. 109.
106. MOLAL, D 44/1852/88.
107. *Ibid.,* 2,405.
108. Ede Wertheimer, *Gróf Andrássy Gyula élete és kora,* I, Budapest, 1910, p. 86.
109. MOLAL, D 44/1852/548, 988, 1,128 and 1853/1.
110. *Pesti Napló,* 16 October 1851.
111. *Ibid.,* 6 October 1851; MOLAL, D 44/1852/1,769 res.
112. *Pesti Napló,* 18 October 1851.
113. *Ibid.,* 10 November 1851.
114. Szögyény-Marich, *op. cit.,* II, p. 49.
115. MOLAL, D 44/1852/3,087; Molnár, *op. cit.,* II, p. 24.
116. MOLAL, D 44/1852/1,582 res. and 3,154; Hanák, *op. cit.,* p. 29; Medgyesi, *op. cit.,* p. 184.
117. *Pesti Napló,* 29 May 1852.
118. *Ibid.,* 3 June 1852.
119. *Ibid.,* 23 June 1852.
120. *Ibid.,* 2 July 1852.
121. Berzeviczy, *Az absolutismus . . . ,* I, pp. 308 f; *Pesti Napló,* 16 August 1852.
122. Medgyesi, *op. cit.,* p. 108.
123. MOLAL, D 44/1852/1690 res.
124. *Ibid.,* 548.
125. *Ibid.,* 1,327, 1,769 res. and 3,154.
126. *Ibid.,* 326.
127. 1853/365; *Pesti Napló,* 1 August 1851.
128. MOLAL, D 44/1852/1,690 res.
129. *Ibid.,* 1,917 res.
130. *Ibid.,* 1,326.
131. *Ibid.,* 700 and 842.
132. *Pesti Napló,* 21 May 1852.
133. Medgyesi, *op. cit.,* p. 99.
134. *Pesti Napló,* 10 December 1852.
135. *Pesti casinó-könyv,* Pest, 1855; *Pesti Napló,* 30 January 1853.
136. Berzeviczy, *Az absolutismus . . . ,* II, p. 403.
137. 3 March 1852.
138. *Pesti Napló,* 20 March 1851 and 27 May 1852.
139. *Ibid.,* 9 April 1850.
140. *Ibid.,* 10 March 1852.
141. *Ibid.,* 5 November and 17 December 1852; 5 January 1853.
142. Berzeviczy, *Az absolutismus . . . ,* II, p. 410.
143. George Barany, "Hungary: From Aristocratic to Proletarian Nationalism," *Nationalism in Eastern Europe,* (eds.) Peter F. Sugar and Ivo J. Lederer, Seattle and London, 1971, p. 277.
144. Gyula Szekfű, *Három nemzedék és ami utána következik,* Budapest, 1934, p. 170.
145. Brenman, *op. cit.,* p. 96.

146. Emil Niederhauser, *A jobbágyfelszabadítás Kelet-Európában,* Budapest, 1962, p. 149; Sándor, *op. cit.,* pp. 27 f; Jászi, *op. cit.,* p. 195; Szekfű, *Három . . .* , p. 169.

147. Galgóczy, *op. cit.,* p. 94.

148. Haynau's 12 July circular to all Hungarian *Főispáns* instructed these officials to keep the Old Conservatives under constant observation and discreetly block their anti-governmental activities (Szögyény-Marich, *op. cit.,* II, p. 64; Asbóth, *op. cit.,* p. 123).

149. Vilmos Sándor, *A tőkés gazdaság kibontakozása Magyarországon, 1849–1900,* Budapest, 1958, p. 12.

150. Hóman, *op. cit.,* pp. 220–227; George Barany, *Stephen Széchenyi and the Awakening of Hungarian Nationalism, 1791–1841,* Princeton, 1968, p. 152.

152. Mihály Horhy imported British harvesting equipment for his Jakabszállás estate (*Pesti Napló,* 4 August 1852). A shipment of agricultural machinery arrived at Hont County in October, 1852 (*Ibid.,* 9 November 1852).

152. *Ibid.,* June 1852.

153. Galgóczy, *op. cit.,* pp. 163 ff and 346.

154. *Ibid.,* pp. 361 ff.

155. *Pesti Napló,* 29 October and 20 November 1852.

156. Dessewffy cited in Medgyesi, *op. cit.,* p. 89.

CHAPTER FOUR:
THE GENTRY IN OPPOSITION

1. Szekfű, *op. cit.,* p. 169.

2. György Szabad, "A kiegyezés előtörténetéhez," *Történelmi Szemle,* Vol. XIV, Nos. 1–2 (1971), p. 256.

3. Leslie C. Tihany, "The Austro-Hungarian Compromise, 1867–1918: A Half Century of Diagnosis; Fifty Years of Post-Mortem," *Central European History,* Vol. II, No. 2 (June, 1969), p. 124; Galgóczy, *op. cit.,* p. 102; Hóman, *op. cit.,* p. 211; Hanák, *op. cit.,* p. 76; Bárány, *Széchenyi . . .* , p. 152.

4. *Ibid.,* pp. 152 f.

5. Of the entire nobility five per cent was Rumanian belonging mostly to the lesser nobility and ten per cent was German distributed among all three layers: aristocracy, gentry and lesser nobility. Both groups were rapidly magyarized along with the few nobles of Slavic origin (Szekfű, *op. cit.,* p. 70).

6. Henrik Marczali, *Hungary in the Eighteenth Century,* Cambridge, 1910, pp. 102 f; Thomas Spira, "The Growth of Magyar National Awareness under Francis I," unpublished doctoral dissertation, Department of History, McGill University, 1969, pp. 40 f.

7. Ernő Lakatos, *A magyar politikai vezetőréteg, 1848–1918,* Budapest, 1942, p. 43.

8. Móric Tomcsányi, *Magyarország közjoga,* Budapest, 1943, p. 163; István Hajnal, "Az osztálytársadalom," *Magyar művelődéstörténet,* V, (eds.) S. Domanovszky *et al.,* Budapest, n.d., pp. 165 ff.

9. Király, *op. cit.*, pp. 32 f and 141; Hóman, *op. cit.*, pp. 209 f and 227 f; Barany, *Széchenyi* . . . , p. 150.

10. Pál Sándor, *A jobbágykérdés az 1832/36-os országgyűlésen,* Budapest, 1948, p. 52.

11. Mihály Horváth, *Huszonöt év Magyarország történelméből, 1823–1848,* III, Budapest, 1886, pp. 298 f. The Kossuth regime eliminated the entail and suspended all related court cases (Bernát, *op. cit.*, p. 37).

12. Spira, "The Growth . . . ," pp. 30 f and 174.

13. László Ungár, "Kapitalisztikus gazdálkodás," *Magyar művelődéstörténet,* p. 215; Iván T. Berend and György Ránki, *Economic Development in East-Central Europe in the 19th and 20th Centuries,* New York and London, 1974, pp. 32 f; Galgóczy, *op. cit.*, p. 106; Bernát, *op. cit.*, p. 79; Niederhauser, *op. cit.*, p. 125; Spira, "The Growth . . . ," pp. 32 f.

14. *Pesti Napló,* 16 March 1850.

15. *Ibid.*, 16 and 17 May 1850.

16. During the reign of Maria Theresa the size of a serf holding was limited. Any land beyond the maximum was called remainder land and was to be returned to the lord.

17. *Pesti Napló,* 18 and 11 November 1850.

18. Bernát, *op. cit.*, p. 273.

19. Sándor, *Parasztságunk* . . . , p. 68.

20. MOLAL, D 51/1850/6,856, 10,069 and 10,842.

21. L. Bogyay, Zala County Chief, to Gábor Dőry, Fehérvár District Chief, Zalaegerszeg, 16 March 1850, Oszkár Sashegyi (ed.), *Munkások és parasztok mozgalmai Magyarországon 1849–1867, Iratok,* cited hereafter as *Iratok.*

22. Berend, *op. cit.*, p. 33.

23. Rights to manufacture and sell alcoholic beverages, milling, selling of meat, hunting, fishing, store opening rights, etc.

24. S. Szarka, Vas County Chief, to Ignác Rohonczy, Royal Commissioner, 29 March 1849, Szombathely, *Iratok,* pp. 80 ff; G. Papp, Chairman of the Robot and Tax Commission, to Geringer, 31 July 1850, Buda, *ibid.*, p. 119; Geringer to Bach, 2 April 1850, Pest, MOLAL, D 55/1850/6,255.

25. In one year from the Kassa District alone 2,000 letters of complaint against the gentry were forwarded to Franz Joseph (MOLAL, D 44/1853/162).

26. Berzeviczy, *Az absolutismus* . . . , II, p. 361.

27. MOLAL, D 55/1850/6,255.

28. Aurél Kecskeméthy, *Magyarország összpontosítása Ausztriában,* Pest, 1851, p. 22; Charles Loring Brace, *Hungary in 1851; with an Experience of the Austrian Police,* London, 1852, p. 116; *Figyelmező,* 28 November 1849; *Pesti Napló,* 14 March 1850; and 5 July 1850; *Gazdasági Lapok,* 11 July 1850.

29. Hóman, *op. cit.*, p. 447; Szekfű, *op. cit.*, p. 173; Molnár, *op. cit.*, II, p. 25; Lukács, *op. cit.*, p. 28; Gracza, *op. cit.*, p. 1,318.

30. Macartney, *op. cit.*, p. 487; Kann, *op. cit.*, I, p. 131; Forster, *op. cit.*, p. 117.

31. Pál Sándor, *A XIX század végi agrárválság Magyarországon,* Budapest, 1958, p. 149; *Pesti Napló,* 26 November 1851 and 15 October 1852.

32. György Szabad, *A tatai és gesztesi Eszterházy-uradalom áttérése a robotrendszerről a tőkés gazdálkodásra,* Budapest, 1957, p. 551.

33. MOLAL, D 55/1850/6,255; Sándor, *Parasztságunk* . . . , p. 40.
34. Berend, *op. cit.*, p. 45.
35. *Gazdasági Lapok*, 22 September 1850; Sándor, *Parasztságunk* . . . ,
pp. 54 f; Hanák, *op. cit.*, p. 60.
36. Brace, *op. cit.*, pp. 124 f.
37. Baranya County Chief to Antal Augusz, 31 January 1850, Pécs, *Iratok*,
pp. 22 f; MOLAL, D 44/1852/3,296.
38. Sándor, *Parasztságunk* . . . , p. 131.
39. *Iratok*, pp. 22 f.
40. F. Swieceny, Kassa District Ministerial Commissioner and Lt. Gen.
Bordolo to Geringer, Kassa, 7 May 1850, *Ibid.*, pp. 24 f.
41. *Pesti Napló*, 1 July 1850.
42. Before 1848 the serf was fined 10 kr. for missed foot *robot* and 20 kr.
for *robot* with draft animals. The payment for overtime *robot* was 20 per cent
higher (H. Ditz, *A magyar mezőgazdaság*, Pest, 1869, p. 108). In Pest County
a harvester earned 40 kr. and a female hoer 15 kr. daily. A woman could earn
18 and a young boy 8 kr. for a day's work (*Magyar Hírlap*, 16 September
1852). In the northern areas of the country labor cost was usually 20 per cent
below the national average (Pest County Chief to Koller, Ministerial Commissioner, 27 May 1850, Pest, *Iratok*, pp. 38 f; *Pesti Napló*, 1 July 1850;
Bernát, *op. cit.*, p. 135). The average wage per day for adult males hovered
around 30 kr.
43. *Az absolutismus* . . . , II, p. 359.
44. MOLAL, D 44/1852/1,582 res.
45. *Op. cit.*, p. 271.
46. Cost of food articles: bread, 3 kr. per pound; pork, 13 kr. per pound;
bacon, 21 kr. per pound; beef, 4 to 10 kr. per pound; eggs, 9 kr. per dozen; pair
of boots, 5 forints; suit, 8 forints (*Pesti Napló*, 13 November 1851; 24 June,
10 September 1850; 17 March, 11 October, 4 August 1852).
47. "In the second half of the nineteenth century in Hungary of the medium
size estates from 500 to 1,000 cadastral hold (1 cadastral hold = 0.57 hectare)
the entire property was leased in 25 per cent of the cases, a part of the property
in 22.5 per cent. In the category of large estates over 1,000 cadastral hold, the
entire property was leased to tenants in 22 per cent of the cases, while in
another 18.6 per cent only a part of the property was let" (Berend, *op. cit.*,
p. 45). There were only a few isolated cases of land left uncultivated, e.g., in
Pest-Pilis (MOLAL, D 77/1851/6,711) and Sáros counties (MOLAL, D 44/
1852/1,582 res.).
48. MOLAL, D 64/1849/1,142; D 77/1849/2,130; D 79/1850/79 and 100.
49. Brenman, *op. cit.*, p. 265; Kálmán Kenessey, *Egy-két őszinte szó
társadalmi viszonyainkat érdeklőleg*, Pest, 1857, p. 34; MOLAL, D 44/1852/
279, 2,851 and 3,215.
50. Geringer to Bach, 28 September 1852, Buda, MOLAL, D 51/1852/
1,954 pr.; D 44/1853/1,431.
51. *Ibid.*, 1852/1,689 res.; István Nagy, *A mezőgazdaság Magyarországon
az abszolutizmus korában (1849–1867)*, Budapest, 1944, pp. 97 ff, *Pester
Zeitung*, 12 March 1852.
52. The Government terminated the moratorium in 1854. The slump came
three years later.

53. Berzeviczy, *Az absolutismus* . . . , II, p. 399.

54. Hanák, *op. cit.,* p. 76.

55. Gyula Oláh, "A társadalmi élet 1848 után," *Vasárnapi Újság,* Vol. LXIV, No. 25 (1917), p. 400.

56. *Pesti Napló,* 31 August 1850; András Diószegi *et al., Irodalmunk az önkényuralom és a kiegyezés előkészítése korában (1849–1867),* Volume I of *A magyar irodalom története 1849–1905,* (eds.) István Király *et al.,* Budapest, 1963, p. 10.

57. *Hölgyfutár,* 19 and 31 January, 7 February and 7 March 1850; Paton, *op. cit.,* p. 217.

58. MOLAL, D 77/1851/4,189; D 44/1852/521 and 567; *Pesti Napló,* 3, 18, 19, 22 and 24 February 1851, 29 January 1852.

59. Mór Jókai, *Politikai divatok,* Pest, 1863, and *Szerelem bolondjai,* Pest, 1869; Pál Gyulai, *Egy régi udvarház utolsó gazdája,* Pest, 1857.

60. MOLAL, D 36/1850/383; D 44/1852/138, 528, 567, and 3,673.

61. *Ibid.,* 3,259.

62. *Ibid.,* Augusz Antal Tolnai Ker. Főbiztos (Antal Augusz, District Chief Commissioner of Tolna District), D 68/1850/3,327; Ede Tóth, *Mocsáry Lajos élete és politikai pályakezdete (1826–1874),* Budapest, 1967, pp. 66 f; Steier, *Haynau* . . . , pp. 23, 27 and 66.

63. MOLAL, D 44/1852/1,787 res.

64. *Ibid.,* D 55/1850/6,255; Berzeviczy, *Az absolutismus* . . . , I, p. 134.

65. Geringer to Bach, 27 February 1852, Buda, MOLAL, D 51/1852/pr.; D 44/1853/1,431.

66. *Ibid.,* 1852/182, 528, 1,229, 1,304, 1,787, 2,851 and 2,996; Brace, *op. cit.,* pp. 116 ff.

67. MOLAL, D 44/1853/1,262.

68. *Ibid.,* D 79/1850/85 and 94.

69. *Ibid.,* D 51/1853/69.

70. George Handlery, "Revolutionary Organization in the Context of Backwardness: Hungary's 1848," *East European Quarterly,* Vol. VI, No. 1 (March, 1972), p. 59.

71. MOLAL, D 51/1852/937 pr.

72. *Ibid.,* D 44/1853/963.

73. Sándor, *Parasztságunk* . . . , p. 68; Szabad, *A tatai* . . . , p. 326.

74. MOLAL, D 44/1852/1,479; *Pesti Napló,* 3 September and 2 August 1850.

75. Király, *op. cit.,* p. 32.

76. Geringer to Bach, 2 April 1850, Pest, MOLAL, D 55/1850/6,255.

77. *Ibid.,* D 79/1850/118; D 44/1852/543; Antal Csengery to his father, 28 February 1851, Pest, *Csengery Antal hátrahagyott iratai és feljegyzései,* Budapest, 1928, pp. 430–433. Kossuthite propagandists misled the foreign public by stating, for example, that in 1852 the whole Hungarian nation looked with undivided and unlimited confidence towards Kossuth (C. F. Henningsen, *The Past and Future of Hungary: Facts, Figures, and Dates, Illustrative of Its Past Struggle, and Future Prospects,* Cincinnati, 1852, p. 51). About Henningsen's friendly relationship with Kossuth see Kossuth to Pulszky, 13 March 1851, *Népek tavasza: ismeretlen levelek, naplójegyzetek*

a magyar szabadságharc és emigráció korából, (ed.) Tivadar Ács, Budapest, 1944, pp. 20–23.

78. *Forradalom után,* Pest, 1850; *Még egy szó a forradalom után,* Pest, 1851.

79. Casinos opened their gates gradually after the Revolution (*Pesti Napló,* 4 April, 22 May, 27 June 1851, 7 January and 12 October 1852, 30 January 1853).

80. Brace, *op. cit.,* pp. 126 f.

81. *Az új földesúr,* Budapest, 1968 (1862), pp. 6 ff.

82. Kossuth to Pulszky, 21 March, 1851, Ács, *op. cit.,* p. 26.

83. See Table I.

84. MOLAL, D 36/1850/333.

85. *Ibid.,* D 44/1852/145, 268 and 852; *Hölgyfutár,* 19 January 1850; György Vadnay, "Zemplén-vármegye a forradalom után," *Adalékok Zemplén-vármegye történetéből,* Vol. VI, Nos. 3–4 (1906), p. 91.

86. "Pannonia vergisst Deinen Tod nie; als Klagen leben sie (Hungary forgets thy death never. As accuser [sic!] they shall live)," Brace, *op. cit.,* p. 216; *Pesti Napló,* 31 December 1850; MOLAL, D 44/1853/842 and D 77/1850/15,929.

87. Molnár, *op. cit.,* II, p. 26.

88. MOLAL, D 51/1852/119pr. and D 44/1852/87, 88, 288 and 1,222.

89. The initial reaction was positive (*Ibid.,* 1,128, 1,479, 1,616 and 1,760 res.; *1847 vagy 1848? Tájékoztatásul,* Debrecen, 1861, p. 5).

90. MOLAL, D 44/1852/1,616, 1,760 res. and 1,653 res.

91. *Ibid.,* 2,115 and 2,289.

92. *Ibid.,* 2,547.

93. Berzeviczy, *Régi emlékek,* p. 67.

94. MOLAL, D 44/1852/2,547.

95. *Ibid.,* 1853/1,054; D 51/1851/565 and 691.

96. *Ibid.,* D 44/1853/1,177 and 1,764.

97. *Ibid.,* 1852/633, 852 and 1,479; *Hölgyfutár,* 10 June 1850.

98. *Pester Morgenblatt,* 7 September 1850; *Pesti Napló,* 3 and 7 September 1850.

99. *Op. cit.,* p. 440.

100. MOLAL, D 44/1853/700; "Visszaemlékezések," *A Hét,* Vol. VII, No. 18 (1896), p. 229.

101. Macartney, *op. cit.,* p. 481; Hanák, *op. cit.,* p. 31; Molnár, *op. cit.,* II, p. 26.

102. MOLAL, D 44/1852/88 and 2,546.

103. *Ibid.,* D 51/1850/2,047; K.K. Ministerial-Commissariat Oedenburg D 86/1850/1,541.

104. *Pesti Napló,* 10 July 1850.

105. *Ibid.,* 20 April, 3 October, 4 December 1850 and 2 September 1851.

106. Hóman, *op. cit.,* p. 450; Berzeviczy, *Az absolutismus* . . . , I, p. 84; Sashegyi, *Az abszolutizmuskori* . . . , pp. 24 and 37.

107. Király, *op. cit.,* p. 33; Molnr, *op. cit.,* II, p. 27.

108. MOLAL, D 44/2,405 and 1,691 res., Appendix 212 präs.

109. Apponyi to Forgách, 5 July 1849, Nagyszombat, *Iratok,* p. 89.

110. MOLAL, D 44/1852/145 res.; *Pesti Napló,* 24 February 1851.

111. MOLAL, D 44/1852/1261, 1,916 res. and 1853/31.
112. *Hölgyfutár,* 18 March 1850.
113. MOLAL, D 44/1853/162 and 1,054; *Pesti Napló,* 13 May 1850; Ferenc Pölöskei and Kálmán Szakács (eds.), *Földmunkás és szegényparaszt-mozgalmak Magyarországon, 1848-1948,* Budapest, 1962, p. 51; Szabad, *A tatai . . . ,* p. 326.
114. MOLAL, D 44/1852/88, 1,850 and 2,405 and 1853/1,054.
115. 5 July 1850, 28 February 1852, 10 January 1851.
116. MOLAL, D 44/1852/2,405; *Visszaemlékezések,* p. 230.
117. MOLAL, D 44/1853/1.
118. Hóman, *op. cit.,* p. 444.
119. MOLAL, D 79/1850/109.
120. György Komoróczy, *Debrecen története a felszabadulásig,* Debrecen, 1955, p. 75.
121. MOLAL, D 77/1850/92 and 2,085.
122. *Ibid.,* 1849/4,998, D 44/1852/2,290; *Pesti Napló,* 5 July 1850.
123. MOLAL, D 44/1851/10, 1852/169, 565, 567, 1509 res., 1,916 res., 1,698 res.,2,405, 2,547, 3,239, 3,296, 1853/700 and 963; D 68/1851/4,129; *Pesti Napló,* 2 May 1850.
124. MOLAL, D 36/1849/304; Péter Hanák, "Hungary in the Austro-Hungarian Monarchy," *Austrian History Yearbook,* Vol. III, Pt. 1 (1967), p. 300; Molnár, *op. cit.,* p. 26.
125. *Pester Zeitung,* 25 May 1850; *Magyar Hirlap,* 14 May 1850, *Pesti Napló,* 8 May 1850.
126. MOLAL, D 68/1850/2,010.
127. *Pesti Napló,* 22 May 1850.
128. *Ibid.,* 12 July 1850.
129. *Ibid.,* 1 May 1850.
130. *Ibid.,* 28 August 1850.
131. *Ibid.,* 17 June 1850.
132. *Ibid.,* 7 June 1850.
133. *Ibid.,* 22 April 1850.
134. *Ibid.,* 8 and 26 June 1850.
135. *Ibid.,* 13 August 1850.
136. MOLAL, D 36/1850/310; D 44/1852/3,576; *Pesti Napló,* 30 August 1851; *Der Wanderer,* 14 February 1852.
137. Lajos Warga, *A keresztyén egyház történelme,* Sárospatak, 1908; Zsilinszky, *op. cit.*
138. Áron Kiss, *Török Pál élete,* Budapest, 1904, pp. 127-131.
139. 6 December 1850.
140. *Pesti Napló,* 18 December 1850.
141. *Ibid.,* 5 May 1850.
142. *Ibid.,* 8 and 17 May and 31 August 1851; Kiss mentions in this connection Count Sámuel Teleki (*op. cit.,* p. 132).
143. *Pesti Napló,* 14 October 1851; Bíró, *op. cit.,* p. 330.
144. MOLAL, D 44/88, 279, 326, 565, 567, 633, 836, 1,054, 1,261, 1,509, 1,582 res., 2,561, 2,365, 1,824, 3,259, 3,576 and 1853/31.
145. István Sőtér, *Eötvös József,* Budapest, 1967, *passim.;* György Szabad

"Eötvös József a politika útjain," *Századok,* Vol. CV, Nos. 3– (1971), pp. 658 ff.

146. *Tűzön át az égbe,* Pest, 1850; *Egy magyar nábob,* Pest, 1854; *Kárpáthy Zoltán,* Pest, 1855.

147. *Fidibusz,* 1850; *Aggteleki barlang,* 1851; *Nagyapó,* 1851.

148. Diószegi, *et al., A magyar irodalom története 1849-től 1950-ig,* Vol. IV of *A magyar irodalom története,* (ed.) István Sőtér, Budapest, 1965, pp. 41 ff.

149. 12 and 14 June, 23 July 1850; 25 March 1852.

150. *Ibid.,* 19 August 1850.

151. Diószegi, *A magyar irodalom* . . . , p. 30.

152. Jánossy, *op. cit.,* p. 411; Lukács, *op. cit.,* pp. 59 ff.

153. Károly Edvi Illés, "Rózsa Sándor," *Budapesti Hírlap,* 15 July 1890; "Az összeesküvő Krivácsy," *Esti Újság,* 2 November 1903; Lukács, *op. cit.,* p. 123.

154. Jánossy, *op. cit.,* p. 442.

155. Sándor Veress, *A magyar emigráció keleten,* I, Budapest, 1878–1879, p. 249.

156. Lukács, *op. cit.,* pp. 61 ff.

157. Jánossy, *op. cit.,* pp. 426 and 465.

158. "Gál Sándor terve az erdélyi felkelésről (1851)," *Hadtörténeti Közlemények,* Vol. XXVI, Nos. 1–2 (1925), pp. 179–183; Veress, *op. cit.,* p. 251.

159. Jánossy, *op. cit.,* pp. 466 and 469.

160. *Pesti Napló,* 2 December 1851.

161. Mihály Boross, *Élményeim 1848–1861,* II, Székesfehérvár, 1881–1882, p. 272.

162. *Az absolutismus* . . . , I, p. 348.

163. Forster, *op. cit.,* p. 1173; Medgyesi, *op. cit.,* p. 89; Zoltán Ferenczy, *Deák élete,* II, Budapest, 1904, p. 204; Dominic C. Kosáry, *op. cit., A History of Hungary,* New York, 1971 (reprint of 1941 edition), p. 257; Szekfű, *op. cit.,* p. 182; Kann, *op. cit.,* I, p. 131.

164. Deák, *op. cit.,* II, pp. 38 ff; Lukács, *op. cit.,* p. 29.

165. MOLAL, D 44/1853/427.

166. Deák to Szögyény-Marich, 1 May 1851, Deák, *op. cit.,* II, p. 384.

167. Szögyény-Marich, *op. cit.,* II, pp. 30 ff and 227 f.

168. *Pesti Napló,* 24 September 1850; Domokos Kosáry, "Kemény és Széchenyi 1849 után," *Irodalomtörténeti Közlemények,* Vol. LXVII, No. 2 (1963), p. 154.

Bibliography

Research Aids

Ausztriai levéltári anyagról készüult mikrofilmek az Országos Levéltár filmtárában [Microfilms on Austrian Archival Materials in the Film Library of the National Archives], (ed.) Iván Borsa, Budapest, 1960.

Bibliographie d'oeuvres choisies de la science historique hongroise 1945–1959, (eds.) E. Niederhauser *et al.*, Budapest, 1960.

Bridge, F. R., *The Habsburg Monarchy 1804–1918 Books and Pamphlets Published in the United Kingdom between 1804 and 1967; A Critical Bibliography*, London, 1967.

Budapest történetének bibliográfiája 1686–1950 [Bibliography of the History of Budapest 1686–1950], 5 vols., (eds.) J. Zoltán and L. Berza, Budapest, 1966.

Csehszlovákiai levéltári anyagról készült mikrofilmek az Országos Levéltár filmtárában [Microfilms on Czechoslovakian Archival Materials in the Film Library of the National Archives], (ed.) Iván Borsa, Budapest, 1963.

Ember, Győző, *Az 1848/49-i minisztérium levéltára* [The Archives of the Ministry of 1848–1849], Budapest, 1950.

Fényes, Elek, *Az ausztriai birodalom statisztikája és földrajzi leírása* [Statistics and Geographical Description of the Austrian Empire], Pest, 1857.

Galgóczy, Károly, *Magyarország-, a Szerbvajdaság s Temesi Bánság mezőgazdasági statisticája* [Agricultural Statistics of Hungary, the Serbian Voivodina and the Banat of Temesvár], Pest, 1855.

Hanák, Péter, "Recent Hungarian Literature on the History of the Austro-Hungarian Monarchy, 1849–1918. A Historiographical Survey," *Austrian History Yearbook,* Volume 1 (1965), pp. 151–163.

Handschriftliche Quellen in der Széchényi-Bibliothek 1789–1867, Budapest, 1950.

Jugoszláviai levéltári anyagról készült mikrofilmek az Országos Levéltár filmtárában. [Microfilms on Yugoslavian Archival Materials in the Film Library of the National Archives], (ed.) Iván Borsa, Budapest, 1963.

Katalog der ungarischsprachigen, gebundenen Manuskripte zur Geschichte der Neuzeit, 3 vols., Budapest, 1956.

Kereszty, István, *A magyar és magyarországi időszaki sajtó időrendi áttekintése 1705–1867* [Chronological Survey of the Magyar and Hungarian Contemporary Press 1705–1867], Budapest, 1916.

Magyar életrajzi lexikon [Hungarian Biographical Encyclopedia], 2 vols., (ed.) Ágnes Kenyeres, Budapest, 1967.

A magyar gazdasági szakirodalom könyvészete [Bibliography of the Literature on Special Topics dealing with the Hungarian Economy], 5 vols., (eds.) F. S. Szabó *et al.,* Budapest, 1956–1961.

Magyar könyvészet 1945–1960 [Hungarian Bibliography 1945–1960], 4 vols., Budapest, 1964.

A magyar munkásmozgalmi sajtó bibliográfiája 1848–1948 [Bibliography of the Hungarian Workers' Movement Press 1848–1948], 4 vols., Budapest, 1951–1959.

Magyar nemzeti bibliográfia [Hungarian National Bibliography], Budapest, 1946–1968.

Magyar történelmi kronológia, Az őstörténettől 1966-ig [Hungarian Historical Chronology from Ancient History to 1966], (ed.) Péter Gunst, Budapest, 1968.

Magyar történeti bibliográfia 1825–1867 [Hungarian Historical Bibliography 1825–1867], 5 vols. (eds.) Z. I. Tóth *et al.,* Budapest, 1950–1959.

Országos Levéltár 10. Gyűjtemények [National Archives, No. 10. Collection], (eds.) Z. Dávid *et al.,* Budapest, 1956.

Országos Levéltár 11. Bécsi levéltárakból kiszolgáltatott iratok [National Archives, No. 11, Documents Released by Viennese Archives], (ed.) Oszkár Paulinyi, Budapest, 1956.

Petrik, Géza (ed.), *Magyarország bibliográphiája 1712–1860* [Bibliography of Hungary 1712–1860], 4 vols., Budapest, 1891.

Romániai levéltári anyagról készült mikrofilmek az Országos Levéltár filmtárában [Microfilms on Rumanian Archival Materials in the Film Library of the National Archives], (ed.) Iván Borsa, Budapest, 1964.

Sashegyi, Oszkár, *Az abszolutizmuskori levéltár* [The Archives of the Age of Absolutism], Budapest, 1965.

Szinnyei, József, *Magyar írók és munkái* [Life and Works of Hungarian Writers], 14 vols., Budapest, 1891–1914.

A történeti statisztika forrásai [Sources of Historical Statistics], (ed.) József Kovacsics, Budapest, 1957.

PRIMARY SOURCES

Manuscripts

Magyar Országos Levéltár, Az Abszolutizmuskori Levéltár [Hungarian National Archives, the Archives of the Age of Absolutism].

D 4 K.K. Ministerium des Cultus und Unterrichtes.

D 8–9 K.K. Armeé-Ober-Commando Feldmarschall Alfred Fürst zu Windischgrätz; Politische und administrative Section.

D 36–38 K.K. (III) Armeé Commando für Ungarn und Siebenbürgen: Polizei Section.

D 39–48   K.K. Militär- und Civil-Gouvernement für Ungarn, D 44:
           Polizei Section.

D 51–55   Der Bevollmächtigte Kais. Commissär für die Civilangelegen-
           heiten in Ungarn Karl Freiherr von Geringer, from 1851: K.K.
           Statthalterei für Ungarn.

D 56   K.K. Ober-Landes-Commissariats-Directorat.

D 59   K.K. Disciplinar Comité.

D 62–63   Pester K.K. Staatsprüfungs-Commission.

D 64   Rohonczy Ignác, Soproni Ker. Főbiztos [Ignác Rohonczy,
           Chief Commissioner of the Sopron District].

D 65   Cseh Ede Pécsi Ker. Ideiglenes Főbiztos [Ede Cseh, Provi-
           sional Chief Commissioner of the Pécs District].

D 67   Dőry Gábor Fehérvári Ker. Főbiztos [Gábor Dőry, Chief
           Commissioner of the Fehérvár District].

D 68   Augusz Antal Tolnai Ker. Főbiztos [Antal Augusz, Chief
           Commissioner of the Tolna District].

D 77   Szentiványi Vince Pesti Ker. Főbiztos [Vince Szentiványi,
           Chief Commissioner of the Pest District].

D 79–80   Uray Bálint Debreceni Ker. Főbiztos [Bálint Uray, Chief
           Commissioner of the Debrecen District].

D 81   Jósa Péter Nagyváradi Ker. Főbiztos [Péter Jósa, District
           Chief Commissioner of the Nagyvárad District].

D 87–88   K.K. Ministerial Commissariat Kaschau.

D 231   K.K. Landes-Baudirection für Ungarn.

D 232   K.K. Ministerial Commissär Ritter F.v. Mitis.

D 233   K.K. Districtual Bauamt zu Pressburg.

D 234   K.K. Districtual Bauamt zu Oedenburg.

D 279,235 K.K. Districtual Bauamt zu Kaschau.

D 237   K.K. Bezirksbauamt zu Grosswardein.

Országos Széchényi Könyvtár, Kézirattári Növendéknapló, 1924 Nos. 35 and
38, 56 letters, Simor János to Lajos Haynald [National Széchényi Library,
Manuscript Diary for Scholars, Nos. 35 and 38, 1924].

Contemporary Accounts

Newspapers 1849–1853

Vienna:

Az ausztriai birodalmat illető birodalmi törvény- és kormánylap
Der Wanderer
Wiener Zeitung

Pest-Buda:

Figyelmező
Gazdasági Lapok

Hölgyfutár
Magyar Hírlap
Pester Morgenblatt
Pester Zeitung
Pesti Napló
Religio

BOOKS AND ARTICLES

Ács, Tivadar (ed.), *Népek tavasza. Ismeretlen levelek, naplójegyzetek a magyar szabadságharc és emigráció korából* [Peoples' Spring. Unknown Letters, Diary Notes from the Age of the Hungarian War of Independence and Emigration], Budapest, 1943.

Alleruntertänigster Vortrag des treugehorsamsten provisorischen Ministers des Innern Alexander Bach, betreffend die allerhöchste Genehmigung der Grundzüge für die Organisation der politischen Verwaltungsbehörden, Vienna, 1849.

Andics, Erzsébet (ed.), *A Habsburgok és Romanovok szövetsége: az 1849. évi magyarorsági cári intervenció diplomáciai előtörténete* [The Alliance of the Habsburgs and the Romanovs: Diplomatic Pre-History of the Tsarist Intervention in Hungary in 1849], Budapest, 1961.

―――― , *A nagybirtokos arisztokrácia ellenforradalmi szerepe 1848–49-ben* [The Counter-Revolutionary Role of the Great Landowning Aristocracy in 1848–1849], 3 vols., Budapest, 1965.

[Asbóth, János], *1849–1866 Adalékok a kényuralom ellenes mozgalmak történetéhez. Az Asbóth-család irataiból* [1849–1866 Data to the History of Movements against Absolutism. From the Documents of the Asbóth Family], Pest, 1871.

Balassa, Imre, (ed.), *Világostól Josephstadtig 1849–1856 Földy János naplótöredékeiből* [From Világos to Josephstadt 1849–1856 From the Diary Fragments of János Földy], Budapest, 1939.

[Bíró, Mihály], *Önvédelem* [Self-defence], Marosvásárhely, 1870.

Boross, Mihály, *Élményeim 1848–1861* [My Experiences 1848–1861], 2 vols., Székesfehérvár, 1881.

Brace, Charles Loring, *Hungary in 1851: with an Experience of the Austrian Police,* London, 1852.

Büntető törvény bűntettek, vétségek és kihágások iránt bűntető bíróságok illetőségét tárgyazó rendeletek és sajtórendtartás 1852. máj. 27-éről az ausztriai birodalom számára [Criminal Law Concerning Crimes, Offences and Transgressions and Ordinances Describing the Jurisdiction of Criminal Courts as well as Press Regulations for the Austrian Empire, 27 May 1852], Buda, 1852.

Császári nyiltparancs 1850. évi augustus 2-ről az ideiglenes törvénnyel a jogügyletek, okiratok, irományok és hivatalos cselekvényekről fizetendő illeték tárgyában, kiható Magyar-, Horváth-Tótországokra a tengermellékkel együtt, nem különben a szerb vajdaság, temesi bánság, s a katonai határőrvidékre [Imperial Rescript of 2 August 1850 with Provisional Law Concerning the Payment of Dues for Legal Affairs, Documents and Writings and Official Actions. Applicable to Hungary, Croatia, Slavonia as well as the Littorial and not exempted the Serbian Voivodina, the Bánát of Temesvár and the Military Borders], Buda, 1850.

Csengery, Lóránd (ed.), *Csengery Antal hátrahagyott iratai és feljegyzései* [The Papers and Notes of Antal Csengery], Budapest, 1928.

Deák, Farkas, *Fogságom története* [The Story of My Captivity], Pest, 1869.

Deák Ferencz beszédei [Speeches of Ferenc Deák], 6 vols., Budapest, 1882–1898.

Deák Ferencz emlékezete. Levelek [In Remembrance of Ferenc Deák. Letters], Budapest, 1890.

Die Direkten Steuern in Österreich und ihre Reform, (ed.) K.K. Finanzministerium, Vienna, 1860.

Documentált felelet Kemény Zsigmondnak, Forradalom után czimű munkájára egy megbukott diplomatától [Documented Reply from a Failed Diplomat to Zsigmond Kemény on his Work Entitled *After the Revolution*], Pest, 1850.

1847 vagy 1848? Tájékoztatásul. Több képviselő' [1847 or 1848? For Information from Several Members of Parliament], Debrecen, 1861.

Engel-Janosi, Friedrich (ed.), *Die politische Korrespondenz der Päpste mit den österreichischen Kaisern 1804–1918,* Vienna and Munich, 1964.

[Eötvös, József br.], *Magyarország különállása Németország egységének szempontjából. Írta egy magyar államférfiú* [The Separation of Hungary from the Point of View of German Unity. Written by a Magyar Statesman], Pest, 1961.

Eötvös, József, *A XIX. század uralkodó eszméinek befolyása az álladalomra* [The Influence of the Dominant Ideas of the Nineteenth Century on the State], 2 vols., Budapest, 1851.

Falk Miksa és Kecskeméthy Aurél levelezése [The Correspondence of Miksa Falk and Aurél Kecskeméthy], (ed.) Dávid Angyal, Budapest, 1925.

Falk, Miska, *Kor- és jellemrajzok* [Period and Character Sketches], Budapest, 1903.

Fiath, Ferenc B., *Életem és élményeim* [My Life and Experiences], 2 vols., Budapest, 1878.

Frankenburg, Adolf, "Egykorú naplójegyzetek 1851-től 1861-ig" [Contemporary Diary Notations from 1851 to 1861], *Pesti Hírlap,* 23 and 24 August 1883.

Gyüjteményét a' Magyarország számára kibocsátott legfelsőbb Manifestumoмok és Szózatoknak, valamint a' cs. kir. hadsereg főparancsnokai által. Magyarországban kiadott hirdetményeknek [Collection of the Highest Manifestoes and Addresses Issued for Hungary as well as Announcements published in Hungary by High Command of the Royal and Imperial Army], Buda, 1849.

Gyulai, Pál, *Egy régi udvarház utolsó gazdája* [The Last Master of an Old Manor House], Pest, 1857.

Gyulai Pál levelezése 1843-tól 1867-ig [The Correspondence of Pál Gyulai from 1843 to 1867], (ed.) Sándor Somogyi, Budapest, 1961.

Hám János szatmári püspök és kinevezett prímás emlékiratai 1848/49-ből [The Memoirs of János Hám, Bishop of Szatmár and Appointed Primate, from 1848/49], (ed.) János Scheffler, Budapest, 1928.

Henningsen, C. F., *The Past and Future of Hungary: Facts, Figures, and Dates, Illustrative of Its Past Struggle, and Future Prospects*, Cincinnati, 1852.

Hőke, Lajos, "Egy hivatalnok emlékeiből" [Recollections of a Civil Servant], *Fővárosi Lapok*, 8, 10 and 11 August 1875.

Horváth, Jenő (ed.), *Origins of the Crimean War; Documents Relative To the Russian Intervention in Hungary and Transylvania, 1848–1849*, Budapest, 1937.

Horváth, Zoltán, *Teleki László 1810–1861* [László Teleki 1810–1861], 2 vols., 1964.

Ideiglenes polgári perrendtartás, Magyar-, Horváth-Tótország, s Szerbvajdaság és Temesi Bánság számára [Provisional Civil Court Procedure for Hungary, Croatia, Slavonia, the Serbian Voivodina and the Bánát of Temesvár], Vienna, 1852.

Die Indirecten Abgaben Österreichs in den Jahren 1847, dann 1850 bis 1859, (ed.) K.K. Finanzministerium, Vienna, 1860.

Jánossy, Dénes, *A Kossuth emigráció Angliában és Amerikában 1851–1852* [The Kossuth Emigration in England and the United States of America 1851–1852], 2 vols., Budapest, 1948.

Jókai, Mór, *Az új földesúr* [The New Landlord], Budapest, 1968 (1862).

———, *Egy magyar nábob* [A Hungarian Nabob], Pest, 1854.

———, *Kárpáthy Zoltán* [Zoltán Kárpáthy], Pest, 1855.

———, *Politikai divatok* [Political Modes], Pest, 1863.

———, *Szerelem bolondjai* [Fools of Love], Pest, 1869.

———, *Tűzön át az égbe* [Through Fire to Heaven], Pest, 1850.

Kalchberg, Johann, *Mein Politisches Glaubensbekenntnis*, Leipsig, 1881.

Károlyi, Árpád (ed.), *Németujvári Gróf Batthyány Lajos első magyar miniszterelnök főbenjáró pöre* [The High Treason Trial of Count Lajos Batthyány of Németujvár, First Prime Minister of Hungary], 2 vols., Budapest, 1932.

Kecskeméthy, Aurél, *Magyarország összpontosítása Ausztriában* [The Incorporation of Hungary into Austria], Pest, 1851.

Kecskeméthy Aurél naplója 1851–1878 [The Diary of Aurél Kecskeméthy, 1851–1878], (ed.) Miklós Rózsa, Budapest, 1909.

Kemény, Zsigmond, *Forradalom után* [After the Revolution], Pest, 1850.

———, *Még egy szó a forradalom után* [One More Word After the Revolution], Pest, 1851.

Kenessey, Kálmán, *Egy-két őszinte szó társadalmi viszonyainkat érdeklőleg* [One or Two Frank Words Concerning Our Social Conditions], Pest, 1857.

Koltay-Kästner, Jenő (ed.), *Iratok a Kossuth-emigráció történetéhez 1859* [Documents to the History of the Kossuth Emigration, 1859], Szeged, 1949.

Koós, Ferenc, *Életem és emlékeim 1828–1890* [My Life and Recollections 1828–1890], 2 vols., Brassó, 1890.

Kossuth, Lajos, *Irataim az emigrációból a villafrancai béke után* [My Papers from the Emigration since the Peace of Villafranca], 3 vols., Budapest, 1881.

Kovács, Márk, "Az egyháziak személyes mentessége ügyében" [On the Case of the Personal Immunity of Clerics], *Religio,* Vol. II, No. 8 (1850), pp. 1–2.

Kübeck, Max von, (ed.) *Tagebücher des Karl Friedrich Freiherrn von Kübeck von Kubau,* 2 vols., Vienna, 1906.

Lonovics, József, *A Josephinismus és az egyházat illető legújabb császári rendelvény* [Imperial Patent Concerning Josephinism and the Church], Vienna, 1851.

A magyar munkásmozgalom kialakulása 1848–1890 [The Development of the Hungarian Workers' Movement 1848–1890], Vol. I of *A magyar munkásmozgalom történetének válogatott dokumentumai* [Selected Documents of the History of the Hungarian Workers' Movement], Budapest, 1951.

Mailáth, Johann, *Gedrängte Geschichte des österreichischen Kaiserstaates bis auf die neueste Zeit,* Vienna, 1851.

Márkfi, S., "1850," *Religio,* Vol. II, No. 1 (1850), p. 1.

Mayr, Josef Karl, (ed.), *Das Tagebuch des Polizeiministers Kempen von 1848 bis 1859,* Vienna and Leipzig, 1931.

[Meyer, Bernhard Fischer von] Anonymus, *Rückblick auf die jüngste Entwicklungs-Periode Ungarns,* Vienna, 1857.

Mitteilungen aus dem Gebiete der Statistik, Vol. V, Book 3, (ed.) Direktion der Admin. Statistik, Vienna, 1855.

Paton, A. A., *The Goth and the Hun, or, Transylvania, Debreczin, Pesth, and Vienna in 1850,* London, 1851.

Podmaniczky, Frigyes B., *Naplótöredékek 1824–1887* [Diary Fragments 1824–1887], 4 vols., Budapest, 1888.

Rapant, Daniel, *Slovenské povstanie roku 1848/49,* 3 vols., Bratislava, 1954.

Récsi, Emil, *A telekadó rendszer Magyarországban az 1850. márcz. 4. cs. pátens szerint* [The Real Estate System in Hungary according to the Imperial Patent of 4 March 1850], Pest, 1850.

Sashegyi, Oszkár (ed.), *Munkások és parasztok mozgalmai Magyarországon 1849–1867. Iratok* [The Movements of Workers and Peasants in Hungary 1849–1867. Documents], Budapest, 1959.

Somssich, Pál, *Das legitime Recht Ungarns und seines Königs,* Vienna, 1850.

Steier, Lajos, *Haynau és Paskievics* [Haynau and Paskevich], 2 vols., Budapest, 1937.

———, *A tót nemzetiségi kérdés 1848/49-ben* [The Slovak Nationality Question in 1848/49], 2 vols., Budapest, 1934.

Sz . . . től [by SZ.], *A közérzület Magyarhonban 1850* [Public Mood in Hungary 1850], Pest, 1850.

Sz. I., *Szláv törekvések és a magyar elem* [Slav Efforts and the Magyars], Pest, 1850.

Szepessy, S., "Politikai hirdetmények az egyházi szószéken" [Political Announcements from the Pulpit], *Religio,* Vol. I, No. 39 (1849), p. 1.

Szigligeti, Ede, *Aggteleki barlang* [The Cave at Aggtelek], Pest, 1850.

———, *Fidibusz,* Pest, 1850.

———, *Nagyapó* [Grandpa], Pest, 1851.

Szilágyi, Sándor, *Rajzok a forradalom utáni időkből* [Sketches from the Post-Revolutionary Times], Budapest, 1876.

Szögyény-Marich, László, *Szögyény-Marich László emlékiratai* [The Memoirs of Chancellor László Szögyény-Marich], 2 vols., 1903–1917.

Szombathy, Ignácz, *Austriai honismeret, különös tekintettel Magyarországra* [Austrian Geography with Special Regard to Hungary], Székesfehérvár, 1855.

Tanrendszerterv a gymnásiumokat és reáliskolákat illetőleg közzétéve a bécsi cultus-és oktatásministérium által tömött kivonatban fogalmazva [Curriculum Plan for High Schools and Real Schools Published in Summary Form by the Viennese Ministry of Culture and Education], Buda, 1850.

Toldy Ferenc összegyűjtött munkái [Collected Works of Ferenc Toldy], 8 vols., Pest, 1868–1874.

Tompa Mihály levelezése [The Correspondence of Mihály Tompa], 2 vols., (ed.) Gyula Bisztray, Budapest, 1964.

Vadnay, György, "Az első zsandár-tisztek Zemplénben" [The First Gendarme Officers in Zemplén], *Adalékok Zemplén-vármegye történetéhez,* Vol. VII, No. 2 (February, 1901), pp. 59–60.

———, "Közigazgatásunk a forradalom után" [Our Public Administration after the Revolution], *Adalékok Zemplén-vármegye történetéhez,* Vol. VIII No. 8 (August, 1902), pp. 252–253.

———, "Zemplén-vármegye a forradalom után" [Zemplén County after the Revolution], *Adalékok Zemplén-vármegye történetéhez,* Vol. VI (1900), pp. 251–255, 285–286, 316–317, 345–347.

———, "Zemplén-vármegye az elnyomatás alatt" [Zemplén County during the Oppression], *Adalékok Zemplén-vármegye történetéhez,* Vol. XII (1906), pp. 38–41, 88–91, 152–155, 159–222; Vol. XIII (1907), pp. 55–60, 152–159.

"Visszaemlékezések" [Recollections], *A Hét,* Vol. VII, No. 18 (1896), p. 331.

Waldapfel, Eszter V., (ed.), *A forradalom és szabadságharc levelestára* [Letter Collection of the Revolution and War of Independence], 4 vols., Budapest, 1965.

Walter, Friedrich (ed.), *Die österreichische Zentralverwaltung,* 6 vols., Graz, 1950–1964.

———, *Aus dem Nachlass des Freiherrn Carl Frederick Kübeck von Kübau, Tagebücher, Briefe, Aktenstücke (1841–1855),* Graz, 1960.

Zsedényi, Ede, *Verfassung von 4 März und die erbliche Pairie,* Vienna, 1850.
_____ , *Über die Verantwortlichkeit des Ministeriums,* Vienna, 1850.

SECONDARY SOURCES

Books

Acsády, Ignác, *A magyar jobbágyság története* [The History of Hungarian Serfdom], Budapest, 1948.

Andics, Erzsébet, *Az egyházi reakció 1848-49-ben* [The Clerical Reaction in 1848-1849], Budapest, 1949.

Asbóth, János, *Magyar conservativ politika* [Hungarian Conservative Politics], Budapest, 1875.

Barany, George, *Stephen Széchenyi and the Awakening of Hungarian Nationalism 1791-1841,* Princeton, 1968.

Beksics, Gusztáv, *I Ferencz József és kora* [Franz Joseph I and His Times] in *A magyar nemzet története* [The History of the Hungarian Nation], X, Budapest, 1898.

_____ , *Kemény Zsigmond, a forradalom és a kiegyezés* [Zsigmond Kemény, the Revolution and the Compromise], Budapest, 1883.

Berend, Iván T. and Ránki, György, *Economic Development in East-Central Europe in the 19th and 20th Centuries,* New York and London, 1974.

_____ , *A monopolkapitalizmus kialakulása és uralma Magyarországon 1900-1944* [The Development and Reign of Monopoly Capitalism in Hungary 1900-1944], Budapest, 1958.

Bernát, Gyula, *Az abszolutizmus földtehermentesítése Magyarországon* [The Freeing of the Land by the Regime of Absolutism in Hungary], Budapest, 1935.

Berzeviczy, Albert, *Az abszolutismus kora Magyarországon 1849-1865* [The Age of Absolutism in Hungary 1849-1865], 4 vols., Budapest, 1922.

_____ , *Régi emlékek 1853-1870* [Old Memories 1853-1870], Budapest, 1907.

Bibl, Viktor, *Von Revolution zu Revolution,* Vienna, 1924.

Bíró, S. et al., *A magyar református egyház története* [History of the Hungarian Reform Church], Budapest, 1949.

Brenman, Andrew Hindall, "Economic Reform in Neuzeit Austria, 1825-1859," unpublished doctoral dissertation, Department of History, Princeton University, Princeton, 1965.

Büchler, Sándor, *A zsidók története Budapesten a legrégibb időktől 1867-ig* [History of the Jews of Budapest from Ancient Times to 1867], Budapest, 1901.

Charmatz, R., *Minister Freiherr von Bruck,* Leipzig, 1916.

Corti, A., *The Reign of the House of Rothschild,* New York, 1928.

Crankshaw, E., *The Fall of the House of Habsburg,* London, 1963.

Czörnig, Carl von, *Österreich's Neugestaltung 1848-1858,* Stuttgart and Augsburg, 1858.

Dezsényi, Béla, *Az időszaki sajtó története a Dunatáj országaiban* [History of the Contemporary Press of the Danube Area Countries], Budapest, 1947.

Diószegi, András, *et al., A magyar irodalom története 1849-től 1905-ig* [History of Hungarian Literature from 1849 to 1905], Volume IV of *A magyar irodalom története* [History of Hungarian Literature], (ed.), István Sőtér, Budapest, 1963.

———, *Irodalmunk az önkényuralom és a kiegyezés előkészítése korában (1849-1867)* [Our Literature in the Age of Absolutism and Preparation for the Compromise (1849-1867)], Part One of *A magyar irodalom története 1849-1905* [History of Hungarian Literature 1849-1905], (ed.) István Király *et al.,* Budapest, 1963.

Ditz, H., *A magyar mezőgazdaság* [The Hungarian Agriculture], Pest, 1869.

Eckhart, Ferenc, *A jog-és államtudományi kar története 1667-1935* [History of the Faculty of Legal and State Sciences 1667-1935], Budapest, 1936.

———, *A püspöki székek és a káptalani javadalmak betöltése Mária Terézia korától 1918-ig* [The Filling of Vacant Episcopal Sees and Chapter Benefices from the Time of Maria Theresa until 1918], Budapest, 1935.

Eisenmann, Louis, *Le Compromis Austro-Hongrois de 1867,* Paris, 1904.

Engel-Janosi, Friedrich, *Der Freiherr von Hübner 1811-1892, Eine Gestalt aus dem Österreich Kaiser Franz Josephs,* Innsbruck, 1933.

Faragó, Miksa, *A Kossuth-bankók kora* [The Age of the Kossuth Bank Notes], Budapest, [1912].

Fekete, Miklós, *Híres alföldi betyár Rózsa Sándor viselt dolgai, perbefogatása és elítéltetése* [Past Deeds, Trial and Sentencing of the Famous Highwayman of the Hungarian Plain Sándor Rózsa], Pest, 1859.

Ferenczy, Zoltán, *Deák élete* [Life of Deák], 3 vols., Budapest, 1904.

Forster, Florence A., *Francis Deák, Hungarian Statesman: A Memoir,* London, 1880.

Fournier, H., *Österreich-Ungarns Neubau,* Vienna, 1917.

Friedjung, Heinrich, *Österreich von 1848-1860,* 2 vols., Stuttgart, 1908.

Frommelt, K., *Die Sprachenfrage im österreichischen Unterrichtswesen 1848-1859,* Graz, 1963.

Gracza, György, *Az 1848-49-iki magyar szabadságharc története* [History of the Hungarian War of Independence of 1848-1849], 5 vols., Budapest, 1898.

Grossmann, Zsigmond, *A magyar zsidók a XIX. század közepén, 1849-1870* [The Hungarian Jews at the Middle of the 19th Century 1849-1870], Budapest, 1917.

Győry, Tibor, *Az orvostudományi kar története 1770-1935* [History of the Medical Faculty 1770-1935], Budapest, 1936.

Hajdú, János, *Eötvös József báró első minisztersége* [The First Ministership of Baron József Eötvös], Budapest, 1933.

Hanák, Péter (ed.), *Magyarország története az abszolutizmus és a dualizmus korában 1849–1918* [History of Hungary in the Age of Absolutism and Dualism], [Manuscript], Budapest, 1969.

Hanák Péter, *et al.*, *Magyarország története 1848–1918, Az abszolutizmus és a dualizmus kora* [History of Hungary 1848–1918, The Age of Absolutism and Dualism], Budapest, 1972 [1973].

Hentallér, Lajos, *A balavásári szüret* [Grape Harvest at Balavásár], Budapest, 1894.

Hermann, Egyed, *A magyar katolikus papság az osztrák katonai diktatúra és az abszolutizmus idején* [The Hungarian Catholic Clergy during the Austrian Military Dictatorship and Absolutism], Gödöllő, 1932.

Hóman, Bálint and Szekfű, Gyula, *Magyar történet* [Hungarian History], 5 vols., Budapest, 1936.

Horváth, Mihály, *Huszonöt év Magyarország történelméből 1823–1848* [Twenty-five Years from the History of Hungary 1828–1848], 3 vols., Budapest, 1886.

Jankovich, Vince, *Korrajzok és eszmetöredékek az 1850–1867 évszakról* [Sketches and Random Thoughts about the Years 1850–1867], Balassagyarmat, 1871.

Jaszi, Oscar, *The Dissolution of the Habsburg Monarchy*, Chicago and London, 1964 (1929).

Jirkovsky, Sándor, *A magyarországi pénzintézetek története az első világháború végéig* [History of Financial Institutions in Hungary until the End of the First World War], Budapest, 1945.

Kann, Robert A., *The Multinational Empire: Nationalism and National Reform in the Habsburg Monarchy 1848–1918,* 2 vols., New York, 1970.

Keleti, Károly, *A telekadó és kataszter közgazdasági és statisztikai szempontból* [Real Estate Tax and Cadastral from the Standpoint of the Economy and Statistics], Budapest, 1868.

Keleti, Károly, *Visszapillantás Magyarország közgazdaságának egynegyed századára* [A Backward Glance at Hungary's Quarter Century Economy], Budapest, 1875.

Kemény, Gábor G., *A balavásári szüret* [The Grape Harvest at Balavásár], Budapest, [1945].

Király, Béla K., *Hungary in the Late Eighteenth Century. The Decline of Enlightened Despotism,* New York, 1969.

Kiss, Áron, *Török Pál élete* [Life of Pál Török], Budapest, 1904.

Kiszling, Rudolf, *Fürst Felix zu Schwarzenberg, der Erzieher Kaiser Franz Josephs,* Graz, 1952.

Komoróczy, György, *Debrecen története a felszabadulásig* [History of Debrecen until the Liberation], Debrecen, 1955.

Kornis, Julius, *Education in Hungary,* New York, 1932.

Kosary, Dominic C., *A History of Hungary,* New York, 1971 (1941).

Kovács, Endre, *A Kossuth-emigráció és az európai szabadságmozgalmak* [The Kossuth Emigration and the European Freedom Movements], Budapest, 1967.

Kovács, Máté (ed.), *A könyv és a könyvtár a magyar társadalom életében 1849-1960* [The Book and Library in the Life of Hungarian Society 1849-1960], 2 vols., Budapest, 1968.

Kramar, Zoltan, "The Road to Compromise, 1849-1867: A Study of the Habsburg-Hungarian Constitutional Struggle in Its Terminal Phase," unpublished doctoral dissertation, Department of History, University of Nebraska, 1967.

Lakatos, Ernő, *A magyar politikai vezetőréteg 1848-1918* [The Hungarian Political Elite, 1848-1918], Budapest, 1942.

Lakatos, Ottó, *Arad története* [History of Arad], 3 vols., Arad, 1881.

Lengyel, Alfréd, *Győr megye történetének írásos emlékei (1001-1918)* [Written Sources of the History of Győr County (1001-1918)], Győr, 1965.

Lingelbach, William E., *Austria-Hungary,* New York, 1971.

Lónyai, Menyhért, *Hazánk földterületi és adóviszonyai* [Land and Tax Affairs of Our Country], Pest, 1861.

_____ , *Közügyekről. Nemzetgazdászati újabb dolgozatok* [On Public Affairs, Latest Essays on the National Economy], Pest, 1863.

Lóránth, Mária, *Adatok az úrbéri kárpótlás történetéhez 1849-1853* [Data to the History of *Robot* Compensation 1849-1853], Budapest, 1927.

Lukács, Lajos, *Magyar függetlenségi és alkotmányos mozgalmak 1849-1867* [Hungarian Independence and Constitutional Movements 1849-1867], Budapest, 1955.

Macartney, C. A., *The Habsburg Empire 1790-1918,* London, 1968.

Marczali, Henrik, *Hungary in the Eighteenth Century,* Cambridge, 1910.

März, Eduard, *Österreichische Industrie- und Bankpolitik in der Zeit Franz Josephs I,* Vienna, 1968.

Marx, Julius, *Die Wirtschaftlichen Ursachen der Revolution von 1848 in Österreich,* Graz and Köln, 1965.

Matlekovits, Sandor, *Die Zollpolitik der Österreichisch-Ungarischen Monarchie von 1850 bis zur Gegenwart,* Budapest, 1877.

May, Arthur J., *The Habsburg Monarchy 1867-1914,* New York, 1968 (1951).

Medgyesi-Mitschang, Sylvia, "The Influence of the Hungarian Aristocracy upon Franz Joseph from 1851 to 1861," unpublished doctoral dissertation, Department of History, University of St. Louis, St. Louis, Mo., 1971.

Meszlényi, Antal, *A magyar katholikus egyház és az állam 1848/49-ben* [The Hungarian Catholic Church and the State in 1848-1849], Budapest, 1928.

Miskolczy, Julius, *Ungarn in der Habsburger-Monarchie,* Vienna and Munich, 1959.

Mód, Aladár, *400 év küzdelem az önálló Magyarországért* [400 Years of Struggle for an Independent Hungary], Budapest, 1951.

Molnár, Erik *et al.* (ed.), *Magyarország története* [History of Hungary], 2 vols., Budapest, 1967.

Müller, Paul, *Feldmarschall Fürst Windischgrätz, Revolution und Gegenrevolution in Österreich,* Vienna and Leipzig, 1934.

Murarik, Antal, *Az ősiség alapintézményeinek eredete* [The Origin of the Fundamental Institutions of the Entail], Budapest, 1938.

Nagy, István, *A mezőgazdaság Magyarországon az abszolutizmus korában (1849–1867)* [The Agriculture in Hungary during the Age of Absolutism (1849–1867)], Budapest, 1944.

Nagy, József, *A Heves megyei munkásmozgalom kezdeti szakasza (1850–1914)* [The Early Phase of the Labor Movement in Heves County (1850–1914)], Eger, 1956.

Nagy, Miklós, *Világostól Trianonig* [From Világos to Trianon], Budapest, 1926.

Niederhauser, Emil, *A jobbágyfelszabadítás Kelet-Európában* [The Liberation of the Serfs in Eastern Europe], Budapest, 1962.

Papp, Ferenc, *Báró Kemény Zsigmond* [Baron Zsigmond Kemény], 2 vols., Budapest, 1923.

Pesti Casino-Könyv, [Pest Casino Book], Pest, 1855.

Pethő, Sándor, *Világostól Trianonig* [From Világos to Trianon], Budapest, 1925.

Pogány, Mária, *Tőkés vállalkozók és kubikos bérmunkások a Tiszaszabályozásnál a XIX. sz. második felében* [Capitalistic Entrepreneurs and Construction Wage Laborers at the Channeling of the Tisza River during the Second Half of the 19th Century], Budapest, 1966.

Pölöskei, Ferenc and Szakács, Kálmán (eds.), *Földmunkás és szegényparasztmozgalmak Magyarországon, 1848–1918* [Agricultural Labor and Poor Peasant Movements in Hungary 1848–1918], 2 vols., Budapest, 1962.

Pólya, Jakab, *Agrárpolitikai tanulmányok. Minimum. Homstead. Örökösödési jog* [Essays in Agricultural Politics. Minimum. Homestead. Law of Inheritance], Budapest, 1886.

Pribram, K. *et al., Materialien zur Geschichte der Preise und Löhne in Österreich,* Vienna, 1938.

Priester, Eva, *Kurze Geschichte Österreichs: Aufstieg und Untergang des Habsburgerreiches,* Vienna, 1949.

Ráday, Béla, *Rózsa Sándor az alföldi rablóvezér élete és kalandjai* [Life and Adventures of Sándor Rózsa, Leading Highwayman on the Hungarian Plain], Budapest and Szeged, 1902.

Redlich, Josef, *Das österreichische Staats- und Reichsproblems: Geschichtliche Darstellung der inneren Politik der Habsburgischen Monarchie von 1848 bis zum Untergang des Reiches,* 2 vols., Leipzig, 1924–1926.

Redlich, Joseph, *Emperor Francis Joseph of Austria, A Biography,* Hamden, Conn., 1965.

[Renner, Karl] Springer, Rudolf, *Grundlagen und Entwicklungsziele der österreichischen-Monarchie,* Vienna, 1906.

Révész, László, *Die Anfänge des ungarischen Parlamentarismus,* Munich, 1968.

Révész, Imre, *Fejezetek a Bach-korszak egyházpolitikájából* [Chapters from the Ecclesiastical Policies of the Bach Regime], Budapest, 1957.

Rigberg, Benjamin, "The Federal Movement in the Habsburg Domains 1840–1871," unpublished doctoral dissertation, Department of History, University of Pennsylvania, Philadelphia, 1946.

Rock, Kenneth Willett, "Reaction Triumphant: The Diplomacy of Felix Schwarzenberg and Nicholas I in Mastering the Hungarian Insurrection, 1848–1850. A Study in Dynastic Power Principles and Politics in Revolutionary Times," unpublished doctoral dissertation, Department of History, Stanford University, 1968.

––––––, "Rejuvenation by Edict: The Habsburg Example after 1848," manuscript paper delivered at the Rocky Mountain Social Science Association's Annual Conference, April 28–29, 1972, Salt Lake City, Utah.

Rogge, William, *Österreich von Világos bis zur Gegenwart,* 3 vols., Leipzig, 1872.

Rothenberg, Gunther E., *The Military Border in Croatia 1740–1881. A Study of an Imperial Institution,* Chicago and London, 1966.

Sándor, Pál, *A jobbágykérdés az 1832/36-os országgyűlésen* [The Question of Serfdom before the Diet of 1832–1836], Budapest, 1948.

––––––, (ed.), *Parasztságunk a Habsburg önkényuralom korszakában 1849–1867* [Our Peasantry during the Era of Habsburg Absolutism 1849–1867], Budapest, 1951.

––––––, *A XIX. század végi agrárválság Magyarországon* [Agricultural Depression at the End of the 19th Century in Hungary], Budapest, 1958.

Sándor, Vilmos, *A tőkés gazdaság kibontakozása Magyarországon 1849–1900* [The Development of Capitalistic Economy in Hungary 1849–1900], Budapest, 1958.

Schadelbauer, Karl, *Amtliche Stimmungberichte 1850/51 und 1859/60,* Innsbruck, 1960.

Schlitter, Hanns, *Versäumte Gelegenheiten. Die oktroyirte Verfassung vom 4. März 1849. Ein Beitrag zu ihrer Geschichte,* Zurich, Leipzig and Vienna, 1920.

Sőtér, István, *Eötvös József,* Budapest, 1967.

Spira, György, *A magyar forradalom 1848–49-ben* [The Hungarian Revolution in 1848–1849], Budapest, 1959.

Spira, Thomas, "The Growth of Magyar National Awareness under Francis I," unpublished doctoral dissertation, Department of History, McGill University, Montreal, 1969.

Stölzl, Christoph von, *Die Ära Bach in Böhmen: Sozialgeschichtliche Studien zum Neoabsolutismus 1849–1859,* Munich and Vienna, 1971.

Szabad, György, *Forradalom és kiegyezés válaszútján 1860–61* [At the Crossroads of Revolution and Compromise 1860–1861], Budapest, 1967.

————, *A tatai és gesztesi Eszterházy-uradalom áttérése a robotrendszerről a tőkés gazdálkodásra* [The Change-over from the *Robot* System to Capitalistic Production at the Eszterhazy Estates of Tata and Gesztes], Budapest, 1957.

Szabó, István, *Tanulmányok a magyar parasztság történetéből* [Studies on the History of Hungarian Peasantry], Budapest, 1948.

Závay, Gyula, *A magyar kamarai intézmények és a budapesti kamara története 1850–1925* [History of the Institution of Chambers of Commerce and of the Budapest Chamber 1850–1925], Budapest, 1927.

Szekfű, Gyula, *Három nemzedék és ami utána következik* [Three Generations and What Comes After], Budapest, 1934.

Szemere, Bartholomew, *Hungary from 1848 to 1860*, London, 1860.

A Kossuth emigráció szolgálatában. Tanárky Gyula naplója (1849–1866) [In the Service of the Kossuth Emigration. The Diary of Gyula Tanárky (1849–1866)], (ed.) Jenő Koltay-Kästner, Budapest, 1961.

Tapié, Victor-L., *The Rise and Fall of the Habsburg Monarchy*, New York, 1971 (1969).

Taylor, A.J.P., *The Habsburg Monarchy 1809–1918. A History of the Austrian Empire and Austria-Hungary*, London, 1964.

Tomcsányi, Móric, *Magyarország közjoga* [Hungary's Constitutional Laws], Budapest, 1943.

Török, Pál, *Pest-Buda 1850-ben* [Pest-Buda in 1850], Budapest, 1944.

Tóth, Zoltán, I., *Magyarok és románok. Történelmi tanulmányok* [Hungarians and Rumanians. Historical Studies], Budapest, 1966.

Tóth, Ede, *Mocsáry Lajos élete és politikai pályakezdete (1826–1874)* [The Life and Early Political Career of Lajos Mocsáry (1826–1874)], Budapest, 1967.

Tschuppik, K., *The Reign of the Emperor Francis Joseph*, London, 1930.

Varga, Zoltán, *Báró Podmaniczky János (1786–1883) életrajza* [The Biography of Baron János Podmaniczky (1786–1883)], Budapest, 1933.

Veress, Sándor, *A magyar emigrátió keleten* [The Hungarian Emigration in the East], 2 vols., Budapest, 1878–1879.

Venetianer, Lajos, *A magyar zsidóság története a honfoglalástól a világháború kitöréséig* [The History of the Hungarian Jewry from the Conquest to the Outbreak of the World War], Budapest, 1922.

Warga, Lajos, *A keresztyén egyház történelme* [The History of the Christian Church], Sárospatak, 1908.

Wertheimer, Ede, *Gróf Andrássy Gyula élete és kora* [The Life and Times of Count Gyula Andrássy], 3 vols., Budapest, 1910.

Winter, Eduard, *Revolution, Neoabsolutismus und Liberalismus in der Donaumonarchie*, Vienna, 1969.

Zimmermann, Franz, *Das Ministerium Thun für die Evangelischen im Gesamtstaate Österreich 1849 bis 1860*, Vienna, 1926.

Zolger, Ivan, *Der Staatsrechtliche Ausgleich zwischen Österreich und Ungarn*, Leipzig, 1911.

Periodical Literature and Articles in Collection

Asbóth, János, "A conservativek a forradalom után" [The Conservatives after the Revolution], *Jellemrajzok és tanulmányok korunk történetéhez* [Character Sketches and Studies to the History of Our Age], Budapest, 1892, pp. 120–142.

Barany, George, "Hungary: From Aristocratic to Proletarian Nationalism," *Nationalism in Eastern Europe*, (eds.) Peter F. Sugar and Ivo J. Lederer, Seattle and London, 1971, pp. 259–319.

――――, "Hungary: The Uncompromising Compromise," *Austrian History Yearbook*, Vol. III, Pt. 1 (1967), pp. 234–259.

Body, Paul, "Baron Joseph Eötvös and his Critique of Nationalism in the Habsburg Monarchy, 1848–1854," *Historian*, Vol. XXVIII, No. 1 (1965), pp. 19–47.

Braun, Róbert, "Az abszolutizmus hetven évvel ezelőtt" [The Absolutism Seventy Years Ago], *Szocializmus*, Vol. XII, No. 1 (1922), pp. 165–173.

Burian, Peter, "The State Language Problem in Old Austria (1848–1918)," *Austrian History Yearbook*, Vols. VI–VII (1970–1971), pp. 81–103.

Diószegi, István, "A Deák-párt és a német egység" [The Party of Deák and the German Unity], *Századok*, Vol. CIV, No. 2 (1970), pp. 227–250.

Eckhart, Ferenc, "Egy nagy magyar főpap életéből" [From the Life of a Great Hungarian Bishop], *A Bécsi Magyar Történeti Intézet Évkönyve*, Vol. II (1932), pp. 272–284.

Edvi Illés, Károly, "Rózsa Sándor," *Budapesti Hirlap*, 16 July 1890, appendix.

Eperjessy, Géza, "A Pest megyei céhes ipar 1686–1872" [The Guild Craft of Pest County 1686–1872], *Pest megye multjából. Tanulmányok* [From the Past of Pest County. Studies], (eds.) F. Keleti *et al.*, Budapest, 1965, pp. 274–285.

Erdei, Ferenc, "A szabad parasztság kialakulása" [The Formation of Free Peasantry], *Sorsunk*, Vol. III, Nos. 7–12 (1943), pp. 691–697.

"Gál Sándor terve az erdélyi felkelésről" [The Plan of Sándor Gál for the Transylvanian Uprising], *Hadtörténeti Közlemények*, Vol. XXVI, Books 1–2 (1925), pp. 179–187.

Hajnal, István, "Az osztálytársadalom" [Class Society], *Az új Magyarország* [The New Hungary] (eds.) Sándor Domanovszky *et al.*, Vol. V of the *Magyar művelődéstörténet* [History of Hungarian Civilization], pp. 163–200.

Halász, Imre, "A magyar konzervativek az abszolut korszakban" [The Hungarian Conservatives in the Age of Absolutism], *Nyugat*, Vol. X, No. 21 (1917), pp. 660–674.

Hanák, Péter, "Hungary in the Austro-Hungarian Monarchy: Preponderancy or Dependency? ", *Austrian History Yearbook*, Vol. III, Pt. 1 (1967), pp. 260–302.

Handlery, George, "Revolutionary Organization in the Context of Backwardness: Hungary's 1848," *East European Quarterly*, Vol. VI, No. 1 (March, 1972), pp. 44–61.

Hidas, Peter, "The Russian Intervention in Hungary," *War and Society in the Nineteenth Century Russian Empire* (eds.) J. G. Purvis and D. A. West, Toronto, 1971, pp. 73–83.

Kosáry, Domokos, "Abszolutizmus és kiegyezés" [Absolutism and Compromise], *Demokrácia és köznevelés* [Democracy and Public Education], Budapest, 1945, pp. 368–388.

_____ , "Kemény és Széchenyi 1849 után" [Kemény and Széchenyi after 1849], *Irodalomtörténeti Közlemények*, Vol. LXVII, No. 2 (1963), pp. 149–170.

"Krivácsy az összeesküvő 1851" [The Conspirator Krivácsy 1851], *Esti Újság*, 2 November 1903, p. 2.

Oláh, Gyula, "A társadalmi élet 1848 után" [Social Life after 1848], *Vasárnapi Újság*, Vol. LXIV, No. 25 (1917), p. 400.

Pech, Stanley Z., "The Czechs and the Imperial Parliament in 1848–1849," *The Czech Renascence of the Nineteenth Century*, (eds.) Peter Brock and H. Gordon Skilling, Toronto, 1970, pp. 201–213.

Révész, László, "Die Bedeutung des Neoabsolutismus für Ungarn," *Der Donauraum*, Vol. XIV (1969), pp. 142–159.

Rock, Kenneth W., "Schwarzenberg versus Nicholas I Round One; the Negotiation of the Habsburg-Romanov Alliance against Hungary in 1849," *Austrian History Yearbook*, Vols. VI–VII (1970–1971), pp. 109–141.

_____ , "Reply," *Austrian History Yearbook*, Vols. VI–VII (1970–1971), p. 165.

Rothenberg, Gunther, E., "The Habsburg Army and the Nationality Problem in the Nineteenth Century, 1815–1914," *Austrian History Yearbook*, Vol. III, Pt. 1 (1967), pp. 70–90.

Sárközi, Zoltán, "A Budapesti Kereskedelmi és Iparkamara hivataltörténete" [Administrative History of the Chamber of Commerce and Craft of Budapest], *Levéltári Szemle*, Vol. XVII, No. 1 (January–April, 1967), pp. 55–109.

Sashegyi, Oszkár, "Magyarország beolvasztása az ausztriai császárságba" [The Incoporation of Hungary into the Austrian Empire], *Levéltári Közlemények*, Vol. XXXIX, No. 1 (1968), pp. 63–104.

Szabad, György, "Eötvös József a politika útjain" [József Eötvös on the Roads of Politics], *Századok*, Vol. CV, Nos. 3–4 (1971), pp. 658–669.

_____ , "A kiegyezés előtörténetéhez" [On the Prehistory of the Compromise], *Történelmi Szemle*, Vol. XIV, Nos. 1–2 (1971), pp. 254–259.

_____ , "Nacionalizmus és patriotizmus konfliktusa az abszolutizmus korában [The Conflict of Nationalism and Patriotism in the Age of Absolutism], *A magyar nacionalizmus kialakulása és története* [The Development and History of Magyar Nationalism], (ed.) E. Andics, Budapest, 1964, pp. 143–164.

Szabó, Ferenc, "Betyárvilág Orosháza környékén a szabadságharc után" [Reign of Highwaymen in the Neighborhood of Orosháza after the War of Independence], *A Szántó Kovács Múzeum Évkönyve* [The Yearbook of the Szántó Kovács Museum], 1959, pp. 41–76.

Tihany, Leslie C., "The Austro-Hungarian Compromise 1867–1918: A Half Century of Diagnosis; Fifty Years of Post-Mortem," *Central European History,* Vol. II, No. 2 (June, 1969), pp. 114–138.

Ungár, László, "Kapitalisztikus gazdálkodás" [Capitalistic Agricultural Management], *Az új Magyarország* [The New Hungary] (eds.) Sándor Domanovszky *et al.,* Vol. V of the *Magyar művelődéstörténet* [History of Hungarian Civilization], pp. 201–236.

Wenzel, Gusztáv, "Endlicher István emlékezete" [In Memory of István Endlicher], *Új Magyar Múzeum,* Book IV (1851), pp. 197–200.

INDEX

A

Absolutist Centralists 29, 30, 31, 32, 33, 34, 40, 41, 42, 43, 44, 45, 59, 60, 63, 64, 84, 85
Administration; *see* Civil service
Agricultural policies; *see* Liberal Centralists — agricultural policies
Albrecht, Archduke Frederich Rudolf 40, 41, 42, 43, 57, 59, 76
Amnesties 9, 27, 42, 52, 73
Andrássy, Count György 48, 52, 58
Andreansky, Sándor 52
Apponyi, Count György 46, 47–48, 49, 50, 53, 56, 57, 58
April Memorandum, 1850 56–57, 77
Armies, Hungarian *Honvéd* 6, 8, 9, 17, 27, 51, 52, 71, 73, 80
Armies, Imperial, Austrian 6, 7, 8, 9, 10, 11, 12, 13, 14, 15, 17, 23, 24, 27, 28, 31, 32, 34, 43, 44, 47, 48, 50, 51, 52, 59, 67, 73, 76

B

Babarczy, Antal 51
Bach, Alexander 2, 5, 6, 11, 12, 13, 14, 23, 25, 26, 28, 30, 31, 32, 33, 40, 41, 42, 51, 52, 54, 55, 57, 60, 62, 67, 81
Bach hussars 34, 40, 76
Bánffy, Simon 54
Banking 17, 38, 39, 68
Batthyány, Count Lajos 53
Bérczy, Károly 54
Bernát, Gyula 69
Berzeviczy, Albert 57, 69, 81
Bíró, Mihály 80
Bishops' Conference, April, 1949 21–22
Bruck, Charles Louis von 5, 29, 36
Bureaucracy; *see* Civil service
Burits, General Baron Johan 51

C

Catholic Church of Hungary 21, 22, 23, 26, 27, 29, 32, 40, 43, 44, 45, 54, 55, 56, 63, 84, 85
Chambers of commerce and craft 24, 37
Civil Code of Austria 29, 37, 44, 71
Civil service 1, 5, 6, 10, 11, 12, 13, 14, 25, 28, 29, 31, 40, 41, 42, 44, 52, 60, 72, 74, 75, 76, 77, 80, 81, 85
Civil service, purge of 10, 11, 12, 49
Civil war; *see* Revolutions, Hungary, 1848–1849
Coburg-Gotha, Prince 62
Concordate 44
Conservative Party 47, 53, 60
Constitutions, Hungarian; *see* Hungary. Constitution
Constitutions, Kremsier, 1849; *see* Kremsier constitution, 1849
Constitutions, March, 1849 3, 4, 5, 6, 12, 13, 15, 25, 26, 27, 28, 29, 30, 32, 33, 42, 45, 49, 50, 51, 54, 60, 83, 84
Corvée; see robot
Counterrevolutions — Hungary 6, 7, 8, 9, 10, 21, 26, 42, 43, 44, 53, 83, 85
Croats in Hungary 61, 76
Csáky, Count László 43
Csengery, Antal 54, 74
Csorics, F.M.L. Anton Frh. von 24, 32, 34
Currency crisis 16–17
Czindery, Count László 62

D

Deák, Francis 81–82, 85
Definitivum, 1853–1860 45, 60

Dessewffy, Count Emil 47, 48, 49, 52, 53, 56, 58, 59
Dynasty; *see* Habsburg, House of

E

Economic policies; *see* Liberal Centralists — economic policies
Educational policies; *see* Liberal Centralists — educational policies
Eötvös, Baron József 24, 79, 82
Erdélyi, János 54
Erkel, Ferenc 79
Esterházy, Prince Pál 47, 59, 62

F

Falk, Miksa 54
Ferdinand I, emperor of Austria 72
Fesztetics, Count György 59
Franz Joseph, emperor of Austria 2, 4, 6, 7, 8, 9, 11, 21, 22, 23, 24, 27, 28, 29, 30, 31, 32, 34, 38, 41, 42, 43, 44, 45, 51, 53, 55, 56, 57, 59, 60, 61, 67, 72, 73, 74, 78, 84, 85
Franz Karl, Archduke 21

G

Gál, Sándor 81
Gendarmes, gendarmerie 9, 13, 14, 21, 67, 72, 74, 76, 77
Geringer, Baron Charles 6, 11, 12, 13, 16, 19, 20, 23, 24, 25, 26, 27, 35, 44, 72
Germanization of Hungary 41, 42, 45, 72, 76
Germans in Hungary 23, 33, 41, 61, 74
Germany — foreign policy; *see* Liberal Centralists, foreign policy
Ghyczy, Emil 48
Görgey, General Artur 6, 72
Gould, Walter 80
Greek Orthodox Church 44
Grünne, Count Carl 32, 42, 44
Gyulai, Pál 27, 54

H

Habsburg, House of 1, 2, 3, 26, 28, 47, 51, 59, 71, 83, 84, 85
Hám, János, Primate of Hungary 21, 22, 23, 55
Hapsburg, House of; *see* Habsburg, House of
Haynau, Field Marshal Julius 6, 7, 8, 9, 10, 11, 15, 16, 17, 23, 26, 27, 28, 53, 55, 78, 83
Haynau's Terror; *see* Counterrevolutions — Hungary
Hierarchy; *see* Catholic Church of Hungary
Honvéd army; *see* Armies, Hungarian *Honvéd*
Honvéd(s) 6, 9, 81
Hübner, Baron Joseph Alexander 48
Hungarian Constitution; *see* Hungary. Constitution
Hungary. Constitution 11, 30, 46, 50, 54, 57
Hungary — press; *see* press, Hungarian

I

Imperial Constitution, March 1849; *see* Constitutions, March 1849
Imperial Parliament; *see* Reichstag, of Austria

J

Jászi, Oscar 10
Jesuits 32, 44
Jews in Hungary 10, 21, 23, 24, 25, 27, 37, 39, 41, 44, 56, 62, 63, 69, 72, 74
Jókai, Mór 54, 73, 79
Joseph, Archduke Palatine 24
Joseph II, emperor of Austria 1, 21
Josephinism 20, 21, 22
Jósika, Sámuel 47, 48, 52, 53, 56, 58

Jubál, Károly 80
Judicial reforms; see Liberal Centralists — judicial reforms

K

Károlyi, Count György 61
Károlyi, György 61, 62
Kemény, Zsigmond 54, 72, 79, 82
Kempen, Field Marshal Baron Johann Franz 7, 31, 41, 42
Klauzál, Gábor 82
Kollar, János 23
Korizmics, László 66
Kossuth, Lajos 6, 8, 25, 27, 44, 47, 48, 50, 51, 53, 67, 71, 72, 73, 79, 80, 81, 85
Kossuth's Honvéd Army; see Armies, Hungarian Honvéd
Krauss, Baron Philipp von 5, 17, 28, 30, 43
Kremsier Constitution, 1849 3
Kübeck, Carl Frederich von 28, 29, 30, 40, 44, 49, 50, 59
Kuzmany, K. 23

L

Liberal Centralists — agricultural policies 15, 16, 34, 35, 39, 40, 61, 62, 67
Liberal Centralists — economic policies 2, 4, 14, 15, 16, 17, 18, 27, 34, 35, 36, 37, 38, 39, 40, 45, 49, 63, 67, 83, 85
Liberal Centralists — educational policies 18, 19, 20, 24, 40, 42, 78, 83
Liberal Centralists — financial policies 15, 16, 17, 18, 34, 35, 36, 39, 40, 68
Liberal Centralists — foreign policy — Germany 1, 5, 6, 34, 36
Liberal Centralists — judicial reforms 4, 12, 32, 33, 83
Liberal Centralists — nationality policy 2, 6, 10, 11, 12, 19, 20, 24, 25, 26, 27, 33, 37, 72, 74, 76, 83

Liberal Centralists — and the middle classes 1-2, 3, 5, 16, 32, 83
Liberal Centralists and the press 25, 44, 57; see also Press, Hungarian
Liszt, Franz 79
Lónyai, Count Menyhért 58
Lukács, Lajos 82
Lukács, Mór 82

M

Macartney, C. A. 75
Magyarization 74
Mailáth, György Jr. 48, 54, 60
Makk, József 80, 81
Maria Dorothy, Archduchess 24
Maria Theresa, empress of Austria 47
Mazzini, Giuseppe 81
Medgyesi-Mitschang, Sylvia 54, 57
Meszlényi, Mrs. Jenő 80
Military; see Armies, Imperial, Austrian
Money supply; see Currency crisis

N

Nationality policy; see Liberal Centralists — nationality policy
Nicholas I, Tsar of Russia 7, 52, 53

O

Old Conservatives 26, 48, 49, 50, 51, 52, 53, 54, 55, 56, 57, 58, 59, 60, 61, 63, 77, 78, 82, 84, 85

P

Pálffy, Count Móric 14
Palmerston, Lord Henry John Temple 7
Pandúr(s) 13, 14
Paskevich, General Ivan Feodorovich 7, 52, 73
Passive resistance 68, 70, 72, 73, 74, 75
Paton, Andrew Archibald 5, 53

Pázmándy, Dénes 48
Peace Party 71
Peasantry and the Hungarian ruling class 31, 40, 48, 57, 64, 66, 67, 69, 71, 72, 73, 75, 76, 77, 80, 82, 85
Peasantry and the Liberal Centralists 5, 15, 35, 40, 61, 72
Perczel, Mór General 9
Pipitz, Hofrat J. von 49
Political administration; see civil service
Pompéry, János 54
Prela, Viale 55
Press, Hungarian 8, 9, 10, 12, 13, 16, 17, 21, 22, 25-27, 40, 42, 43, 44, 53-55, 56, 57, 60, 61, 66, 77, 79, 81, 84; see also Liberal Centralists and the press
Protestant Churches of Hungary 10, 21, 23, 24, 27, 44, 56, 78, 85
Protmann, Josef 44, 76, 80
Provisorium, 1851-1853 33-34, 35, 37, 39, 40, 41, 44, 45, 54, 63, 64

R

Radetzky, Count Joseph 17
Railroads; see Transportation — railroads
Rauscher, Cardinal Joseph Othmar von 32
Reichsrat, Imperial Council of Austria 4, 28, 29, 30, 82
Reichstag of Austria 2, 3, 28, 48, 83
Revolutions, Hungary 1848-1849 1, 8, 9, 10, 12, 14, 15, 16, 17, 20, 22, 24, 25, 27, 37, 39, 47, 48, 53, 55, 56, 57, 64, 65, 66, 67, 70, 71, 72, 73, 80, 81, 82, 85
Road construction; see Transportation, road construction
Robot (corvée) 2, 15, 16, 35, 38, 64, 66, 67, 68, 71
Rohonczy, Ignác 52
Roman Catholic Church; see Catholic Church of Hungary
Rothschild, Anselm 36, 38

Rousseau, Baron Leopold 50
Rózsa, Sándor 80
Rudnyánszky, Bishop József 55
Rumanians in Hungary 72
Russian intervention in Hungary, 1848-1849 6, 7, 15, 27, 39, 40, 52, 73

S

Sándor, Count Móric 62
Schmerling, Baron Anton 7, 12, 29, 33, 43, 81
Schwarzenberg, Prince Felix 1, 2, 3, 5, 7, 11, 14, 29, 30, 31, 32, 48, 49, 51, 52, 56, 57, 84
Scitovszky, Primate János 23, 25, 53, 55, 56, 59
Sennyey, Baron Pál 59
Serbs in Hungary 9, 61, 72, 75, 76
Serfs, emancipation of 15, 30, 39, 57, 61, 66
Sina, House of 38
Slovaks in Hungary 23, 41, 61, 72, 75
Somssich, Pál 54, 56, 61
Sophia, Archduchess 32
Stadion, Count Philipp 3, 5, 48
Sylvester Patents 30-31, 40, 45, 60
Szabad, György 18, 69, 70, 75
Szapáry, Count Gyula 59
Széchen, Antal 47, 48, 51, 53, 56
Széchényi, Count István 62
Szekfű, Gyula 61, 76
Szentiványi, Vince 25, 52, 53, 56, 60
Szigligeti, Ede 79
Szilágyi, Ferenc 21, 26
Szirmay, István 52
Szögyény-Marich, László Sr. 29, 30, 41, 50, 81

T

Terror, revolutionary, 1848-1849 8-9
Thinnfeld, Ferdinand von 5
Thun, Count Leo 19, 20, 22, 23, 24, 29, 30, 32, 42-43, 78

Tocqueville, Alexis de 7
Torkos, Mihály 61
Török, János 80
Transportation — railroads 35, 37, 38
Transportation, road construction 38–39
Transportation, water 18, 38
Trefort, Ákos 82

U

Ukrainians in Hungary 72, 75
Urházy, György 54
Ürményi, József 47, 54, 58, 61

V

Vahot, Imre 54
Vay, Baron Miklós 43
Vida, Károly 25, 53
Vormärz 47, 61, 64, 66

W

War of Independence; see Revolutions, Hungary, 1848–1849
Welden, Lt. Gen. Baron Ludwig 51, 52
Wenzel, Gusztáv 54
Windischgrätz, Field Marshal Prince Albert 17, 21, 25, 27, 47, 48, 50, 51, 52, 55, 59, 63, 68, 84
Wirkner, Lajos 57

Z

Zichy, Count Ferenc 29, 30, 46, 52, 60
Zichy, Count Herman 60
Zichy, Edmund 51
Zichy, Mihály 62
Zichy-Ferraris, Count Felix 51, 52
Zsedényi, Ede 47, 55, 61, 78